Unreal Beliefs

Mind, Meaning and Metaphysics

Series Editors:
Johannes L. Brandl, University of Salzburg, Austria
Christopher Gauker, University of Salzburg, Austria
Max Kölbel, University of Vienna, Austria
Mark Textor, King's College London, UK

The Mind, Meaning and Metaphysics series publishes cutting-edge research in philosophy of mind, philosophy of language, metaphysics and epistemology.

The basic questions in this area are wide-ranging and complex What is thinking and how does it manage to represent the world? How does language facilitate interpersonal cooperation and shape our thinking? What are the fundamental building blocks of reality, and how do we come to know what reality is?

These are long-standing philosophical questions but new and exciting answers continue to be invented, in part due to the input of the empirical sciences. Volumes in the series address such questions, with a view to both contemporary debates and the history of philosophy. Each volume reflects the state of the art in theoretical philosophy, but also makes a significant original contribution to it.

Editorial Board:
Annalisa Coliva, University of California, Irvine, USA
Paul Egré, Institut Jean-Nicod, France
Olav Gjelsvik, University of Oslo, Norway
Thomas Grundmann, University of Cologne, Germany
Katherine Hawley, University of St. Andrews, United Kingdom
Øystein Linnebo, University of Oslo, Norway
Teresa Marques, University of Barcelona, Spain
Anna-Sophia Maurin, University of Gothenburg, Sweden
Bence Nanay, University of Antwerp, Belgium
Martine Nida-Rümelin, University of Freiburg, Switzerland
Jaroslav Peregrin, Czech Academy of Sciences, Czech Republic

Tobias Rosefeldt, Humboldt University of Berlin, Germany
Anders Schoubye, University of Edinburgh, United Kingdom
Camilla Serck-Hanssen, University of Oslo, Norway
Emily Thomas, Durham University, United Kingdom
Amie Lynn Thomasson, Dartmouth College, USA
Giuliano Torrengo, University of Milan, Italy
Barbara Vetter, Humboldt University of Berlin, Germany
Heinrich Wansing, Ruhr University of Bochum, Germany

Titles in the series include:
Knowledge and the Philosophy of Number, by Keith Hossack
Names and Context, by Dolf Rami
The Metaphysics of Contingency, by Ferenc Huoranszki
Fragmenting Reality, by Samuele Iaquinto and Giuliano Torrengo
Unreal Beliefs, by Krzysztof Poslajko

Unreal Beliefs

An Anti-Realist Approach in the Metaphysics of Mind

Krzysztof Poslajko

BLOOMSBURY ACADEMIC
LONDON • NEW YORK • OXFORD • NEW DELHI • SYDNEY

BLOOMSBURY ACADEMIC
Bloomsbury Publishing Plc, 50 Bedford Square, London, WC1B 3DP, UK
Bloomsbury Publishing Inc, 1359 Broadway, 12th Floor, New York, NY 10018, USA
Bloomsbury Publishing Ireland, 29 Earlsfort Terrace, Dublin 2, D02 AY28, Ireland

BLOOMSBURY, BLOOMSBURY ACADEMIC and the Diana logo are
trademarks of Bloomsbury Publishing Plc

Copyright © Krzysztof Poslajko, 2024

Krzysztof Poslajko has asserted his right under the Copyright, Designs and
Patents Act, 1988, to be identified as Author of this work.

For legal purposes the Acknowledgements on pp. viii–ix constitute an
extension of this copyright page.

Series design by Louise Dugdale
Cover image © Mykola Mazuryk / Adobe Stoc

All rights reserved. No part of this publication may be: i) reproduced or transmitted in
any form, electronic or mechanical, including photocopying, recording or by means of
any information storage or retrieval system without prior permission in writing from the
publishers; or ii) used or reproduced in any way for the training, development or operation
of artificial intelligence (AI) technologies, including generative AI technologies. The rights
holders expressly reserve this publication from the text and data mining exception as per
Article 4(3) of the Digital Single Market Directive (EU) 2019/790.

Bloomsbury Publishing Inc does not have any control over, or responsibility for,
any third-party websites referred to or in this book. All internet addresses given
in this book were correct at the time of going to press. The author and publisher
regret any inconvenience caused if addresses have changed or sites have
ceased to exist, but can accept no responsibility for any such changes.

A catalogue record for this book is available from the British Library.

Library of Congress Cataloging-in-Publication Data
Names: Poslajko, Krzysztof, author.
Title: Unreal beliefs : an anti-realist approach in the metaphysics of mind / Krzysztof Poslajko.
Description: 1. | London : Bloomsbury Academic, 2024. | Series: Mind, meaning and metaphysics | Includes bibliographical references and index. |
Summary: "Krzysztof Poslajko offers a novel version of an anti-realist view about beliefs, rejecting the extreme proposal of eliminativism that claims beliefs do not exist. He argues we should rather say that beliefs exist, but they are not real. By arguing for the antirealist view as a revision of our common-sense view about the nature of mind, Poslajko makes the case for adopting a pragmatic metaphilosophy when we deal with philosophical questions about belief"– Provided by publisher.
Identifiers: LCCN 2023050015 (print) | LCCN 2023050016 (ebook) | ISBN 9781350354760 (hardback) | ISBN 9781350355002 (paperback) | ISBN 9781350354784 (epub) | ISBN 9781350354777 (ebook)
Subjects: LCSH: Belief and doubt.
Classification: LCC BD215 .P68 2024 (print) | LCC BD215 (ebook) | DDC 121/.6–dc23/eng/20240430
LC record available at https://lccn.loc.gov/2023050015
LC ebook record available at https://lccn.loc.gov/2023050016

ISBN: HB: 978-1-3503-5476-0
PB: 978-1-3503-5500-2
ePDF: 978-1-3503-5477-7
eBook: 978-1-3503-5478-4

Series: Mind, Meaning and Metaphysics

Typeset by Integra Software Services Pvt. Ltd.

For product safety related questions contact productsafety@bloomsbury.com.

To find out more about our authors and books visit www.bloomsbury.com
and sign up for our newsletters.

Contents

Acknowledgements   viii

1	Introduction	1
2	Existing anti-realist approaches	11
3	The deflationary gambit	33
4	Belief realism and anti-realism reconsidered	51
5	Inspirations	73
6	Reasons for non-realism	91
7	Minimal non-realism and common sense	115
8	Possible charges	137
9	Consequences	165
10	Conclusion	181

References   184
Index   197

Acknowledgements

Various people and institutions have supported me in writing this book. In 2014–19, I held a grant entitled 'Forms of mental anti-realism' from the National Science Centre, Poland, devoted to analysis of various forms of anti-realism about the mental. Working on this grant led me to the somewhat vain idea that in order to present my own views on the metaphysical status of propositional attitudes, I would need to write a full book.

In 2018, I was a visiting scholar at the Centre for Philosophy of Natural and Social Science of the London School of Economics (funded by the European Society for Philosophy of Science). This stay allowed me to work on the nature of natural kinds in the context of folk psychology. The very process of writing the first parts of the book was greatly eased by a stay at the University of Aberdeen in 2019, funded by the Bednarowski Trust, and supported by the Polish National Agency of Academic Exchange, under grant No. PPI/APM/2018/1/00022. Invaluable help during this stay came from Nigel Dower. The aforementioned grant from the Polish National Agency of Academic Exchange (coordinated by Pawel Banas) has also generously covered the costs of proofreading the early versions of the book. My home institution, Jagiellonian University, provided me with a sabbatical in 2019 and reduced my teaching load in the academic year 2020–1.

I am very grateful to Max Kölbel, Chris Gauker, and the rest of the editorial board of the Mind, Meaning and Metaphysics series at Bloomsbury for their encouragement during the writing and publishing process.

Important inspirations for various ideas in this book came from conversations with Szymon Bogacz, Brice Bantegnie and Jedrzej Grodniewicz. Also, brief (and probably forgotten by the other party) conversations with Christian List, Robert Matthews and Frances Egan greatly helped me to clarify my thinking on several important matters.

I have had the good fortune to present various ideas related to this book at several meetings of the Polish Semiotic Society in Warsaw, where I can always count on encouragement combined with helpful criticism. I am eternally grateful to all the people who have participated in these meetings and created a wonderful philosophical atmosphere. My warmest thanks go to Tadeusz

Ciecierski and Joanna Komorowska-Mach, whose personal and philosophical support cannot be over-appreciated.

My home department of philosophy at Jagiellonian University has provided a great environment in which to work on this book. I am grateful to my present and former colleagues and students for many inspiring conversations, especially Pawel Banas, Bartosz Janik, Leopold Hess, Zuzanna Krzykalska, Stanisław Ruczaj, Jan Rostek, Szymon Sapalski and Ewa Grzeszczak. I am extremely indebted to Katatrzyna Kijania-Placek for her constant efforts to make the Philosophy of Language and Mind section of Jagiellonian University Philosophy Department a great place to work.

I am also very grateful to the reviewers at Bloomsbury, especially Tadeusz Zawidzki, who, at the end of the process, de-anonymized himself in his role as Reviewer 2. His detailed and insightful comments helped me vastly improve the final version of the book.

Finally, my greatest thanks go to my wife and kids, who have provided me with constant support, while gently reminding me that there is more to life than academic philosophy.

I have avoided quoting any of my previously published work *in extenso* in this book, but it is worth noting that the basic ideas behind the first four chapters have been already presented, albeit in a different form and different wording, in my paper 'How to Think about the Debate over the Reality of Beliefs', published in Review of Philosophy and Psychology, 2022, 13(1), 85–107.

1

Introduction

1.1 Objectives

Ordinary people talk a lot about what people believe, and contemporary 'analytic' philosophers have thought and written a lot about this talk. The question of whether beliefs – along with other propositional attitudes – are real is of prominent importance to philosophy, and it was subject to intense debate in philosophy of mind 30–40 years ago. Consensus has it that this debate has been resolved in the affirmative. Most philosophers of mind accept arguments that our epistemic endeavours (including regarding the nature and existence of beliefs) make no sense unless beliefs are real, and these philosophers regard the ontological commitments of belief realism as relatively uncontroversial. This book argues that this consensus depends on an unjustified conflation of two questions: (1) whether beliefs exist, and (2) whether beliefs are real, which I take to be the same as the question of whether they constitute natural properties (in a technical sense, borrowed from Lewis [1983]).

Once these questions are distinguished, it becomes possible to present a plausible version of anti-realism about beliefs, which I call 'minimal non-realism'. The core of this view is the conjunction of three main claims: the first is that beliefs do exist (at least in a deflationary sense of existence); the second is that we have good reasons to think that beliefs are not real in the sense of naturalness; the third is that the folk take beliefs to be real, thus the folk concept must be reformed.

Framing the debate about the reality of beliefs as a debate about the naturalness of beliefs – not as a debate about their existence – will allow us to see the proposed version of anti-realism as a plausible position. Even a cursory glance at the state of the debate shows that there is a strong presumption in favour of realistic positions; however, in my opinion we gave up on anti-realism prematurely. To undermine the current consensus, it is important to try to delineate the distinction between realism and anti-realism in non-ontological terms: we need to stop asking whether beliefs exist and start wondering whether they are real.

My hope is that the proposed account will make the issue of realism in the domain of beliefs tractable: by adopting a new outlook on the debate we should be able, at least in principle, to settle the issue of whether beliefs are real. This new framework will also, hopefully, make it possible to introduce some theoretical unity into the philosophical debates about the metaphysics of beliefs. The answer to the question of whether beliefs are real would depend on whether they meet certain criteria of naturalness. For example, do they function in causal explanations? Do they constitute natural kinds? Are they connected to more natural vocabulary?

The second main aim of this book is to provide motivation for adopting the minimal non-realist position. I will, among other things, show that this position is at least worthy of consideration, as anti-realism understood in this way avoids the popular inconsistency argument that is levelled at traditional irrealism about beliefs. Although I genuinely consider the question of whether beliefs are real to be an epistemically open issue, I think that there are some important reasons to claim that the anti-realist option is the more viable one. Admittedly, these reasons are mainly negative in nature: the idea is to show that claims that constitute the general realistic approach to beliefs lack support, or there are serious reasons to doubt them. I do not claim to present a once-and-for-all argument for my preferred view. Still, providing reasons – even if only tentative – for preferring the minimal non-realist approach should be seen as important as this might change the perception of belief anti-realism from being considered a theoretical non-starter to a viable option.

The third aim of this book is to inquire into the relation between the minimal non-realist approach and common sense. I will argue that the proposed minimal non-realist position comes into conflict with the commonsensical picture of the mental sphere. However, this should not lead us to discard anti-realism; on the contrary, the idea is to show that anti-realism might be seen as a viable revision of the ordinary concept of 'belief', which is, arguably, a defective one. This proposal is motivated by the currently much-discussed idea of conceptual engineering; of particular importance as points of inspiration are Haslanger's approach to gender and Vargas's proposal regarding free will. By adopting such a conceptual revision, we might be able to adopt the preservationist approach to the notion of belief (i.e. to advocate keeping the term 'belief' in our discourse) and, at the same time, to appreciate the kernel of truth which was present in the original eliminativist position.

The view I develop here has some important consequences for the metaphysics of mind. First, it leads to a certain view on the relation between folk psychology and contemporary cognitive science: if we accept the proposed revision of the concept of belief (and, perhaps, other folk-psychological categories), then we should see folk psychology as being largely independent of cognitive science (and vice versa). The other important consequence is of a methodological nature: minimal non-realism implies that when confronted with the question of whether a certain state should qualify as a case of belief, we should focus on pragmatic and normative considerations. This means that we should try to answer the question of whether using the word 'belief' in such a case would be the right decision. We should not, however, expect such questions to have objective answers which can be established either by means of *a priori* analysis or by deference to science.

1.2 The importance of beliefs to philosophy

Although the concept of 'belief' lacks a universally accepted definition, there are certain assumptions regarding this concept that seem more or less uncontroversial for most philosophers. It is customary to introduce this concept by examples: so, according to at least one news outlet, Donald Trump believes that exercise will kill you, whilst I believe that writing a philosophy book might be a worthwhile effort (and it might be hard to say which belief is more controversial). Such examples usually serve to illustrate the fact that in typical cases we might analyse belief attributions as having a relational structure: a belief attribution, on the face of it, seems to describe a relation of believing which holds between a subject and a content of belief that is described by a 'that phrase'. Thus, the sentence 'I believe that writing a philosophy book is a worthwhile effort' is seen in this analysis as describing my relation to certain propositional content, namely that writing a philosophy book is a worthwhile effort.

Talk of beliefs is ubiquitous in common speech: we routinely talk about what we and other people believe. Beliefs are also part and parcel of some branches of science; notably, they are a subject of interest in social sciences (like sociology or political science) that are interested in knowing what people believe. Certain branches of psychology are also devoted to the study of beliefs: in social psychology, the study of attitudes is of primary importance (and that often includes the attitude of believing), whereas one of the most studied phenomena in developmental psychology is the development of the capacity to attribute beliefs to others. These processes of attribution are sometimes taken to illuminate the very phenomenon of belief.

In neither of these sciences, however, do beliefs play as prominent a role as in contemporary analytic philosophy. For philosophies of language and mind, as well as for philosophy of action and epistemology – as they have been conducted in this broad tradition – the concept of 'belief' is of utmost importance. Most importantly, philosophers often think that folk-psychological explanations of actions are based on so-called 'practical syllogism', the idea of which is that an explanation of an intentional action should consist in attributing a belief–desire pair to a subject. In particular, an example of such an explanation has the following form: if a subject intentionally does A, we attribute to them the desire to achieve B and the belief that by doing A they will achieve B. In this way, beliefs directly enter into the explanations of actions.

Philosophers are often reminded that our folk-psychological practice is far richer than belief-involving explanations based on practical syllogism: we describe and explain ourselves and others by appealing to character traits, emotions and so on (see, e.g., Alvarez 2017, Andrews 2008, 2015, Spaulding 2018). Still, for many philosophers the idea of 'folk psychology' is the idea of something that is based on 'belief' as a central notion; this notion plays an important role in many areas of philosophy, including philosophy of action, speech acts theory, etc.

In my opinion, this centrality of belief for analytic philosophy stems from the fact that beliefs are usually conceptualized in a way which ascribes to them some philosophically crucial features. Beliefs are commonly thought to do two things at once: they are considered to be internal mental states that are able to causally determine our behaviour; they are also considered to be bearers of semantic properties. Zawidzki aptly summarizes this consensus: 'Philosophers typically understand propositional attitudes and other mental states as concrete, unobservable causes of behavior. In addition, propositional attitudes are mental states with semantic properties: they represent the world as being a certain way, and this representation can be either satisfied or not, for example, in the case of beliefs, true or false' (Zawidzki 2013, p. 11).

Beliefs are thought to have content: 'that clauses' in belief attributions are considered to specify propositions which are believed. This feature of content possession makes it possible for beliefs to have truth conditions and enter into logical relations: a belief can entail another belief or be inconsistent with other beliefs. In this way, beliefs do seem to serve as a bridge between the 'space of reasons' (to borrow the famous phrase from Sellars [1956]) and the realm of causes. The difficulty of bridging the two was evident in analytic philosophy from the very outset, as was the idea that we might be able to fill the lacuna with the notion of belief.

'How does a thought act?', asks Frege in his seminal essay 'The Thought'. Frege's answer is:

> By being apprehended and taken to be true. This is a process in the inner world of a thinker which can have further consequences in this inner world and which, encroaching on the sphere of the will, can also make itself noticeable in the outer world. If, for example, I grasp the thought which we express by the theorem of Pythagoras, the consequence may be that I recognise it to be true and, further, that I apply it, making a decision which brings about the acceleration of masses.
>
> (Frege 1956, p. 310)

The problem that Frege faces in this paragraph is a common one. If we take contents/propositions ('thoughts') to be abstract, then even if we do not wholly buy into Fregean Platonism, we have a hard time in explaining how such abstract contents or propositions can have any causal influence on the physical world. The Fregean answer is seemingly the standard one: 'thoughts' can act because they can be 'apprehended and taken to be true'. Translating this answer into more modern jargon, we get the familiar idea that propositions should be seen as contents of beliefs, and beliefs play an explanatory role with regard to our behaviour. Thus, contents enter the realm of causes in virtue of the fact that our actions in the physical realm are (at least partly) explained by reference to content-bearing states.

That many analytical philosophers have implicitly bought into this picture should come as no surprise. Analytic philosophy, at least in some quarters, has been deeply invested in the idea of gaining insights into the structure of thoughts by some sort of logical analysis (conducted by either formal or informal methods). If beliefs really are what we suppose them to be, then it is possible to gain insight into the causes of our behaviour by means of analysis of abstract contents. This is a substantial theoretical advantage.

This picture presumes that beliefs are real – that indeed we do have such internal, causally efficacious states which serve as bearers of content. However, this could be and has been questioned. Thus, the question of whether beliefs are real was, as we should presently see, at some point one of the most central issues of analytic philosophy of mind.

1.3 State of the debate and motivation

The debate over the reality of beliefs occupied the centre stage of the philosophy of mind in a period spanning from approximately the 1970s until (at most) the early 2000s. Obviously, there were previous serious attempts to provide an account of beliefs (Ryle's [1949] analytic behaviourism is one such attempt), but it was in this period that the question of the reality of beliefs was most hotly debated. The debate involved major figures in philosophy of mind of that time: Fodor, the Churchlands, Dennett, Davidson, Rorty and many others.

In his 'Real Patterns' (1991), Dennett provides an influential description of the positions in this debate. He distinguishes three major camps: on the extremes, he describes the 'industrial-strength realism' of Fodor and the 'eliminative materialism' of the Churchlands; in the middle, he places his own and Davidson's 'mild-realist' position and Rorty's 'mild irrealism'. The main claim of Fodor-style realism (see Fodor 1985 for the classic exposition) is that belief attributions should be treated as literally true in the sense that when we attribute a belief to a person, we point to some concrete state which is realized in the brain of the person in question. On the other hand, eliminative materialists (see Churchland 1981) see beliefs as being simply non-existent. Adherents to middle-ground theories try by different means to secure the existence of beliefs without affirming the controversial presuppositions of strong realism.

Contemporary philosophy of mind seems to have moved past this debate. Obviously, it is not that philosophers have stopped caring about beliefs completely – new ideas about the metaphysics of beliefs are still being developed (and more will be said on them below) – but the issue seems to be far less central than it was when the author of this book was in primary school. I can speculatively point to two reasons why this has happened. First, the general methodology of the philosophy of mind has shifted: it has become more customary to engage directly with the deliverances of cognitive science than to try to solve the issue of the metaphysical status of entities postulated within the folk framework. In this way, the belief–realism debate might be seen as having been partly transformed and partly replaced by the debate about representationalism in cognitive science. Such a view on the most recent developments of philosophy of mind is endorsed, for example, by Rupert, who distinguishes between the first generation of philosophers interested in the issue of naturalization of content with relation to folk psychology, and the 'second generation of naturalistic theorists of mental content (…) [who] have, on the whole, been inclined to pursue a theory of representational content as part of the theoretical foundations of cognitive science, putting folk psychology largely to one side' (Rupert 2018, p. 206).

The other reason for the relative lack of interest in the issue of belief realism is that the anti-realist position in this area is now commonly seen as unworkable (this decline in interest was conceded by Churchland himself [see Churchland 2007]). Once the threat of eliminativism had vanished from the scene, the need to provide positive justification for adopting the realist view, whether in the mild or the extreme version, waned. One might get the impression that the realist position is sometimes taken to have won as a result of a sort of philosophical walkover: as the extreme version of anti-realism is treated as a non-starter, there is little pressure to engage in disproving it.

What then are the motivations for trying to tackle this problem once again? First, despite the diminished interest in the debate, there have been some interesting developments in the theory of beliefs, such as the development and subsequent discussion of neo-dispositionalism, championed notably by Schwitzgebel (see, e.g., his 2002), and the rise of interest in mental fictionalism (see Joyce 2013, Toon 2016, Wallace 2016).

In philosophy of mind, more broadly construed, there is also continuing interest in the question of realism. First, there is the ongoing issue concerning the question of representationalism in the philosophy of cognitive science, with the eliminativist party still playing an important role in this debate. This issue is related but not identical to the question of the reality of beliefs. Slightly less related is the question of the reality of phenomenal consciousness: there is growing interest in the position, called 'illusionism' (see Frankish 2016), which claims that our conviction that we have phenomenal states is mistaken. While this conception is not universally accepted (to say the least), it has generated enough attention to warrant the claim that the issue of realism with regard to phenomenal states is a serious one.

Most importantly, I believe that advances in general metaphysics make it possible to frame the question of realism about beliefs more carefully than it was originally. Contemporary analytic metaphysics provides us with ways to make some fine-grained distinctions which might be used to present anti-realism about beliefs in a more palatable way.

I think the original eliminative materialist position was, in a way, a huge intellectual step forward: the idea that our pre-theoretic conception of the human mind might be fundamentally mistaken has potentially far-reaching consequences and might be much better supported than most contemporary philosophers of mind are willing to admit. However, I also think that the original eliminative materialist position is impossible to defend wholesale as it has too many flaws and contains too many indefensible assumptions. This does not mean that we should reject the intuitions that drove the original theory. We might, instead, critically assess the way various philosophers have tried to express their scepticism about the reality of beliefs while still appreciating the basic intuitions that motivated their approaches.

1.4 Plan of the work ahead

The book proceeds as follows. First, I will provide a brief description of the already formulated anti-realist positions about beliefs and the controversies they generated. This overview has no claim to being exhaustive: the debates about the reality of beliefs would require an in-depth historical study which the author of this book feels unable to deliver. I will instead focus on what I think were the reasons that made the anti-realist proposals unpopular. I will start with a brief discussion of non-cognitivism about beliefs and show why this mainly hypothetical position never really gained traction. I will then describe eliminative materialism and present three major objections to that theory: the 'cognitive suicide' argument, the argument from reference and the argument from common sense. I will show that, despite appearances to the contrary, it is the last argument that should be considered the most fatal to eliminativism. I will also discuss mental fictionalism in order to see to what extent it can avoid the problems of eliminativism.

The main take-away from Chapter 2 will be the conclusion that what makes the original eliminative materialist (and other classic anti-realist) position unacceptable is largely its commitment to an ontological (in the Quinean sense) way of framing its central thesis. Eliminativists claim that beliefs do not exist, the direct consequence of which is their adherence to irrealism about belief discourse, i.e., to the idea that belief attributions can never be true. But this is what makes the idea of denying the reality of beliefs so hard to swallow.

Consequently, in Chapters 3 and 4 I will present a way of expressing anti-realism about beliefs which involves neither the negative ontological claim about beliefs nor irrealism about belief attributions. In Chapter 3, I will lay the ground for this approach by presenting what I call a 'deflationary gambit': the idea that we should accept the deflationary/minimalist approach to ontology and accept that many things that are considered ontologically problematic do actually exist. However, accepting this idea does not do away with the issue of realism: the other part of the deflationary gambit is the idea that it is possible to make a distinction between realism and anti-realism without using existence claims. I will argue that, in the context of the belief debate, the best way to do so is by employing David Lewis's distinction between natural and non-natural properties.

In Chapter 4, I will characterize this distinction in more detail: I will show which criteria might be used to decide if beliefs should be seen as real. These criteria include constituting natural kinds; figuring in causal explanations; and being connected to more natural properties. I will provide the characteristics of ideal-type realism and anti-realism concerning beliefs, as conceptualized within the proposed framework.

Chapter 5 is devoted to showing how some of the previously developed positions in the metaphysics of beliefs can be made to fit the proposed framework, and how some of them might be seen as being predecessors and sources of inspiration for the version of anti-realism I endorse. I will focus on three main conceptions of beliefs which might be seen as less or more anti-realist. The first is the (neo-)dispositionalist one, developed historically by Ryle and more recently by Schwitzgebel. The second is the interpretivist approach, most famously endorsed by Davidson and Dennett. The third is the eliminativist view, at least in some milder formulations; I focus on the versions of eliminativism that were presented by Stich and by Chomsky. I close Chapter 5 by looking at what might be seen as the paradigmatic realist outlook on beliefs, namely the representationalist theories of belief; I focus on the contemporary psychofunctionalist version of representationalism, which provides a useful reference and contrast point to the position I develop.

Chapter 6 is devoted to providing justification for preferring the anti-realist position as I have described it. I will present arguments for claiming that beliefs do not meet the criteria for naturalness. First, I will try to establish that belief attributions do not track genuine similarities, and beliefs do not form natural kinds. Second, I will show that they do not function in genuine causal explanations: this will require engaging with the recent attempts to defend mental causation, especially with the interventionist picture of mental causation. Thirdly, by way of showing problems with the naturalization of content project, I will argue that there is little connection between a description in terms of belief and a description in terms of more fundamental vocabulary. I will also offer some reflection on the epistemic status of the arguments I present, and on why – despite these arguments' limitations – the minimal non-realist position might be seen as the rational option to take.

Chapter 7 is perhaps the most original (read: theoretically risky) part of the book. I will attempt to show that such an anti-realist position, although theoretically feasible and supported by some plausible arguments, comes into conflict with the common-sense view on belief. Crucially, I will try to demonstrate that this should not be seen as a problem for anti-realism; this position should be seen as a justified revision of the folk concept of belief. I will strengthen the case for revision with some analogies, notably the analogy with the concepts of free will and gender. Lastly, I will show how this revisionary account of the anti-realistic position allows us to see that the original eliminative materialist position contained a kernel of truth in that eliminativists were right when they claimed that our folk outlook on beliefs is flawed. Yet, I will argue that we should favour revision over elimination.

Chapter 8 deals with some possible objections to minimal non-realism. First, I will show how this position differs from the fictionalist view, even if there are certain important affinities. Next, I will deal with the issue of whether the proposed anti-realist view leads to semantic nihilism. I will specifically engage with the notorious Boghossian-Wright argument which aimed to show that any form of anti-realism about beliefs undermines our ability to make a meaningful realism vs anti-realism distinction. Subsequently, I will try to dispel the worries that stem from the 'success argument' for the reality of folk-psychological categories. I will also critically engage with the argument that proceeds from the alleged austere character of folk psychology to the rejection of anti-realism in this domain. Moreover, I will try to offer some thoughts on the idea that we might save realism about beliefs by adopting a non-naturalist view of the nature of intentional properties. Finally, I will deal with the possible suggestion that the category of belief should be seen as a socially constructed natural kind.

In Chapter 9, I present a brief discussion of the consequences of minimal non-realism concerning the category of 'belief'. First, I deal with the question of whether the position I develop generalizes to other folk-psychological categories. Second, I point to the picture of the relation between folk psychology and cognitive science that stems from the approach I have developed: on the proposed account, these two become largely independent of each other. Finally, I show that minimal non-realism leads to adopting a pragmatic metaphilosophical approach to many debates concerning the notion of belief – most importantly, the debate about the boundaries of belief. This metaphilosophical pragmatism implies that many debates which have been considered substantial should rather be seen as being a matter of conceptual decisions regarding how we want to use the notion of belief. Chapter 10 provides a summary of the developed position.

2

Existing anti-realist approaches

2.1 Non-cognitivism about attitudes

I will start my review with a relatively unpopular position, namely the conception according to which we should adopt a non-cognitivist stance towards ascriptions of belief (and other propositional attitudes) (my account and criticism of this view are expanded upon in my earlier paper; see Poslajko [2024]). To an extent, this is a purely hypothetical theory: it is not easy to point to any particular philosopher who would actually subscribe to such a view. Still, this hypothetical position has attracted the attention of several philosophers, including Bar-On (2012), Jackson (1999), Wright (1995, 2002), and Toppinen (2015). The idea of applying non-cognitivism to belief ascriptions seems to stem from a simple argument: the first premise is that by ascribing beliefs we are making normative claims; the second premise is that normative statements should be seen through non-cognitive lenses. The natural conclusion is that we should see belief ascriptions as being non-cognitive.

I think that engaging with this position – despite its relative unpopularity – is important, as it offers perhaps the most radical way of denying the reality of beliefs. In such an approach, we would repudiate the idea that statements in which we attribute beliefs aim to describe the world as it is: these statements would be taken to perform some other functions. Consequently, these statements cannot be seen as candidates for truth, therefore there would be no point in asking whether there is anything in reality that corresponds to belief attributions. In this way we could entirely avoid the problem of metaphysics of belief (many philosophers have pointed out that one of the principal attractions of the original non-cognitivist position in meta-ethics was that it made it possible to avoid problems that are usually associated with realist accounts of normative facts [see, e.g., Chrisman 2010]). So, let us look at the proposal in more detail, starting with the premises that might lead to the adoption of this particular view.

It will be shown that as long as the discussed position is based on the classical expressivist rejection of the truth-aptness of normative statements, expressivism is a non-starter. Additionally, I will argue that a more contemporary version of expressivism that is based on quasi-realism fares better, but this position is also contentious.

The idea that belief ascriptions involve normative elements is as popular as it is controversial. Its proponents claim that ascriptions of beliefs essentially involve some 'ought claims'. This view might be spelled out in two main ways (see Zangwill 2010). The first is that many propositional attitudes have satisfaction conditions: there is a sense in which, for example, a belief aims to be true. In this sense we might say that some oughts are applied to ascriptions of belief as we might be entitled to say that someone ought or ought not to hold a particular belief. If one believes something that is true, then one has the belief one ought to have; however, if one has a false belief, then some philosophers would be ready to say that this is a belief that one ought not have.

The second idea is that there are norms of rationality which govern the relations between the propositional attitudes held by a single subject. The ought claims applied to beliefs (and other attitudes) are thought to be true in virtue of these norms: if one has beliefs that violate these standards of internal consistency, then perhaps it is right to say that the subject in question has certain beliefs they ought not have. The idea of the normativity of attitudes is subject of ongoing discussion and I have no ambition of trying to settle it here (see Glüer & Wikforss [2018], McHugh & Whiting [2014], for useful overviews of this debate): my aim is only to see whether one can motivate a legitimate form of mental anti-realism by this premise.

The other thought that motivates non-cognitivism about belief is the idea that ought claims should be seen as non-cognitive, i.e., they do not aim to describe states of affairs; instead, they serve to express non-cognitive mental states such as desires (the classic exposition of such-understood non-cognitivism can be found in Ayer 1936). The crux of non-cognitivism is the claim that sentences in which we make normative claims are not truth-apt: they cannot be legitimately described as true or false as they cannot be seen as expressions of mental states which aim to truly describe the world.

These two premises taken together lead to a position according to which ascriptions of beliefs should not be treated as aiming to describe reality; instead, they should be seen as expressions of non-cognitive mental states. Consequently, they cannot be assessed with regard to their logical value. So, when I ascribe to Mark a belief that London is not pretty, then I am not attempting to describe Mark's internal states; rather, I am expressing my own non-cognitive state of mind, and this expression should not count as either true or false (at least on the classical expressivist account of normative statements).

This does not seem very intuitively plausible, to say the least. Worse still, such a theory faces a serious theoretical obstacle. Traditional non-cognitivism was founded on a psychological distinction between beliefs and desires or, more broadly, between cognitive and non-cognitive mental states. The problem is that if one wished to apply non-cognitivist anti-realism to the area of folk psychology, then such a theorist would undermine the basis of their own claims. This is because one would be forced to deny the reality of a folk-psychological distinction between beliefs and desires. In this way, psychological non-cognitivism becomes a self-undermining theory. This is a somewhat oversimplified version of the popular argument against non-cognitivism about attitudes (more elaborate versions can be found in Wright [1995, 2002] and Bar-On [2012]), and the question of whether the argument is actually sound is much more complex than this characterization suggests.

However, such complexities seem to be mainly irrelevant nowadays; this is mainly because classical non-cognitivism is nearly universally rejected as a theory of normativity, even by meta-ethicists of an expressivist persuasion (see, e.g., Blackburn 1993). Most contemporary expressivists reject the central claim of Ayer's version of expressivism and no longer assert that normative statements cannot be described as being true or false. On the contrary, most contemporary expressivists now accept that truth can be predicated of normative statements (although in deflationary sense, see Blackburn 1993 or Gibbard 2012).

Whether some version of sophisticated expressivism which allows normative statements to be truth-apt can be applied to belief talk is a vexed question. There have been many sceptical voices about the possibility of applying the quasi-realist framework to the realm of beliefs (and other propositional attitudes) (see, e.g., Evans & Shah 2012). The problem with the possible quasi-realist approach to propositional attitudes seems to stem from the fact that it seems any form of quasi-realism must be committed to the substantial reality of the realm of attitudes. This, in turn, is the consequence of the fact that the distinction between what is real and what is quasi-real is cashed out (at least partly) in terms of distinct psychological attitudes. This issue of the cogency of attitudinal quasi-realism is complex, mainly because it is hard to see exactly what constitutes the distinction between the real and the quasi-real; for this reason, it might be hard to exactly formulate a quasi-realism position about attitudes, and the debate tends to be fairly technical. I have tried to present my approach to this issue elsewhere (Poslajko 2024) – mainly with negative results.

However, for our present purposes a detailed discussion of this position is not required because even if the idea of applying the quasi-realist view to the area of beliefs were feasible, this would not save us from metaphysical concerns over the status of these attitudes. One of the main attractions of the classical expressivist position – with its commitment to denying the truth-aptitude of normative statements – was that it carried a promise of avoiding the hard questions about normative reality. If normative statements aren't true or false as they do not aim to describe anything, then there is no issue with asking questions about putative normative facts. In this way, ontological questions about the normative domain were thought to be avoided.

However, once the contemporary expressivists reject non-cognitivism, this way of avoiding the issue is closed. Most of the contemporary discussions about the reality of beliefs are framed in a way that assumes that statements about attitudes might be true or false. A classic example of an anti-realist approach that adopted this assumption is eliminative materialism, which will be discussed presently.

2.2 Eliminative materialism

Eliminative materialism is by far the most well-known (which in this context does not mean 'popular') version of anti-realism concerning beliefs. Unlike non-cognitivism, it does not shy away from saying that belief attributions have truth-values or from making ontological claims about beliefs. In both cases, the claims of eliminative materialism are bold and simple: in its purest form, eliminative materialism is committed to the claim that all elementary attributions of beliefs are false and beliefs do not exist.

The expositions of eliminative materialism which are now considered classic are Churchland's (1981) and Stich's (1983). Their position had some important predecessors, including Quine's (1960) repudiation of talk about propositional attitudes as an 'essentially dramatic idiom' (Quine 1960, p. 218) which should have no place in strict scientific theorizing, as well as Rorty's (1965) eliminativism about sensations, which popularized the idea of adopting the eliminativist approach to the mental as an attractive alternative to the identity theory. More recently, the eliminativist approach to the issue of beliefs has been endorsed by Rosenberg (2015) and Chomsky (2000; a more detailed discussion of Chomsky's views on eliminativism can be found in Collins (2007); further analysis of Chomsky's original position will be provided in Chapter 5, section 3).

In what follows, I will present a rough-and-ready characterization of the basic tenets of eliminative materialism, but I am fully aware that such a characterization might not do full justice to the arguably complex and subtle views of the historical proponents of this position. Nonetheless, it is a simplified version of a position that has received substantial yet negative attention in the philosophical literature, and for this reason this standard version of eliminativism will be the starting point of the present discussion.

According to the standard account, eliminativism is a version of error theory about belief discourse (see, e.g., Miller 2016). In contrast to non-cognitivists, error theorists see a given area of discourse as aiming to represent reality; moreover sentences belonging to this discourse are considered to be truth-evaluable. As it happens, however, these representational attempts fail, therefore all elementary statements from this area of discourse should be said to be false (a classic exposition of error theory is Mackie's [1977] approach to morality). The simplified version of eliminative materialism is just an application of this general definition to the discourse about belief (and to folk psychology in general).

This standard version of eliminative materialism is usually thought to follow from the following reasoning, which was presented by Churchland (1981): First, Churchland assumes that folk psychology should be seen as a theory, and 'belief' should be seen as a theoretical term that is defined by its role in this theory. Second, according to Churchland, if we were to assess this theory according to the standards all genuine theories should meet, we would be forced to say that it fails this assessment miserably as it does not progress, is not compatible with other more mature theories (like neuroscience) and has a hard time explaining certain important phenomena (like mental illnesses). According to Churchland, this shows that the proto-theory of folk psychology deserves to be deemed false. Therefore, we should conclude that beliefs, as theoretical posits of a false theory, do not exist and should be eliminated from our use.

It is important to note that at least three different theses are being put forward here. The first one is ontological: the claim that beliefs do not exist (e.g., Daly [2013] claims that this ontological thesis is central to eliminative materialism). The other two theses are claims concerning the elimination of the notion of belief: the first is that the term 'belief' should be eliminated from the folk discourse; the other is that this term should be eliminated from mature cognitive science (these two versions of the general eliminative thesis were usefully distinguished by Collins [2007], who dubs them 'futuristic' and 'meta-scientific').

Much of the dismay that was caused by Churchland's pronouncement can probably be traced back to the implausibility of the futuristic aspect of his conception. It is hardly believable that we would suddenly stop using folk-psychological vocabulary due to the putative discovery of the falsity of folk psychology even if we discovered that folk psychology were false: folk discourses are full of references to objects which we know do not exist (think of the 'celestial sphere', which we know is not a 'real thing', yet we still talk as if we believed that the stars move round the earth in the celestial sphere). However, to my mind, the most philosophically important part of eliminativism is the ontological claim that there are no beliefs. Controversies regarding the feasibility of eliminating belief talk from folk discourse and science should not be treated as central (although the problem of elimination will be briefly discussed in the section devoted to mental fictionalism).

The other important yet controversial presupposition of the original eliminativist view was its insistence that folk psychology is a theory. This way of seeing the issue made eliminative materialism dependent on the theory–theory approach to mindreading (for a critical discussion of this assumption, see Ramsey 2019). The issue of whether the theory–theory is the right view of mindreading is important in its own right; certainly, it is not the only available explanation of the phenomenon of mindreading (see Slors et al. 2015 for a useful overview of the current state of the mindreading debate). However, the issue of the reality of beliefs (and other propositional attitudes) seems to be largely independent of whether we have some sort of theory 'in our heads' which is responsible for our folk-psychological ability (i.e. the ability to interpret and predict the behaviour of others). Even if there is no grain of truth in the theory–theory approach, the issue of whether beliefs are real is still worthy of consideration. As Ramsey notes, 'Cherubs, presumably, are not part of any sort of quasi-scientific theory, yet this alone is no reason to think they might exist' (Ramsey 2019). This is quite right: ontological and metaphysical questions do not presuppose the existence of a proto-theory about the objects of our ontological interest. In my opinion, the observation that there is such a thing as belief discourse, i.e., the common practice of ascribing beliefs to oneself and others, and the fact that this discourse seems to involve an ontological commitment to beliefs are sufficient rationale to inquire into the issue of the existence of beliefs.

Thus, the crux of eliminative materialism, as I understand it, is simply the claim that there are no beliefs. Even in this theoretically austere version, eliminative materialism is a powerful and controversial thesis. Eliminative materialism's most important idea is that the ontological presuppositions that we make in our folk discourse about human minds and agency are simply false: the things/ states/events we seem to speak about in this discourse (namely beliefs) do not exist. In this way, eliminative materialists draw our attention to an (alleged) ontological/metaphysical error in the way we speak about ourselves and others. This possibility of error is an important philosophical conjecture, even if does not lead to any conclusions about the mechanics of human interactions.

Seen in this way, eliminativism becomes yet another position in the long history of philosophical scepticism. In the European philosophical tradition, there have been many sceptics who aimed to show us that our pre-reflective vision of the world is mistaken. From ancient sceptics who showed us the impossibility of knowledge (see Annas & Barnes 2000), to Hume's attack on causation (Hume 1748/51) and Kripke-Wittgenstein's scruples concerning the concept of meaning (Kripke 1982), philosophers have always been keen to show us that some of the central elements of our worldview are inadequate.

From my personal perspective, this aspect of eliminativism is important, as development (if we want to avoid talking about progress) in philosophy is often spurred by the need to deal with such challenges. Eliminativism about beliefs should be seen as being such a sceptical philosophical challenge that aims to wake us from our dogmatic slumber, in which we unreflectively treat our belief-ascribing practice as being a guide to genuine mental reality. Eliminativists boldly claim that this practice is wrong and our attributions are false. I contend that putting forward this bold claim was an important development in the history of our reflection on the human mind.

2.3 Objections to eliminative materialism

As with all sceptical projects in the history of philosophy, the eliminativists' proposal met with fierce opposition. There have been numerous controversies regarding eliminative materialism, but providing a comprehensive overview of them would be neither possible nor illuminating. Instead of trying to engage in such an impossible project, I will focus on the three counter-arguments which I consider to be the most important: the cognitive suicide argument, the Lycan-Stich argument, and the argument based on common-sense functionalism. These arguments are important in their own right but even more so in the context of this book. First, they directly engage with the ontological claim of eliminative materialism, which I deem to be the most important aspect of this position. Second, I think that by dealing with these arguments we might get to see what exactly the problem is with the eliminativistic way of framing the idea of anti-realism about beliefs, which, in consequence, might justify proposing a better alternative.

2.3.1 Cognitive suicide

Perhaps the most prominent argument against eliminative materialism is the 'cognitive suicide' argument, which was made popular by Baker (1987) and was subsequently picked up on by several philosophers (see, e.g., Boghossian 1990). The gist of the argument is fairly simple: one cannot coherently adopt the idea that beliefs do not exist because the very act of making this eliminativistic claim presupposes the reality of beliefs. There are three main strands in Baker's argument. First, she claims that without accepting beliefs as real one cannot maintain that one accepts the theory of eliminative materialism because accepting any theory seems to presuppose believing in this theory. Second, she maintains that eliminative materialists cannot maintain that their theory is justified because the notion of being justified somehow involves having beliefs. And thirdly, she maintains that eliminativists cannot say that their theory is true because being a believer is a necessary precondition of maintaining that one is in a possession of a true theory about anything.

The first worry, which concerns the putative impossibility of asserting the eliminativist claim, is in my opinion not necessarily fatal for the eliminativist. There are two reasons for this. First, this way of arguing relies on the questionable assumption that the only way to conceptualize any assertion is by assuming that it must be seen as an expression of beliefs. Whilst it is true that most currently accepted theories of assertion accept the view that assertions express beliefs (see, e.g., Pagin 2016), it would be hard to show that it is impossible in principle to provide a characterization of assertion that would not rely on the notion of belief. It seems that such a claim about impossibility is something that would be needed for the assertion-based version of the cognitive suicide argument.

The other reason for scepticism is that this argument only shows why one cannot accept eliminativism – it does not show that eliminativism is not true. That these two questions are distinct has been recently stressed by Streumer (2017) in the general context of the debate about error theory. For Streumer, it might be the case that certain error-theoretic claims (error theory about normativity is a central example for him) are impossible for us to accept, but this does not change the fact that such error-theoretic claims are true. Being true and being believable are two distinct things. Although Streumer does not endorse error theory about psychology, it seems obvious that his general observation is also applicable in this case: there is no reason to suppose that the logical value of the ontological claim about the non-existence of beliefs depends on our ability to accept or assert it.

In a similar vein, one might want to resist the second way of arguing against eliminative materialism, which is based on the notion of justification. If we read this notion in an 'internalist' fashion, i.e., we treat justification as something which metaphorically happens inside people's heads, then eliminativists obviously cannot claim that their theory is justified. This is because they deny that they (or anybody else) possess states with propositional content 'inside their heads' which can be seen as elements of justificatory processes. Nonetheless, this line of disproving eliminativism might be resisted on similar grounds as the previous one. First, it might be said that even if we agree that proponents of eliminativism are not justified, in the internalist sense, in holding their position, this does not lead to the conclusion that their view is false. Additionally, it would be hard to prove that it is impossible for an eliminativist to create an eliminativistically acceptable counterpart of the notion of justification that would not presuppose the existence of folk-psychological content-bearing states.

In my view, the most serious aspect of the cognitive suicide problem is the problem of truth. If it were indeed the case that the eliminativist thesis entailed that nothing is true, including the eliminativist thesis itself, then eliminativism could indeed be considered inconsistent. However, this conclusion (that the eliminativist thesis entails the denial of its own truth) can be challenged. The most popular way of deflecting this argument is by resorting to the deflationary account of truth (this line is proposed by, e.g., Taylor 1994). Regarding the deflationary account of truth, there is no need to make any substantial assumptions about the nature of intentionality or word–world relations. On this account, to say that 'p is true' is equivalent to asserting that p. Deflationism about truth does not presuppose that in order to be able to make true statements one must be in possession of contentful mental states which serve as the vehicles of truth-evaluation. It seems that nothing that eliminativists want to deny is needed to formulate the deflationary view on truth. For the deflationists, truth is a metaphysically thin notion and no substantial psychology is required to make sense of truth-value attributions.

This way of merging eliminativism and deflationism has attracted some criticism (see Boghossian 1990). According to this line of thought, eliminativism about mental content results in the impossibility of anything having truth conditions of any sort. This is a complex and controversial argument (see, e.g., Devitt & Rey 1991 for criticism). I have developed my own critique of this argument elsewhere (see Poslajko 2019): the gist of my response is that eliminativism is indeed incompatible with the notion of substantial representation if we understand it as the capacity of propositional contents to, as it were, match portions of reality. Consequently, if eliminativism were a claim about the failure of the belief discourse to represent reality (in the substantial sense of representation), then this position would be unstable. However, the substantial notion of representation is not the only one we can adopt. We can, in my opinion, adopt a broadly anti-representationalist outlook as an alternative to the representational view of truth conditions; in this way, we can try to express the eliminativist thesis without falling into inconsistency.

There is no space here to get into the technical details of this intricate debate; instead, I want to present the two main conclusions that I think can be drawn from the debate. The first is that arguments against eliminativism of this kind do not constitute direct, self-evident proof that eliminativism is inconsistent. Rather, all such arguments rely on specific philosophical presuppositions which might be challenged. The second conclusion, which is more important in the broad scheme of this book, is that the troubles that eliminativism runs into stem from the fact that it denies the truth of folk-psychological attributions of beliefs. Even though eliminativists might use technical distinctions to defend themselves from the formal charge of inconsistency, the feeling that there is something is wrong with eliminativism cannot be easily dismissed by technical philosophical arguments. However, the claim that something is wrong with eliminativism cannot be justified by arguing that this view is obviously self-defeating. The gut feeling that eliminativism cannot be true must be defended in some other way.

2.3.2 The Lycan-Stich argument

The other popular line of argument against eliminative materialism is the one presented by Lycan (1988) and popularized by Stich (1996) and his collaborators (see Mallon et al. 2009; it is worth noting that Stich changed his position from a proponent to a staunch critic of eliminativism). According to this line of thought, eliminative materialism relies on an unjustified assumption of the descriptivist theory of reference for terms like 'belief'. However, if we adopted an alternative view about the reference of 'belief', then the eliminativist conclusion might be avoided.

It is indeed assumed in the formulation of eliminativism that 'belief' is a theoretical term which belongs to a theory called 'folk psychology'. Stich

(1996) is also correct in pointing out that in the formulation of the eliminativist argument, Churchland – in the vein of Ramsey-Carnap-Lewis's conception of theoretical terms – assumes the descriptivist theory of reference for theoretical terms (according to Stich, the best exposition of this line of thinking can be found in Lewis [1970]).

To put it simply, according to Ramsey-Carnap-Lewis's view, the meaning of a theoretical term is defined by its role in a theory. For example, if we wanted to know what the term 'money' means in neoclassical economics, we would have to collect all the claims that neoclassical economics makes about money before we could make a definite description of it. The consequence of this approach is that money (as defined by neoclassical economics) exists only if there is something which satisfies this description (at least to a large extent). Conversely, if there is nothing that satisfies this description (i.e., these theoretical claims are mostly false), we might say that money (as understood in neoclassical economics) does not exist.

The Churchlandian approach to eliminativism is clearly based on this theory. In his argument, Churchland goes from the alleged falsity of folk psychology to the conclusion concerning the non-existence of beliefs. As he puts it: 'The thesis of eliminative materialism can be expressed (…) as follows: The principles of folk psychology are substantially false, and its ontology is non-existent' (Churchland 1986, p. 219). But this reasoning (if this is the right word here) is valid only if the existence of beliefs hinges on the truth of the theory in which the term 'belief' is embedded, and this extra assumption relies on the descriptivist account of theoretical terms.

However, as Lycan, Stich, and others rightly note, the descriptivist account is not the only possible approach to the issue of semantics of theoretical terms. There is an important alternative to this view, namely the natural-kind terms theory, which was developed by Putnam (1975) and Kripke (1980). On this approach, what constitutes the meaning of a theoretical term is not its role in a theory but rather the chain of reference from its current usage to the kind in question. Take Putnam's example of 'gold': in his view, the term is introduced by a sort of baptism which introduced it into our language (in an idealized case, this baptism would look as if the putative first user had pointed to a portion of gold and said 'let's call this substance "gold"'). Then, by means of participation in the communicative chain with that first usage, we get to refer to anything that belongs to the same natural kind to which the sample used in the original baptism belonged.

The important feature of the Putnam-Kripke approach is that the reference of theoretical terms is not dependent on the content of a given theory. This has two vital consequences: first, it makes it possible to acknowledge the existence of trans-theoretical terms, i.e., terms which refer to the same thing even though the theories in which they function are different. For example, our term 'gold' and the ancient Greek counterpart of this term refer to the same substance, even though our theory about gold is substantially distinct from the ancient Greek one. Second and more importantly, the upshot of the natural-kind terms approach is that the falsity of a given empirical theory does not imply the non-existence of the referent of the terms used in this theory. The ancient Greeks might have had wildly false beliefs about 'gold' (e.g., they did not think it was an 'element'), but this does not mean that they did not refer to anything when they used this term. In fact, they successfully referred to the very same substance as we do; thus, the referential success does not depend on the truth of our theories.

This last feature of the natural-kind terms approach is obviously crucial in the context of the eliminative materialism debate. It seems that if it turned out that the term 'belief' had natural-kind semantics, then the eliminativist reasoning might be easily blocked: even if the premise of Churchland's reasoning – that folk psychology is a largely false theory – were true, its conclusion (that beliefs do not exist) would not follow. It might be the case that our theory about beliefs is mostly false, yet our term 'belief' refers to some cognitive natural kind: this is the suggestion made by Lycan (1988); Stich is more cautious in this respect, as he claims that which theory of reference is right is somehow underdetermined (both generally and in the specific case of the term 'belief'). However, even this more cautious conclusion is bad news for eliminativism: if it is indeterminate which theory of reference is the correct one for 'belief', then we cannot determine whether eliminativism is true (at least, according to Stich).

This way of refuting eliminativism suffers from two important weaknesses. First, it is highly controversial that the term 'belief' has a natural-kind semantics. It cannot be just stipulated by theoretical fiat that 'belief' has direct referential semantics: this claim demands strong justification. Elsewhere (Poslajko 2022), I have tried to show that there are strong reasons to think that 'belief' does not function in this way. I have tried to argue there that the concept of belief is plastic, i.e., it can survive changes in intension and extension and remain the same concept: my claim was that we do not have the intuition that in changing this concept we are constrained by the natural boundaries of this concept; this feature, in my view, precludes 'belief' from having natural-kind term semantics.

The other important thing about Lycan-Stich's argument is that it provides only a way of deflecting a certain (albeit popular) way of arguing for eliminative materialism. It is not intended to provide proof of the truth of belief realism, although there have been voices that suggest that it would be possible to establish the conclusion that beliefs are real on the basis of the assumption that the term 'belief' has natural-kind term semantics (see, e.g., Perez 2004). However, trying to show that beliefs are real solely on the basis of this assumption is not an easy task.

In general, the fact that some term 'X' has natural-kind term semantics does not in itself prove that Xs exist. In order to justify this positive ontological claim, one would also have to show that there is indeed a natural kind which the term 'X' denotes. There are some natural-kind terms which fail to refer to any natural kind (see, e.g., Besson (2012) for an overview of the issue of empty-kind terms). So, in order to justify realism about beliefs based on the idea of natural kinds, it would be necessary to show some evidence for the existence of a natural kind denoted by the term 'belief', but such an argument is hardly present in the literature concerning the Lycan/Stich argument.

Still this argument points to an important lacuna in the original eliminativist position, and if the eliminativist reasoning is to be successful, it has to be improved so as to include the possibility of 'belief' having a natural-kind term semantics. One might reasonably argue for some sort of eliminativistic conclusion regarding beliefs by way of showing that they do not constitute a natural kind (see, e.g., Jenson 2016). Such an argument, if successful, would prove that it is possible to defend eliminativism even in the context of the presupposition that 'belief' has a natural-kind term semantics. The issue of whether beliefs actually constitute a natural kind will be discussed in more detail in Chapter 6, section 1. The conclusion for now, however, is that the Lycan/Stich argument does not provide us with a silver-bullet argument against eliminativism.

2.3.3 Common-sense functionalism

An interesting yet somewhat underappreciated way of arguing against eliminative materialism was developed by proponents of so-called 'common-sense functionalism' (see Jackson & Pettit 1990, 1993). According to this line of thought, it is relatively easy to show that beliefs exist and to disprove the eliminativist claim in this way. According to Jackson and Pettit, in order to show that beliefs exist, one must show that people are truly describable by folk attributions of beliefs. On this approach, being truly describable by folk attributions of beliefs means satisfying the functional role specified by the folk theory of beliefs, which is characterized by appealing to platitudes, i.e., commonly held, trivial convictions about the role beliefs play. An example of a platitude about beliefs might be the conviction that beliefs are things that are often expressed by sincere assertions; another example is that beliefs tend to guide actions when coupled with appropriate desires, and so on.

Consider Jones: he is a person who, when asked, says that London is the best destination for a weekend break; given the chance to spend a weekend outside his hometown, he regularly goes to London to spend two days there, and he does so with visible excitement. In such a situation, it seems that we are perfectly justified in attributing to Jones a belief that London is the best destination for a weekend break. And there are countless similar examples of when we can say with utmost confidence that such and such a person has such and such a belief. If this is true, however, then we can quite easily show that beliefs exist: if it is true that Jones believes that London is the best destination for a weekend break, then there exists at least one belief.

Thus, we might say that people harbour beliefs as long as they satisfy the platitudes of the folk belief theory. This fact is, according to proponents of common-sense functionalism, largely independent of the future developments of neuroscience and cognitive science: this leads to the conclusion that although the truth of belief attributions is partly dependent on the empirical premises (it must be empirically true of people that they satisfy the platitudes of the folk theory of belief), it is somehow impossible that we could 'scientifically discover' that there are no beliefs. Regarding the common-sense functionalists take, the fact that we have beliefs can be established solely by means of establishing the content of the folk-psychological concept of belief and by trivial epistemic observations, no matter what science would say on that matter.

According to this account, the claim that people have beliefs has the status of being a sort of Moorean truth, i.e., it is an example of a claim which is taken to be obvious and trivially true and which cannot be easily denied (for Moore himself, the claim that there are external things had such a character; see Moore (1939)). Moorean truths are peculiar because their epistemic status is by default taken to be higher than any counter-claims that are motivated solely by appeal to philosophical theorizing. In this way, if we take something to be a Moorean truth, then we need to provide very strong reasons to deny it. Even though Moorean truths are not impervious to counter-arguments, such counter-arguments need to be very serious.

Thus, it seems fair to say that common-sense functionalism provides two strong arguments against eliminativism. The first is that the epistemic status of the claim that beliefs exist might be much stronger than the proponents of eliminative materialism suspect. If this is true, then the dialectics of this debate seem to be tilted against eliminativists, who have a heavy argumentative burden on their shoulders as they need to provide arguments which would be strong enough to convince us to reject central elements of our intuitive worldview. The second argument is that considerations concerning the possible future shape of cognitive science might not be the only ones that are relevant to the issue of the reality of beliefs. Reasons pertaining to common sense might also be important here, and it might even be the case that it is common sense that delivers the final argument for the claim that beliefs exist.

The most important conclusion that can perhaps be drawn from the common-sense functionalism proposal is that the claim that beliefs exist should be considered both epistemically secure and somewhat trivial. As a consequence, there is not much point arguing against it. However, as I shall argue in the course of this book, this conclusion need not close the issue of the reality of beliefs.

2.4 Mental fictionalism

Although the original eliminativist position regarding beliefs is not particularly popular nowadays, there has been a surge of interest in the broadly similar position of mental fictionalism. The guiding idea of this position is – to put it in the simplest terms – that we might retain the central insights of eliminative materialism whilst rejecting some of the problematic consequences of the original eliminativistic theory.

This way of motivating mental fictionalism was explicitly endorsed by Wallace, who wrote:

> A mental fictionalist is at heart a mental eliminativist, or mental agnostic. She maintains that common-sense folk psychology is somehow untrue. She may claim that the entities folk psychology quantifies over – belief states, desires, sensations, qualitative feels, propositional attitudes, etc. – either don't exist, or she has reason to doubt that they do. Yet she also maintains that folk psychology is incredibly useful, that ordinary discourse is riddled with it, and as such should not (or could not) be abandoned. Mental fictionalists aim to find a way to keep folk-psychological talk while rejecting the folk-psychological walk.
> (Wallace 2016, p. 407)

In this vein, mental fictionalists (apart from Wallace, this conception is either endorsed or discussed by, among others, Daly 2013, Demeter 2013, Joyce 2013, Toon 2016) retain the idea that our folk-psychological ascriptions of beliefs are somehow metaphysically deficient as there is (or might be) nothing in reality that corresponds to such attributions. However, what they reject from the original eliminativist theory is the idea that mental talk should be banished from our everyday talk because they see folk-psychological belief discourse as extremely useful or simply impossible to eliminate.

However, a question might arise at this point: how is it possible to retain a discourse which we know is not capable of correctly representing the 'parcel of reality' which it purports to represent? In short, if we assume that folk psychology is untrue and that beliefs do not exist, then how can we continue to use belief discourse in our everyday speech?

The answer that the fictionalists propose is quite simple: we might use belief talk even when we are aware of its deficiencies, as long as we treat it as a fictional discourse. This means that we adopt (or we should start to adopt) a certain fiction, namely the fiction of folk psychology, and we treat (or should start to treat) beliefs as existing in the context of this fiction.

There are two ways of conceptualizing what it means to adopt folk psychology as fiction. The first version, which was preferred by Wallace (2016) and was based on the general approach to fictionalism developed by Lewis (1978), consists in the claim that when we utter statements about beliefs (and other mental states) we treat them as implicitly containing a hidden prefix, namely 'According to mental fiction … '. Thus, we are not making any direct claims about any putative mental reality in this way; rather, we are speaking from within a certain fiction.

In the second version of mental fictionalism (see Toon 2016), which is based on Walton's (1993) theory of fiction, assertions about beliefs should be seen as moves in a special mentalistic game of make-believe. We use language as if we claimed that people had internal, causally active mental states, but this practice should be seen as consisting of acts of pretence rather than genuine assertions. Differences notwithstanding, both versions of fictionalism imply that ascriptions of beliefs are not literally true.

To make this idea clearer, consider again Jones, on the basis of whose assertions and behaviour we want to attribute the belief that London is the best weekend destination. According to mental fictionalism, we can still legitimately make this ascription even though we cannot say that is literally true. In the version of mental fictionalism based on prefix theory, the proper reading of such a statement would be something like 'according to folk-psychological fiction, Jones believes that London is the best weekend destination'. According to the pretence theory, we are not making a 'genuine' assertion when attributing this belief to Jones: rather, we are making a move in a game of psychological make-believe; this might be compared to a children's game in which one child is pretending to be an ogre which the other children say is 'devouring' someone. In this sense, when we see someone behaving intelligibly and making certain vocal assertions, we pretend that he has a certain mental state 'inside his head'. Both interpretations allow us to make this ascription without committing us to its literal truth.

As an alternative to eliminativism, mental fictionalism has several important theoretical advantages. First, it explicitly rejects the problematic 'futuristic' element of Churchland's original position, which was commonly thought to be incredible: fictionalism is not committed to the claim that at some point in the future we will stop using the belief idiom. Second, fictionalism makes bigger concessions to common sense: it provides a way of respecting folksy intuitions while adopting the central ontological claim of eliminativism.

However, there seems to be a significant problem with the cogency of mental fictionalism (this fact is noted by, among others, Joyce 2013, Wallace 2016). This issue stems from the fact that fictionalism in general rests on a substantial psychological assumption, namely the claim that there is a difference between two kinds of attitudes: the attitude of (genuine) belief, and the attitude we have towards fiction (this is stressed by, e.g., Joyce 2013).

This distinction is crucial for the feasibility of the fictionalist project. Imagine we wanted to adopt a fictionalist theory about morality but not towards a discourse about macroscopic physical objects. The problem is then that these discourses do not differ on the surface level. We say, in apparently the same manner, that certain objects are round and that certain deeds are evil. Yet, according to the proposed view, we must be able to tell the difference between the two statements as the first is factual and the other fictional. Thus, according to the fictionalist account, the distinction is on the level of the attitudes we harbour towards these statements. According to the fictionalist view, our attitude towards statements about macroscopic objects is different than our attitude towards normative statements. We believe that material objects have properties like mass, shape etc., yet we (merely) accept that actions are good or evil. (Proponents of so-called revolutionary fictionalism, such as Joyce [2001], claim that although we might at the present moment have an attitude of belief towards 'problematic' areas of discourse, we should change our attitude to that of accepting.)

This way of conceptualizing fictionalism generally makes the very idea of mental fictionalism problematic. Mental fictionalism denies that we can truly describe anything when we are using belief discourse, but this theory makes use of the notion of belief. This puts the whole enterprise in a precarious position: it seems that fictionalists simultaneously deny that there are beliefs whilst also presupposing their existence. This way of arguing against a mental fictionalist is a variant of the cognitive suicide argument which plagued classic eliminativist position. However, I believe this reasoning is more problematic for fictionalists than it was for eliminativists. The austere version of the classic eliminativist position, which boiled down to a negative ontological claim about belief, did not in itself have any psychological presuppositions. Yet, the fictionalist attempt to improve eliminativism incurs such theoretical debt and thus becomes more prone to counterarguments. Perhaps it would in principle be possible to formulate a 'purified' version of mental fictionalism that would eschew any psychological commitments, but as of now this is not an option that has been satisfactorily developed. (More detailed and sophisticated analysis of this argument and an attempt to defend fictionalism is provided by Wallace 2016; the issue of fictionalism will be discussed again in Chapter 8, section 1.)

The lesson from this certainly too brief analysis of belief-fictionalism is that it is valuable as a way of trying to overcome some of the strongly counterintuitive consequences of eliminativism. However, this position ultimately fails, and if one wants to retain anti-realism about beliefs, then one needs to do better: a more coherent and more plausible version of anti-realism is needed. But, before we attempt to formulate such a new proposal, let us try to diagnose what went wrong with the previous theories.

2.5 Presumptions of the debate

The conclusion from the previous sections is that although various versions of traditionally conceived anti-realism concerning beliefs fare better than is usually thought, these positions turn out to more or less implausible under close scrutiny. In this section, I want to propose a hypothesis concerning why these conceptions fail.

A somewhat popular opinion has it that the problems that any formulation of anti-realism about beliefs runs into show that this discourse is in some way privileged and there cannot be a coherent way of denying its reality (more on this line of thought in Chapter 8, sections 2 and 2.1). My view on this matter is more pedestrian: I do not think that there is any insurmountable obstacle to the idea of denying the reality of beliefs. Rather, the problems with all the theories discussed in this chapter stem from the way they conceptualize the basic intuition that beliefs are not real.

As I see it, the source of the problems of traditional eliminative materialism was its subscription to Quine-style meta-ontology and methodology of philosophy. It is now commonly accepted that one of Quine's main contributions in this area was his insistence that the philosophical question of realism should be asked in existential terms (Schaffer [2009] is one of the philosophers who stresses this aspect of Quine's legacy). For Quine, the basic question of ontology was, famously, 'what is there?' (Quine 1948). Thus, the philosophical issue of reality should be framed in terms of questions about existence. To be a realist about certain Xs in the Quinean framework is to endorse the claim that Xs exist, whereas to be an anti-realist is to say that Xs do not exist. So, to be a realist about tables is to say that tables exist, and to be an anti-realist about fictional characters is to say that there are no fictional characters.

The other important aspect of the Quinean tradition is that it provides us with a method to establish which putative entities we should include in our ontology. In order to do so, as Quine says, we need to establish our best theory of the world and then check what the ontological commitments of this theory are, i.e., what the entities are over which this theory quantifies. As admirers of desert landscapes, we should include in our ontology only those entities which are ineliminable ontological commitments of our best theories; we should dispose of anything that does not have the status of being a necessary commitment of our best theory.

Despite its admittedly simplistic character, this rather stereotypical description of Quineanism is useful in analysing the eliminativist position. If we see proponents of eliminative materialism as being Quineans in this sense, then their reasoning might be provisionally reconstructed as follows:

1. Beliefs are ontological commitments of folk psychology;
2. Folk psychology is a bad theory;
3. No good theory is committed to the existence of beliefs;
4. Only the ontological commitments of our best theory are to be seen as existing.
Conclusion:
Beliefs do not exist.

Such a 'naive Quinean' reconstruction of the eliminativist position was explicitly discussed by Stich (1983, p. 221-2), who admits being influenced at some point by this line of thinking (although he disavowed it in his 1983 exposition of eliminativism). For Stich, such a way of justifying eliminativism is mistaken as it unjustifiably equates existence with being explicitly mentioned in scientific theories: Stich correctly points out that in many cases we have no truck with treating certain objects and properties as existing, even though they are not quantified over in our best science.

However, Stich still considers science to play an important role in determining ontological questions. He conjectures (Stich 1983) that we might have good reason to disbelieve the existence of belief properties if the folk-psychological classification of mental states were drastically different from the scientific one or if science were capable of showing us that certain empirical presuppositions we make when we attribute beliefs to people would turn out to be false. Despite his repudiation of 'naive Quineanism', Stich (at last in his 1983) remains Quinean in one important aspect: for him, the possible failure of folk psychology would lead to the conclusion that beliefs do not exist. The Quinean aspect of this view is that it accepts the move from a denial that certain existence claims are true relative to some successful science, to a denial that these claims are true simpliciter.

Such an ontological framing of the negative conclusion in the area of belief metaphysics is, in my opinion, what makes this conclusion unpalatable. The direct consequence of the claim that beliefs do not exist is, on a standard reading, the thesis that no simple first-order positive statements about beliefs can ever be true, and that there are no positive facts concerning beliefs; in short, it leads to a version of irrealism about beliefs (for a general definition of irrealism, see Boghossian 1990). Such an irrealist commitment is also shared by non-cognitivism and fictionalism as both these positions lead to the conclusion that attributions of beliefs are not true, and the claim that 'beliefs exist' is also not true. According to expressivism about belief (at least in its classic version), these statements are taken to lack truth-value; most versions of fictionalism about beliefs also lead to the denial that the statements in question can be true in a literal sense. Both these positions are thus versions of Quinean anti-realism in the broad sense as they lead to denial of the positive ontological claim about beliefs.

In all of these theories, such denial of the literal truth of the claim that beliefs exist is linked to the denial that ascriptions of beliefs can ever be true: for classical eliminativists, they are uniformly false; for classical expressivists, they lack truth-value; and, for fictionalists, they are true only relative to a certain fiction. But this idea that ascriptions of beliefs can never be literally true might be seen as the main problematic aspect of these views. To say that we can never truly say of anyone that they have a belief even in the most mundane cases strikes us as utterly counter-intuitive. Although the popular inconsistency charges levelled against the traditional forms of belief anti-realism might be debunked by means of introducing philosophical technicalities, it certainly feels paradoxical to deny that proponents of eliminativism believe their own theory. As Putnam famously quipped, eliminativists contend that 'people only believed that they had beliefs' (see Putnam 1987, p. 16). Because denying the truth of belief ascriptions goes hand in hand with the negative ontological thesis about beliefs, it might be conjectured that the implausible character of belief irrealism is what motivates many philosophers to resist the negative ontological claim about beliefs.

Arguments that are produced against different forms of irrealism about beliefs are mainly negative: they rarely aim to show us positive proof for the claim that there are such states as beliefs. Instead, they show that a fully irrealist view about beliefs is unacceptable for some reason or other; consequently, they want us to reject the negative ontological claim about beliefs.

However, even if we had good reasons to reject both irrealism about beliefs and the negative ontological claim about them, this would not in itself show that there are good reasons to think that there are indeed beliefs in the sense that we have internal, causally active states which are vehicles of propositional contents. Such reasons show only that we cannot accept the claim that beliefs do not exist, nor can we embrace the resulting belief irrealism.

There seems to be room to claim that we are dealing with two separate problems here. The first problem concerns whether we do indeed have certain internal states which can be characterized as beliefs; the second concerns whether the negative ontological claim about beliefs might be coherently and plausibly maintained. Once we see these issues as distinct, we start to see the possibility of questioning the reality of beliefs in a way that is different from how it has traditionally been conceived. The broadly Quinean approach, according to which denying the reality of beliefs equates to claims that beliefs do not exist and that their attributions can never be true, need not be taken as the only game in town.

This conclusion provides the motivation for the central idea of this book: that we should try to express the distinction between realism and anti-realism concerning beliefs in some other way. This new way should preferably not focus on the issue of existence as a defining feature of anti-realism about beliefs. Nor should it question the possibility of making true belief attributions. Even though it seems obvious for many philosophers that the question of realism is inevitably linked to the issue of truth and existence, it seems worthwhile to look for an alternative, given the fact that the traditional approach does not allow us to frame scepticism about beliefs in a satisfactory manner. Such an alternative framework will be developed in the next chapters.

3

The deflationary gambit

The previous chapter's conclusion was that, in order to create a viable form of anti-realism about belief, the idea that beliefs are not real must be decoupled from irrealism about beliefs. This means that what is needed is a formulation of the claim that beliefs are not real that would not commit us to the denial of their existence nor the truth of their ascriptions.

The very idea of such a position might seem unconvincing: how could we claim that beliefs are unreal yet existing? This chapter will be devoted to developing such a position. In my view, it is possible to make the question of whether beliefs are real as intelligible and non-trivial as possible, even if we accept that the statement 'beliefs exist' is true. What is needed is some alternative meta-metaphysical framework to ask the realism question in a way that would not equate the question of realism to the question of existence. The construction of this framework in this chapter will proceed as follows: First, I will present the general deflationary framework which would allow us to secure a positive answer to the question of whether beliefs exist. Second, in this framework I will introduce the general idea of making the distinction between what's real and what's not real, along with some specific examples of proposals of this distinction. Third, I will present my proposal of how to make this distinction in the specific case of beliefs.

3.1 Deflationism in general ontology

The ontological framework that is most pertinent to the aims stated above is contemporary metaontological deflationism, which was proposed, among others, by Schiffer (1996, 2003), Thomasson (2015) and Wright (1992). According to deflationism, questions about existence should be seen as being easy (this is stressed by Thomasson 2015), which means that such questions can be answered by appeal to some epistemically straightforward considerations. This puts deflationism in stark contrast to orthodox Quineanism, which treats ontological questions as substantial. Thomasson (2015, p. 17) observes that in the broadly conceived Quinean tradition, questions about existence are 'epistemically metaphysical' (to use Sider's [2011] phrase): this means that they cannot be resolved by straightforward empirical observation or simple conceptual analysis. The deflationists, on the other hand, want to see existence questions as being trivial (in a non-disparaging sense). For them, establishing a positive existential conclusion is far easier than most philosophers have imagined.

Let us take a closer look at the specific deflationary proposals. The starting point of Wright's version of deflationism is the idea of minimalism about truth-aptitude, namely the claim that all well-formed and disciplined (i.e. governed by rules of usage) statements can be considered true or false. This claim holds true even in discourses that might be considered problematic from the metaphysical point of view, such as normative discourse. The statement 'genocide is evil' might be considered true or false purely on the grounds that this is a well-formed declarative statement and that there are socially acceptable rules for use of statements of this kind. Our scruples about the status of normative facts have nothing to do with this observation. This approach to truth-aptitude has important ontological consequences (this is stressed by Divers & Miller 1995): if we have a minimally truth-apt singular sentence which we consider true, then we have to admit the existence of the object to which the singular term refers. Number terms are an excellent example here: as simple arithmetical statements are truth-apt, and many of them are arguably true (like the statement 'three is a prime number'), we must admit that numbers exist. In this way we prove the existence of numbers by means of a fairly uncomplicated line of reasoning.

Schiffer's (1996, 2003) approach gives the central role to the idea of 'something-from-nothing' transformations. Let us consider the question of whether properties exist. According to Schiffer, we might provide a positive answer quite easily. We start with some uncontroversial premise like 'grass is green', then we observe that this statement is semantically equivalent to the statement 'grass has the property of being green'. The latter statement commits us to the existence of properties, so we are entitled to say that we inferred the existence of properties from an uncontroversial premise. In this way, we get something from nothing: the first statement of our reasoning has apparently fewer ontological commitments than the latter. (It is worth mentioning that Schiffer's approach was originally meant to be a local one that is applicable to the issue of the existence of propositions and of properties. However, as we shall see in the next section, this view might be generalized to other questions, including the question of the existence of beliefs.)

On Thomasson's (2015) account, the process of answering the question about the existence of certain Xs has two parts. First, using the method of conceptual analysis, we must establish what the application criteria for the term 'X' are. Second, we need to empirically check whether these criteria are met; in some cases this would be fairly trivial. Take the example of chairs: if we wanted to prove that chairs exist, we would need to establish the criteria of application of the term 'chair', and then see whether these criteria are met. Both steps are fairly unproblematic, so we might easily establish the existence of chairs. Obviously, in some cases, the empirical element of the inquiry would not be trivial (establishing the existence of black holes is more empirically demanding than establishing the existence of chairs). Still, no metaphysically profound investigation is needed in either case.

All these three approaches, although different in detail, share a similar attitude: existence questions are not to be treated as philosophically problematic. The idea is that there should be a general presumption towards ontological realism, even in cases in which many philosophers would have serious reservations about the existence of certain things/states/properties. One important consequence of this approach is that we should not treat questions about existence as central for philosophical controversies. This might lead us to adopt some sort of philosophical quietism, i.e., the view according to which there are no important and substantial philosophical questions. However, such quietism is, as we will see in the course of this chapter, not a necessary consequence of the deflationary approach.

One thing is important to note here: a deflationary view of existence does not have to lead to the view that entities/facts/properties that exist in the deflationary sense are mind-dependent (or 'created by humans'). If we take Thomasson's example of ordinary objects as instructive, this should be quite obvious. Although chairs are man-made and they belong to the category of artifacts, other ordinary objects, such as rocks, are not. These and similar ordinary objects exist in deflationary sense, yet they are not mind-dependent. For Thomasson it is obvious that such ordinary objects are not modally dependent on human mental states as they exist in possible worlds where there are no humans. Of course, some of the things that exist in a deflationary sense are mind-dependent, but mind-dependence claims are not a necessary feature of deflationism.

3.2 Deflationary approaches and the existence of beliefs

The general deflationary approach to existence questions can be quite easily extended to the category of beliefs. The resulting position would amount to the claim that the question of the existence of beliefs might be solved 'easily' and a positive answer to this question might be established without the need to engage in any epistemically metaphysical inquiry.

The idea of applying the deflationary meta-ontological framework to the issue of existence of beliefs has been explicitly proposed and forcefully defended by Mölder (2010), who applies Schiffer's ideas to this case. In Mölder's framework, mental properties, such as the property of possessing a particular belief, should be seen as being pleonastic properties, i.e., as products of something-from-nothing transformations. For Mölder, the fact that there are mental properties can be established solely on the basis of the observation that mental properties are ascribable to humans.

Mölder's idea is certainly ingenious: his theory is probably the most developed explicit application of the idea of meta-ontological deflationism to the area of beliefs (and other propositional attitudes). Still, I cannot endorse it here in its entirety as his deflationary approach to the existence of mental states is embedded in his broader project, which is a defence of the interpretivist approach to the nature of mental states. This broader project might be deemed controversial for reasons that will be spelled out later. What needs to be stressed here, however, is that these two points are, in principle, distinct: the general deflationary way of answering the existence question about beliefs is, on a conceptual level, separable from any definite theory about their nature. It is only the first deflationary claim that I wish to endorse here. (I will have some more to say about the issues that arise from the second interpretivist claim in Chapter 5, section 2; see also my Poslajko 2020).

The deflationary approach to existence might be seen as being implicitly presupposed by some other theories of beliefs. Common-sense functionalism, which was discussed in Chapter 2, section 3.3, might be treated as a prime example of this. In the common-sense functionalist framework, we need to do two things to establish the existence of beliefs. First, we need to establish the content of the folk-psychological concept of belief; second, we need to check whether actual subjects satisfy the functional roles defined within this folk theory. This idea might be seen as roughly parallel to Thomasson's view on how to answer existence questions. Thus, common-sense functionalism might be seen as being a version of easy ontology *avant le lettre*.

In a sense, all the 'mildly realistic' positions in the metaphysics of beliefs might be seen as being somehow similar to the generally deflationary approach to the issue of the existence of belief: these positions include dispositionalism (Ryle 1949), neo-dispositionalism (Schwitzgebel 2002) and various versions of interpretivism (see Davidson 1970, Dennett 1989). All of these theories try to defend the idea that we might say that beliefs exist, but these theories do so without committing to any problematic metaphysical theses in general, nor to Fodor-style industrial-strength realism (namely, the notion that belief attribution must track some deep mechanisms in the brain) in particular. In this way, these views all qualify as 'easy' approaches to the ontology of beliefs.

To sum up, the deflationary answer to the question of the existence of beliefs would consist, on a most general level, in saying that we only need to engage in trivial conceptual analysis and empirical observations. There is no need for deep metaphysical or scientific 'proofs' in order to establish that ordinary people have beliefs and that the attributions of them which we make in ordinary contexts are truth-apt and often true.

This deflationary story about the existence of beliefs strikes me as generally plausible. The concept of belief is taken from our folksy repertoire, and there is something correct in the idea that the application criteria for such folksy terms involve only trivial empirical observations. Moreover, it seems right that scientific discoveries cannot really refute existential claims about beliefs. The idea that tables should be seen as not existing merely because we discovered that they are composed of micro-particles is extremely suspicious; the application criteria of the term 'table' seem to be more or less independent from the issues of atomic composition and so forth. Similarly, the folksy criteria of the application of the term 'belief' seem to be independent of the discoveries of cognitive science. As Dennett (1989) notes, we competently use folk-psychological jargon without any deep knowledge about neural mechanisms and the like. This strongly suggests that the conditions for the correct application of mental terms are independent of any 'deep' metaphysical and scientific facts.

If we embrace the general deflationary approach to existence – plus the idea that the application criteria for the term 'belief' are superficial – then the conclusion that beliefs exist is perfectly justified. Consider the example of Dave, who is an ardent proponent of conspiracy theories, especially ones concerning the attacks on World Trade Centre. He goes about claiming that 'Bush did 9/11', gathers lots of information supporting the theories, is willing to engage in discussion with anyone on the issue and so on. In such a case, we might be perfectly justified in ascribing to Dave the belief that Bush is responsible for the 9/11 attacks. This attribution seems to be both truth-apt and true; if this is so, there is at least one belief that someone has, namely the belief possessed by Dave. It is quite improbable that our appreciation of the truth of this attribution would be radically challenged by any future developments in cognitive science or neuroscience, or by any metaphysical argumentation. The reason for this immunity of belief attributions, however, is not any putative fact about the metaphysically privileged status of beliefs; rather, the reason is that we should see the truth of belief attributions as being minimal, and we should see the reasoning which leads us to accept the existence of these states as being easy.

Again, the important thing to stress here is that embracing the deflationary approach to the issue of existence of beliefs does not have to lead to the view according to which beliefs are mind-dependent. As was noted in the previous section, the deflationary account of existence does not necessitate any claims about mind-dependence (but it does not exclude them either). The issue of whether beliefs can be seen as mind-dependent will be discussed in the further sections and chapters.

3.3 Saving the differences in the deflationary framework

This book might have ended with the previous section: I might have simply argued that the deflationary approach to existence questions provides us with an easy and elegant solution to the issue of the existence of beliefs and that the threat of eliminativism might consequently be avoided. It would then seem that we should forget about any metaphysical scruples about the reality of beliefs; we should rest assured that much less evidence is needed to establish the claim that beliefs exist than we previously thought.

This would, however, be too hasty a conclusion. What we have established so far is just that the claim 'beliefs exist' should be accepted as true. But, as has been already noted, this claim might be taken to be distinct from the thesis that beliefs are real. Some philosophers might opt for quietism and say that no further philosophical questions about beliefs are needed; however, this is not the only option. We might try to inquire more deeply into the issue of the reality of beliefs.

There is a growing trend in philosophy of attempting to frame the question of realism in a non-ontological manner. According to this line of thought, we should see various potential problematic entities/properties/facts as existing by default and try to ask difficult metaphysical questions in another way. (The distinction between ontology, which is seen as 'easy', and metaphysics, which might be considered substantial, is explicitly drawn by Thomasson [2015], although, for her, metaphysics deals with issues other than the question of realism, e.g., with modal issues.) The gist of the view according to which we might distinguish between the real and the non-real in the broadly deflationary framework is that it is possible to distinguish the elements of our ontology that are 'substantial' from those which are 'lightweight'/'insubstantial'. Deflationary ontology might be extremely inclusive, but there might be important reasons to deny that all its elements have equal philosophical standing. For various reasons, some of them might be treated as not fully real.

One area of philosophical inquiry in which this way of thinking became popular is meta-ethics. As was noted in Chapter 2, section 1, there is little enthusiasm nowadays for the claim that normative statements are simply not truth-apt. Many prominent meta-ethicians of the anti-realist persuasion, especially from the expressivist camp (the most prominent ones being Blackburn [1993] and Gibbard [2012]), now accept the idea that we should treat normative statements as being truth-apt (and often true); they also have no problem admitting that there are normative properties and facts, as we commonly refer to them in our everyday discourse. However, the central idea of quasi-realism is that although normative facts and properties exist, they should be seen as less substantial than ordinary facts. They are not real but quasi-real, and the propositions that refer to them serve different functions than those that we use to describe ordinary facts.

The crucial question which arises within the context of quasi-realism is how to distinguish between the real and the quasi-real: there is a lurking danger that if we cannot make this distinction clear, then quasi-realism would, as it were, collapse into realism (this is pointed out by Dreier 2004). This problem stems from the fact that quasi-realists are committed to embracing all commonly accepted truths about the normative domain. But, if they do so, they must face the question of how their position is different from full-blooded realism.

There are many possible answers to this question. Some philosophers point to the differences between the attitudes that are expressed by normative vs. factual statements (see, e.g., Gibbard 2012). For some others, the difference lies in the functional roles of normative and factual vocabularies (see, e.g., Price 2013). Other theorists try to put this difference in more explicitly metaphysical terms: Blackburn (1993), for example, suggests that the difference might be framed in terms of what he calls the Eleatic principle. He introduces this concept as follows: 'if the convergence in the opinion that p is best explained by the fact that the opinion was caused by the fact that p, then we should treat "p" realistically'

(Blackburn 1993, p. 31–2). Thus, realistic discourses are those in which our opinions about the area in question are explained by the idea of them tracking reality; in discourses which deserve to be treated quasi-realistically, we do not resort to such explanations.

Outside the area of meta-ethics, there are more general metaphysical projects which try to establish the difference between the real and the non-real in ways other than by questioning the existence of 'problematic' entities. Two prominent examples of such approaches can be found in Fine's and Wright's writings.

Fine (2001), unsurprisingly, frames his view on how to distinguish the real from the non-real in terms of grounding, i.e., the relation of metaphysical determination that supposedly obtains between fundamental and non-fundamental facts. In Fine's view, there is a small class of fundamental facts that are real by default, and everything that is fully grounded by these fundamental facts is also real. Facts which are not fully grounded by real facts, i.e., they are at least partially grounded by non-fundamental or otherwise non-real facts, are to be treated as not real. There are two important features of Fine's proposal. First, it is unashamedly metaphysical: the question of realism is not to be reduced on this account to any semantic or pragmatic considerations. Second, he clearly distinguishes the issue of fundamentality from the question of realism: for him it is clear that not only fundamental entities should count as fully real, therefore there is a place for non-fundamental yet real objects in this framework.

Wright's project, presented in his 'Truth and Objectivity' (Wright 1992), is remarkably ambitious: he aims to provide not one but several criteria for distinguishing between realist and anti-realist discourses. The starting point of his discussion is the postulate of accepting minimalism about truth-aptitude with regard to metaphysically problematic discourses. Wright insists, however, that if we agree that a given discourse contains truth-apt statements, there is a further question to be asked: should the truth predicate applicable in a given area of discourse be seen as minimal or substantial? Thus, the central role in Wright's approach to conceptualizing the real/anti-real distinction is played by the notion of truth. The fact of whether in a certain area of discourse the operative concept of truth is minimalist or substantial hinges on further issues: we might need to establish whether truth in that context exceeds assertability, or whether putative facts in a given area are required to explain a convergence of opinions, etc. It would be impossible here to give full justice to the breath of Wright's project, but let us note that this approach has one important aspect: there might not be a single, unique way of establishing whether a certain area of discourse requires substantial truth and should consequently be seen in the realist light.

To sum up, all these examples show that there are several ways in which one might wish to introduce a distinction between real and non-real in the broadly deflationary framework. There still seems to be room to make important metaphysical distinctions about the status of the facts/entities/properties that we include in our permissive ontology. This conclusion is of particular importance in the context of the present book: the idea that we can make room in the deflationary framework for the distinction between what is real and what is not-real can be straightforwardly applied to the case of beliefs. This idea has already been tried out in the literature, so let us take a look at some of the existing attempts to frame the issue of the reality of beliefs in this way.

Wright himself explicitly applied his theory to the area of attitudes (Wright 2002): for him, if one wanted to embrace anti-realism towards this subject, one – on pain of being outright inconsistent – must adopt a view according to which sentences of attitudinal discourse are truth-apt, yet they do not meet the criteria of a fully factual discourse. As Wright puts it:

> The proposal to be reviewed, then, is that the proper outlet for the psychological noncognitivist is minimalism. Such a theorist should allow that psychological discourse is genuinely assertoric and highly disciplined and thereby sustains the introduction over its characteristic claims of a predicate with all the essential features of a truth predicate. But she should insist that nothing is true of psychological discourse that should motivate the interpretation of this predicate in terms of the imagery of correspondence to external, objective matters, in the fashion characteristic of realism.
>
> (Wright 2002, p. 219–20)

Wright presents this possible view as the most plausible version of anti-realism about attitudes. Still, he rejects this option as inconsistent. His argument for this claim is, however, both controversial and complex, and for this reason I will postpone detailed discussion of it for the later part of the book (see Chapter 8, section 2.1). At this point, let me just note two things: first, it is explicitly acknowledged by Wright that it is at least possible to try to formulate anti-realism about attitudes by invoking minimalism; second, it seems reasonable to say that Wright's way of delineating the real/anti-real distinction is, as I will presently argue, not best suited to the job in this particular region of discourse.

As was noted in the previous chapter, some philosophers (see Evans & Shah 2012, Toppinen 2015) have attempted to answer the question of whether it is possible to embrace a quasi-realist view on the status of beliefs (and other propositional attitudes) that is modelled on quasi-realism about the normative. According to such a view, we should see attributions of beliefs as capable of being true or false in a deflationary sense; however, we should see facts about this area as only quasi-real. Again, there have been serious worries about the cogency of such a view, but these cannot be fully discussed here: a more detailed analysis of this proposal and criticism of it can be found in my other work (see Poslajko 2024).

Mölder (2010), whose theory serves as an important source of inspiration for the proposal developed here, might also be interpreted as trying to introduce some sort of distinction between the strongly real and the less real in a deflationary ontological framework. This is because he distinguishes between 'pleonastic' and 'natural' properties; he places beliefs in the former category, which might be seen as being less metaphysically committing. Although Mölder himself does not embrace the label of anti-realism, from an external perspective his views can be seen as leading to the conclusion that beliefs fall into the category of less real properties/states. A more detailed discussion of his position and of interpretivism in general will be presented in Chapter 5, section 2.

The general idea under discussion in these proposals is that it might be possible to claim that beliefs are not real, even if we agree that the deflationary account of existence allows us to secure the truth of the claim that beliefs exist. In other words, these proposals point to the option that we might be able to put forward the view that beliefs fall in the non-real category, while at the same time denying strong irrealism. But the question now arises of whether any of the presented proposals will fit the specific character of the debate about the reality of beliefs.

This question is not easy to answer because the metaphysical landscape is extremely rugged in this region of inquiry: there is a plethora of possible ways in which it would be possible to fill in the details of a general picture in which the deflationary approach to the existence of beliefs would be merged with an anti-realist account of them. Any attempt to provide a comprehensive overview and assessment of such hypothetical proposals would probably require more space than a single book (and would not be particularly illuminating). For these reasons, I will not present such an overview here. Instead, I will take a theoretical shortcut: I will provide a novel account of the real/non-real distinction in the hope that this proposal will be illuminating in the context of the debate about the metaphysics of beliefs.

My proposal on how to think about the real vs non-real distinction has no ambition to be a universally correct one. In fact, I have a strong feeling that it might indeed be the case that distinct discourses require distinct conceptualizations of this divide. What counts as a good marker of realness in the context of the normative discourse might not do the trick in the debate about the reality of mathematical objects. So, on my terms, my proposal will count as a successful one if it allows us to gain significant new theoretical insights into the specific area of the metaphysics of beliefs. In this context, I propose seeing the distinction between the real and the non-real in terms of the distinction between natural and non-natural properties, as defined by Lewis (1983). Although this distinction was not originally intended to serve as a criterion of realism, there are some important reasons to think that it can be used in this context.

3.4 Proposal for the belief debate: Lewis's theory

In what follows, I hope to show that there are significant theoretical advantages to adopting a conceptual framework which merges a deflationary approach to existence with the view according to which the distinction between the real and the non-real (in the specific context of the debate about belief realism) should be seen in terms of the Lewisian distinction between natural and non-natural properties. To name a few of these advantages: first, adopting a conceptual framework allows us to introduce a certain theoretical unity into various debates on the metaphysics of beliefs; second, it helps to formulate the anti-realist position in a coherent manner; and thirdly, it will make the debate about the reality of beliefs more tractable. So, let us present this proposal in more detail.

Lewis (1983) introduced the distinction between natural and non-natural properties in the context of the debate about universals. His main aim was to defend a certain version of nominalism about universals, and to do so in the context of modal realism, namely the conviction that other possible worlds not only exist but are as genuine as the world we happen to inhabit. Lewis is committed to both realism about set theory and possible worlds, and from these commitments it automatically follows (see, e.g., Hall 2016) that transworld sets exist, i.e., sets of objects which exist in different possible worlds, as well as sets of ordered pairs/triples, etc. of such possible objects.

Lewis contends that we might consider such modal sets to be properties and, by way of analogy, sets of ordered pairs/triplets, etc. to be relations. So, simplifying a bit, the property of being green is a set of all green objects that exist in all possible worlds. The relation of 'being older than' is a set of all pairs of possible objects, where the first member of the pair is older than the second, etc.

Such a definition of properties and relations is, according to Lewis, quite useful, as properties understood in this way might be used as semantic values of abstract singular terms such as 'redness'. However, as Lewis rightly notes, this is an abundant view of properties: this view implies that there is an extremely large number of properties and relations, many of which are such that we have never referred to them or thought of them. This is because, for any possible combination of objects across possible worlds, there is a set that contains these and only these objects, which means that there is a property that these objects share. So, for example, there is a property which is exemplified solely by my nose and by Ludwig Wittgenstein's youngest daughter, etc.

The drawback of the abundant conception of properties is that properties as conceptualized within this framework are unable to do some of the theoretical work which they are supposed to do. As Lewis put it:

> Because properties are so abundant, they are undiscriminating. Any two things share infinitely many properties, and fail to share infinitely many others. That is so whether the two things are perfect duplicates or utterly dissimilar. Thus properties do nothing to capture facts of resemblance. ... Likewise, properties do nothing to capture the causal powers of things. Almost all properties are causally irrelevant, and there is nothing to make the relevant ones stand out from the crowd. Properties carve reality at the joints – and everywhere else as well.
>
> (Lewis 1983, p. 1983)

To do the theoretical jobs that Lewis listed, we need a concept of 'sparse properties' (sometimes branded 'truly natural' or 'fundamental') that would be discriminating enough to be exemplified only by those objects which are genuinely similar and that share the same causal powers. Let us assume that 'having a mass of 1 kg' is a sparse property. Then, the objects which shared this property could be said to be truly similar and as sharing some real causal powers (unlike objects which share only abundant properties). The fact that a certain property is a (truly) natural one should be seen as being primitive, although Lewis acknowledges the possibility that less nominalistically inclined philosophers would have a tendency to see these natural properties as genuine universals.

There is a strong supposition that genuinely natural properties would be extremely sparse, i.e., that there would be only few of them; most probably, only fundamental properties of the future complete physical theory would count as truly natural, and the current state of the physical sciences suggests that the future theories will be austere in their vocabularies. One of the main arguments for treating only properties of fundamental physics as perfectly natural is the idea of duplicates: two objects which shared all the fundamental physical properties would be (near-)perfect duplicates, assuming that some form of physicalism is true (Lewis 1983, p. 356–7).

However, a theory which included only perfectly natural properties and treated all other properties on a par would certainly be insufficient for other theoretical needs. For example, properties which are part of special sciences would have to be treated as being non-natural, and their status would then be similar to random collections. Thus, Lewis postulates that we should treat the natural/non-natural distinction as graded. Apart from perfectly natural properties and completely non-natural ones, there is a group of 'less elite' natural properties that are somewhat natural as they are connected to perfectly natural properties via definitional links: this means that a reasonably natural property is one which might be defined in terms of perfectly natural properties via a reasonably short formula. In the case of 'merely abundant' properties, such a definition is either unattainable or would be extremely long and cumbersome.

Lewis intends the natural/non-natural distinction to play a theoretical role not in the context of realism but in the context of the debate about universals (for him, natural and non-natural properties are equally real). However, this idea might also be used to illuminate the realism debate. Conceptualizing the real/unreal distinction in Lewisian terms is certainly a non-standard theoretical move, but it is not entirely new: there have been important and interesting attempts to use this distinction to characterize the issue of realism.

Stoljar (2014) uses the Lewisian framework to provide an interpretation of Chomsky's (2000) infamous London argument. Chomsky claims that if we looked for a 'reference' for terms like 'London', we would have a hard time finding a referent which would be acceptable from the point of view of natural sciences. This is because the boundaries of the physical place called 'London' vary over time and, worse still, in some uses we treat the putative referent of London as something immaterial. Some (Kennedy & Stanley 2009) have claimed that these remarks of Chomsky can be read as the (implausible) claim that London does not exist. However, Stoljar suggests that a more charitable interpretation of Chomsky would be to say that according to Chomsky 'being London' is not a natural property. This interpretation, according to Stoljar, should be extended to Chomsky's scruples about the ontological status of desks: it would be implausible to say that there are no desks, but the claim that the property of being desk is not a natural one has a bigger claim to plausibility. What is important to note here is that Chomsky's target is not only the ontology of desks and cities but also the status of folk-semantic and folk-psychological properties: this aspect of Chomsky's thought will be discussed more deeply in Chapter 5, section 3.

Another example of using the natural vs non-natural properties distinction in the context of the debate on realism can be found in McPherson (2015). He uses the Lewisian distinction to conceptualize the differences between various positions in meta-ethics, especially between those which he characterizes as 'deflationary naturalism' and 'Moorean non-naturalism'. McPherson notices that these two views might be seen as being more or less indistinguishable as they both oppose a straightforward reduction of normative facts to fundamental natural facts, yet they see these facts as existing. However, they seem to be intuitively different: deflationary naturalism sees normative facts and properties as metaphysically insubstantial, whereas Moorean non-naturalism takes them to be metaphysically fundamental. McPherson's suggestion is that in order to appreciate the distinction between these two theories we should see the proponent of the Moorean approach as postulating a distinct 'normative' class of elite properties, whereas the deflationary naturalist sees normative properties as being merely abundant. Thus, by invoking the notion of 'elite properties' we are able to distinguish between positions which postulate deep, metaphysically fundamental normative facts, and those which see normative facts and properties as being metaphysically lightweight.

The Lewisian distinction also plays an important role in Edwards's (2013) account of the difference between deflationary and substantial accounts of truth. Contemporary deflationists (unlike their predecessors) do not claim that there is no such property as being true (see also Damnjanovic 2010 for such a characterization of contemporary deflationism). The deflationists nowadays want to say that what is special about their account of truth is that they see truth as being an insubstantial, purely logical, transparent property, whereas the proponents of inflationary theories (like correspondence or coherence theory) see truth as a substantive property. Edwards raises the question of precisely how we should interpret this difference between substantial and insubstantial properties in this context. The answer is that it is the Lewisian distinction between abundant and sparse properties that is supposed to do the job here. Thus, in Edwards's account, a deflationist is someone who sees truth to be merely an abundant property in Lewis's sense, whereas proponents of the inflationary approach see truth as a sparse/natural property. Obviously, on the inflationary take, truth is to be taken to be a 'less elite' natural property, not a fundamental one: there is little reason to expect that truth would be a fundamental property, but inflationists see 'being true' as a reasonably natural property.

The case of truth is instructive for the purposes of the debate about the reality of beliefs. It would indeed be implausible to say that there is no such property as being true if we took this claim literally as leading to the conclusion that the predicate 'is true' has an empty extension. The claim that no sentence/proposition is true is paradoxical and is patently false from the common-sense point of view. Still, deflationists want to somehow put the reality of the truth-property in question; if Edwards is right, then the most plausible way of doing so is by invoking the notion of abundant and sparse properties.

Thus, in Edwards's reading, deflationists are theorists who are ready to accept the truth of many statements which contain a truth predicate; e.g., they have no problem with saying that the statement '>>Snow is white<< is true' is true. Moreover, they do not hesitate to admit that there is a property of being true because the truth-predicate has an extension. However, they wish to deny that the truth-property has any deep nature. The truth-property is to be seen as a purely logical/transparent one, so its attributions do not track objective similarities, and there is no explanatory benefit in attributing truth. Additionally, the idea of looking for any explanation of this property in terms of more metaphysically fundamental properties is futile. On this point, the deflationists would obviously disagree with inflationists, but their debate would not be trivial.

To sum up, Stoljar, McPherson and Edwards propose that we should see the difference between the real and the non-real as explicable in terms of the distinction between natural and non-natural properties. In this general approach, to be a realist about a certain area of discourse is to say that the discourse in question targets natural properties in Lewis's sense. To be an anti-realist about an area of discourse is to say that although there are properties that the discourse in question is about, these properties are not natural ones in the Lewisian sense.

However, a question now arises: how to square this definition with the idea that the distinction between natural and non-natural properties is graded? This means that there are properties which cannot be classified as being perfectly natural or completely non-natural. The broad category of such 'in-between' properties includes many properties which are of particular philosophical interest. For example, the properties of special sciences which are multiply realizable by fully natural properties are neither perfectly natural nor completely non-natural. They are not perfectly natural as they supervene on the most natural; they are not completely non-natural as they play some important explanatory roles in the special sciences and capture important similarities between higher-level phenomena. The same might be said about some of the 'human kinds', especially those which exhibit the 'looping effect' described by

Hacking (1995): they also cannot be seen as perfectly natural because, in a sense, they are socially constructed; however, neither are they completely non-natural as they have genuine effect on social reality.

So, how can we fit this graded distinction into the binary opposition between the real and the non-real? The answer is that we should treat only reasonably natural properties as real, and those which are not reasonably natural should be treated as not real. But this answer needs to be supplemented by a more robust idea of what differentiates reasonably natural properties from those that cannot be said to be reasonably natural. Following Edwards (2013), I will adopt a view according to which to be a reasonably natural property is to be a property which is not perfectly natural but can still be said to ground objective similarities, be relevant in causal explanations, and be appropriately linked to perfectly natural properties.

So, to be a realist in a particular domain is to claim that the properties that the discourse in question targets are either perfectly or reasonably natural. To be an anti-realist is to say that although the properties which we talk about in given area of discourse exist, they cannot be seen as reasonably natural. This general definition can be straightforwardly applied to the case of beliefs. Thus, a realist about belief is someone who is committed to two claims: first, that beliefs exist; second, that belief attributions track (reasonably) natural properties in Lewis's sense. A minimal non-realist about belief is someone who admits that beliefs exist yet denies that belief attributions track natural properties (in the sense of less elite yet still reasonably natural properties).

Thus, a minimal non-realist about beliefs is someone who admits that many of our mundane attributions of beliefs are truth-apt and are often true. As a consequence, proponents of such a view would say that beliefs exist. Yet, they would try to retain some metaphysical scruples about the category of belief. They want to say that belief attributions do not track any deep facts about our mental lives and that the property of belief is not an elite, natural one. In this way, they wish to retain the ability to disagree with the belief realists without falling into the theoretical problems which plagued other forms of belief anti-realism.

An analogy with the deflationary account of truth might help us see the attraction of such a view about beliefs. Maintaining that no elementary statements belonging to either truth-discourse or belief discourse can be true is counter-intuitive and might be deemed self-defeating. Yet, there seems to be a logical space for some sort of denial of the full reality of both of the phenomena in question: if we do not buy into some sort of transcendentalism, we might think that it is at least plausible to claim that neither the property of being true nor belief properties are metaphysically real. Consequently, if the Lewisian distinction might be used to conceptualize the distinction between deflationism and substantialism in the area of truth, it might as well do the job in the area of beliefs.

Minimal non-realism, defined as the combination of the deflationary approach to the existence of beliefs with the claim that belief properties are not natural, is in my opinion the best expression of the anti-realist intuition about belief. Thus, in my view the best way to see the debate about the status of the reality of belief is to interpret it as dealing primarily with the question of whether belief properties are natural.

The proposal to see the debate about the reality of beliefs in this manner is obviously a revisionary one: to my knowledge, no one has yet explicitly proposed conceptualizing anti-realist intuitions about belief in this way. Still, I am convinced that buying into this framework has important theoretical advantages which will be spelled out in subsequent parts of this book. To do so, however, it is necessary to characterize the proposed position in more detail, and this will be the subject of the next chapter.

4

Belief realism and anti-realism reconsidered

4.1 Criteria for naturalness

Once we adopt the view that the debate about the reality of beliefs is to be understood as a debate on whether belief properties are natural, we must inquire into the issue of how to establish whether a certain property is natural (or not). There are three main features that a given property must have if we are to treat it as a 'reasonably natural one'. First, objects that share such a property should be genuinely similar to each other because natural properties ground objective similarities. Second, natural properties are relevant in causal explanations. Thirdly, reasonably natural properties should be definable in terms of fundamental natural properties.

These criteria, as we will presently see, can be easily translated into important issues in contemporary metaphysics of belief. In this chapter, I will try to show how this translation might look.

4.1.1 Similarities and natural-kindness

The first criterion of the naturalness of a property is that of similarity: natural properties are said to ground objective similarities, therefore objects which share natural properties are objectively similar. If we apply this claim to the issue of belief realism, then we get the following claim: belief properties should be treated as natural if attributions of beliefs track objective similarities, which means that when we attribute the same belief to two persons (or two temporal stages of the same person), we attribute a property which makes these subjects genuinely similar. This issue might be divided into two sub-questions: Do attributions of particular beliefs track objective similarities? Is the category 'belief', understood in a general sense, in the businesses of depicting objective similarities?

The first of these sub-questions can be phrased as follows: when we attribute a belief with the same content to two different subjects, are we describing a genuine similarity between these two subjects? The problematic character of the positive answer to this question was brought to the attention of philosophers by Stich (1983). As he notices, there is a deep problem with the notion of the sameness of content; this notion is essential to the idea that when we attribute the same belief to two subjects (or to two time slices of the same subject), we are describing some important similarity between these subjects.

Stich (1983) claims that we should be sceptical about this very idea; to prove this, he introduces the case of Mrs T, a woman suffering from gradual, progressive memory loss. According to the story, Mrs T, before the onset of her illness, believed that McKinley was assassinated. But, as her illness progresses, she loses many of the beliefs surrounding the one in question: she forgets who McKinley was and what it means to be assassinated, etc. However, she is still willing to claim that McKinley was assassinated. The questions that Stich invites us to consider are the following: Is Mrs T's current belief the same as her interlocutor's, who is not suffering from any sort of cognitive malfunctioning? Is it the same belief as the one she used to have before the onset of her disease?

These questions, according to Stich, have no definite answers. This leads him to the conclusion that there are no strict criteria for saying whether one has the same belief as before (or whether two different subjects share the same beliefs). It is precisely this conclusion that motivates Stich's scepticism about the legitimacy of the category of belief. If there is nothing that determines the fact of having the same belief, then the category in question is not in the business – as Stich concludes – of describing anything real.

Defenders of the representational theory of belief argue for the opposite conclusion (see, e.g., Carruthers 2013), as they see the possession of a particular belief as a matter of being in a determinate representational state. Thus, two subjects who genuinely possess the same belief are objectively similar with respect to the representational properties they share.

If we reflect on this claim, we might appreciate how deep the representationalists' commitment to belief realism is: they not only see belief attributions as being true, but they also see attributions of particular beliefs, which are individuated by their content, as tracking objective similarities in the cognitive architecture of subjects who harbour given beliefs. According to representationalists, if two people (or the same person at different times) have the same belief, this is because there is some sort of internal representational state that they share. Thus, representationalists see attributions of particular beliefs as carving mental reality at its joints (to use a well-worn metaphor).

The more complex issue is the one of whether belief as a category has objective boundaries. The question that arises here is whether the category of belief denotes a natural kind or whether it is, in a way, a constructed category. In philosophy of mind, there is generally a strong tendency to link the issue of realism with the issue of the natural-kindness of mental categories. Most explicitly, this claim has been presented by proponents of so-called scientific eliminativism, such as Machery (2009) or Corns (2016). For the scientific eliminativist, only categories which denote unitary kinds deserve to be included in cognitive science, and psychological categories that do not denote cognitive natural kinds deserve to be eliminated from cognitive science. This eliminativist project differs from the classic eliminativism of Churchland in that it does not postulate the elimination of 'deficient' psychological categories from our folk-psychological parlance. It is somewhat unclear what the ontological consequences of the scientific eliminativist proposal are, as at least some of the proponents of this position (Corns 2016) are hesitant to claim that categories that don't refer to unitary kinds should be eliminated from our ordinary language. It is not my aim here to provide a deep interpretation and assessment of the metaphysics of 'scientific eliminativism', but it is important to note that the issue of natural-kindness is commonly taken to weigh in on the question of realism in philosophy of mind.

Philosophy of psychiatry is another field in which the issue of the objectivity of mental kinds is taken to be related to the question of realism. It is a subject of heated debate whether psychiatric categories are natural kinds or arbitrary constructs (see Cooper 2013 for an overview); it is also disputed whether emotions can be characterized as natural kinds (see, e.g., Griffiths 2004 for a discussion). In all these cases, the central question seems to be the following: are folk-psychological categories in accord with the categorizations that are provided by mature sciences? An important implicit presupposition of these debates is that the realist position about given categories is linked to the idea that these categories have to point to objective kinds. So, a realist about psychiatric categories would claim that there are some objective distinctions between different psychiatric categories.

In my view, it would be utterly unhelpful to tie the issue of natural-kindness to the question of the existence of mental kinds; however, it seems plausible to say that if one wants to retain a stronger version of realism about a given category, then one should include the claim that this category constitutes a natural kind. Although Lewis himself didn't interpret the idea of 'grounding objective similarities', which for him was the hallmark of natural properties in terms of natural kinds, in my view such an interpretation is justified, at least in the context of dealing with the question of the reality of mental categories. Thus, according to my proposal, beliefs should be treated as real if the category of beliefs denotes a natural kind.

There are two main ways in which the idea of a kind being natural is cashed out: mind-independence and projectibility. The idea behind the mind-independence conception (which might be traced back to Mill 1843/1882 and was strongly endorsed by essentialists like Putnam 1975) is as follows: a kind is natural if its boundaries are created, as it were, by nature itself; it is a matter of objective – independent of anyone's opinion – fact that a given object belongs to a given kind. In this way, natural kinds are contrasted with artificial or constructed ones, in which case the fact of an object belonging to a given artificial kind is a matter of some sort of convention.

It is important to note here that the idea of the mind-independence of natural kinds does not exclude the possibility that certain kinds would turn out to have fuzzy boundaries. Biological species, which for many (see, e.g., Putnam 1975) are a paradigmatic example of natural kinds, have fuzzy boundaries, and this is something that, according to evolutionary theory, is a central feature of species. If there is such a process as speciation, then there must be some specimens which cannot be classified as belonging only to 'new' or 'old' species. But this does not make biological species non-natural: the fact that certain animals are in the 'fuzzy' region of a given species is also a natural fact that is determined by mind-independent natural facts (at least, according to biological species realists).

So, if beliefs constitute natural kinds, they also should exhibit this kind of min-independence; if however, they are not such a kind, their boundaries would somehow be constructed. This disagreement about the status of beliefs as natural kinds was aptly expressed by Matthews:

> At one end of the spectrum are the endogenous explanations favoured by nativists such as Fodor. On such explanations, the taxonomy of attitude types reflects the fixed causal-functional architecture of the mind/brain, such that an attitude type is a common-sense psychological natural kind and thus has explanatory and predictive power, just in case it picks out a functionally specified innate structure of the mind/brain. At the other end of the spectrum are the exogenous explanations favored by social constructivists. (…) In the former case, the taxonomy of attitude types would reflect in transparent fashion the endogenously determined causal-functional architecture of the mind/

brain that a developed scientific cognitive psychology might be expected to describe, whereas in the latter case, this taxonomy might reflect only poorly the endogenously determined causal-functional architecture of the mind/brain, since this taxonomy would also reflect exogenous social factors and as such could be expected to vary both cross-culturally and diachronically within any particular culture.

(Matthews 2013, p. 109)

Another possible hallmark of natural kinds is that they function in (preferably multiple) surprising empirical generalizations, i.e., they are highly projectible. This aspect of natural kinds is strongly underlined by proponents of the popular 'property cluster' approach to natural kinds (see, e.g., Boyd 1991). According to the property cluster view, a kind is natural if there is a mechanism that ensures that certain clusters of properties remain connected in the members of this kind. According to an even more liberal view, we do not even need to postulate a mechanism that underlies a cluster's character, as the very existence of empirical generalizations makes the kind in question natural (see Khalidi 2013).

So, for a psychological category to be natural and hence real in the sense defined in this book, it must function in many substantial empirical generalizations. On the other hand, categories which do not constitute natural kinds cannot be expected to be the basis of any significant empirical generalizations. If beliefs constitute natural kinds, then we should be ready to admit that there are interesting empirical generalizations about them which are yet to be discovered. If, however, a given category turns out to not form a natural kind, then we shouldn't expect any significant generalizations to be discoverable about it (this will be expanded upon in Chapter 6, section 1).

To sum up, according to my proposal, the similarity criterion of naturalness works in the following way: according to realists, attributions of beliefs allow us to attribute a property which makes these subjects genuinely similar. Also, the category 'belief', understood in a general sense, denotes a natural kind which is mind-independent and capable of functioning in empirical generalizations. These objective similarities between beliefs with particular content and between states belonging to the general category of 'belief' stem from the fact that belief attributions depict a deep internal cognitive architecture. Anti-realists would deny all these claims.

On both the general plane and in the special case of beliefs, the question of the natural-kindness of psychological categories is sometimes treated as related to the question of the causal-explanatory character of the categories in question: it is usually assumed that to say that a certain mental category constitutes a natural kind is to say that this kind is relevant in causal explanation. In this way, the issue of objective similarity becomes related to the issue of causal relevance, which is another criterion of being a natural property. This criterion will be discussed presently.

4.1.2 Causal efficacy

Another criterion which is often used to distinguish between natural and non-natural properties is that of causal relevance. The idea is that properties which are natural/elite/sparse should be the ones that are used in causal explanations, whereas non-natural properties are, as it were, causally idle and irrelevant in causal explanations. This criterion of reality is directly translatable into one of the major issues in contemporary metaphysics of mind: the problem of mental causation in general, of which the problem of the causal relevance of beliefs is a special case.

The general problem of mental causation has a long history that was initially raised within the context of Descartes's dualism (Descartes himself was pressed on this issue by Gassendi, Arnauld and Princess Elisabeth of Bohemia [see, e.g., Kim 2002]). In the context of dualism, the question of mental causation is simple: how can a mind – being an immaterial substance that is located outside physical space – cause movements of a material spatial body? Cartesian dualism offered no clear answer to this issue, and it truly seems hardly possible that something immaterial could cause a physical body to move. On the other hand, it does seem natural to think that our mental lives play a role in controlling our actions. Thus, the inability of dualism to account for this fact was widely held to be a serious problem of the dualistic positions.

The currently discussed version of the problem of mental causation targets not only substance dualism but also all views which do not see the mind as being strictly identical to the brain; this problem especially plagues the popular position of non-reductive physicalism (Fodor 1974 and Davidson 1970 might be considered classic expositions of this theory). According to this view, each singular mental event should be seen as identical to some singular physical event, yet there is no identity between types of mental and of physical events. So, every instance of my pain is identical to some neural event, while pain in other creatures might be realized by physical events of different types.

The contemporary version of the problem of mental causation that is applicable to non-reductive physicalism was formulated by Malcolm (1968) and popularized in series of books and articles by Kim (see Kim 1989, 1998, 2005). As Kim presents this problem, it arises when we combine three intuitively plausible metaphysical claims. The first is the assumption of non-reductive physicalism, i.e., the claim that mental states such as beliefs supervene on yet are not reducible to physical states. The second is the assumption of causal closure: the claim that every physical event that has a sufficient cause has a sufficient physical cause (this means that the physical world is, as it were, causally complete). The third assumption is that of causal exclusion: it is assumed that, in normal cases, one event can have only one cause; this assumption does not work in cases of overdetermination, like the case of a firing squad, but such cases of genuine overdetermination are considered to be rare.

These assumptions, taken together, cast serious doubts on the idea that mental states (if we consider them to be not strictly identical to brain states) can be treated as causes of actions. Consider the following example: my belief that there is a pack of batteries in the cupboard causes me (at least apparently) to open said cupboard. Let's call this belief M (for mental event) and the opening of the cupboard A (as in action). We would intuitively say that in this example M is the cause of A; however, is this really the case?

From the first assumption of non-reduction, we get the claim that my belief (M) is a higher-level state which supervenes on some physical state of my brain (P). By assumption of causal closure, we must assume that if A has any sufficient cause, it must have, by virtue of being a physical event, a sufficient physical cause. Let's assume, for the sake of simplicity, that my brain state P is such a sufficient physical cause of my action A. But, at this point it would seem that we must say that A has two causes: common sense sees M as the cause of A, but we are also forced to say that P is a sufficient cause of A. However, as the causal exclusion principle teaches us, this event (as any other one) can have only one sufficient cause. And given the choice between M and P, we should judge P to be the actual cause (if it were not, we would violate the causal closure assumption).

Thus, if we treat beliefs (along with other mental states) as being irreducible to mental events, then Kim's argument aims to show that their causal powers are being 'crowded out' by the causal powers of the physical events on which beliefs supervene. Whenever we assume that our belief has played a causal role in producing some of our actions, we find a physical event on which our belief supervenes and which takes on the role of the genuine cause of the action in question. So, my belief that a pack of batteries is in a cupboard turns out not to be the cause of my reaching for said cupboard: the actual cause is one of my brain states.

Kim's (1989, 1998) preferred solution to this problem is to deny that mental states are irreducible to brain events and to embrace some version of strong reductionism (like type identity theory). In my view, however, such a reductionist solution does not seem to be very promising in the case of beliefs. There is currently little reason to suppose that we would be able to find a type of brain event that would be identical to beliefs. This is especially true if we accept the popular view, according to which beliefs are at least partly individuated by their content: a type-identity theory of beliefs would have to show us that for each and every belief with a specific content there must be a distinct neural state corresponding to it. Although it is not *a priori* impossible that this is so, the current evidence for a such strong form of reductionism is scant.

Some other philosophers have attempted to solve the problem of mental causation in general and of causal relevance of beliefs in particular without rejecting the assumption of irreducibility of mental states (including beliefs). Such attempts will be subject to detailed analysis in the further course of the book (see Chapter 6, section 2). At this point, I wish to focus on the relation between the issues of mental causation and realism, both on the general plane and with respect to the category of beliefs in particular.

Kim himself strongly claims that these two issues are related, as he claimed that the failure to defend mental causation would result in eliminativism (Kim 2005). However, in my view, it is hard to justify the transition from the claim that mental states/properties do not have causal powers to the claim that they purely and simply do not exist. (I presented a more detailed argument against this transition in Poslajko 2016; a sceptical appraisal of this transition was also put forward by Demeter 2009, but his general approach and final conclusions are substantially different from mine.)

However, it seems that there is an important connection between the idea that certain entities/properties have genuine causal powers and the idea that these entities/properties are real in a strong sense. In general metaphysics, this was stressed by, among others, Wright (see his remarks about 'the width of cosmological role' in his 1992, especially p. 196–204). In the specific context of the debate about the reality of propositional attitudes, the connection was explicitly expressed by Fodor: 'someone is a Realist about propositional attitudes if (a) he holds that there are mental states whose occurrences and interactions cause behavior and do so, moreover, in ways that respect (at least to an approximation) the generalizations of common-sense belief/desire psychology; and (b) he holds that these same causally efficacious mental states are also semantically evaluable' (Fodor 1985, p. 78).

The issue of realism about beliefs and the question of whether belief properties are natural seem to strongly coincide: in both cases, the positive answer is partly justified by accepting the claim that beliefs play a genuine causal-explanatory role. This conclusion lends more support to the idea that we might transpose the question of belief realism into the question of whether belief properties are natural: as it turns out, the indicators are similar in both cases.

It is important, however, to correctly formulate the issue of the causal relevance of beliefs in order to exclude the issues which seem to have obvious answers. For example, several philosophers (see, e.g., Bennett 2008) have suggested that it would be utterly unhelpful to frame the question of whether beliefs are causally relevant if we understood 'causation' as referring to fundamental causation. According to such philosophers, it is perfectly possible that the only entities that would turn out to be causally active in a fundamental sense would be those postulated by future fundamental physics. In such a case, the claim that beliefs do not play a causal role (in the fundamental sense) would turn out to be trivial. Thus, in order to make the issue non-trivial, we must accept some sense of causation that would be friendly to the notion of there being genuine higher-level causes.

On the other hand, we might say that the idea that 'to be causally relevant' means just 'to be used by a scientist in causal explanations'. In this sense, beliefs would be uncontroversially causally active: it is customary in many sciences to explain humans' actions by resorting to their supposed beliefs (historians explain the actions of historical figures in terms of the beliefs of such figures, etc.).

The whole issue of causal exclusion rests on the assumption that such practices of higher-level sciences can be challenged because careful inquiry can show us that the attributions of causality at the higher-level can be mistaken in the sense that the actual causes of certain phenomena can reside on a lower level than is accepted in day-to-day causal explanations. For example, economists might routinely use macro-economic phenomena as factors in causal explanations, but one can reasonably wonder whether the genuine causes of said phenomena shouldn't be located at the level of the economic activity of individuals. Similarly, one might wonder whether the explanations which are now given at the level of beliefs shouldn't be given at some lower, more appropriate level.

The crucial notions here are those of 'ineliminability' and 'indispensability', as the issue of belief-causation seems to revolve around the question of whether we could do away with causal explanations at the level of beliefs, or is the practice of explaining phenomena such as action by resorting to beliefs indispensable? The question of realism about beliefs seems then to hinge on the issue of whether there is indeed such a notion of causation that would allow us to accept the idea of beliefs being genuine, ineliminable, higher-level causes. If we could justify this, then beliefs would deserve to be called real. If, however, there is no such notion that could be applied to the notion in question, then a mild version of anti-realism seems to be an appropriate option.

4.1.3 Relation to more natural properties

According to Lewis, the last criterion for being a reasonably natural/elite property is that such properties are connected to perfectly natural ones. He expressed this idea in the following passage:

> [P]hysics discovers which things and classes are the most elite of all; but others are elite also, though to a lesser degree. The less elite are so because they are connected to the most elite by chains of definability. Long chains, by the time we reach the moderately elite classes of cats and pencils and puddles; but the chains required to reach the utterly ineligible would be far longer still.
>
> (Lewis 1984, p. 228)

The original Lewisian idea was that the connection between most elite/perfectly natural properties and reasonably natural ones should be seen as being definitional one. This might be considered controversial, as there is some room for scepticism about the idea that, for example, higher-level, multiply realizable properties (such as money) are definable in a reasonable way by reference to the most fundamental physical properties.

However, there is some intuitive appeal to the idea that properties that belong to the category of real-yet-not-fundamental should be somehow connected to perfectly natural ones. In my view, the best way to conceptualize this postulate is to say that properties that are real but not perfectly natural might be somehow explained (rather than strictly defined) by their relation to more fundamental ones. Although the idea that money might be defined in physical terms is debatable (but not *a priori* impossible), the view according to which economic properties should be explainable in terms of some more fundamental ones, if they are to be deemed real, is certainly reasonable: we might, for example, try to explain what money is by reference to more basic notions such as preferences.

There is little temptation to treat belief properties as belonging to the class of the most elite/fundamental natural properties. So, the claim that belief properties are natural should be, on the most plausible reading, treated as the claim that belief properties are reasonably natural ones. Consequently, the belief realist should claim that there exists a reasonably short explanatory link that connects beliefs to more natural/elite properties. Anti-realists about beliefs would, on their part, cast doubt on the idea that such links can be found.

As was indicated in Chapter 1, there are two features that beliefs are commonly thought to have: they are both causes of behaviour and bearers of semantic properties. The causal aspect of beliefs seems to be fairly easily explainable in terms of more fundamental properties: the functional account of belief in terms of input–output relations might be able to provide such a reasonable connection (if we bracket the worries about belief holism).

The semantic aspect is far more problematic from the perspective of the task of linking beliefs to more natural properties. The question that arises here is how we might connect semantic properties of beliefs to more natural properties.

This issue is closely related to one of the most discussed problems in the contemporary metaphysics of mind, namely the problem of the naturalization of content. So, let us characterize this problem in more detail.

A clear and succinct (although slightly dramatic) exposition of the problem of the naturalization of content has been provided by Rosenberg:

> The basic problem that intentionality raises for naturalism has been obvious enough since Descartes or even Plato (…): how can a clump of matter, for example, the brain or some proper part of it, have propositional content, be about some other thing in the universe. What naturalism requires is a purely physical, causal account of intentionality that itself makes no overt or covert appeal to semantical concepts.
> (Rosenberg 2013, p. 3)

A slightly more sober yet similar-in-spirit formulation of the problem is provided by Shea, who writes as follows:

> I will take it that a naturalistic account of mental content must provide illuminating explanatory connections between representational content and properties that are non-semantic, non-mental and non-normative. Furthermore, it must show that content properties supervene on the physical, or at least must be compatible with such supervenience. Reduction is one live option (…), but the naturalising project is not limited to reductive theories. It is a familiar point that many special sciences deal in properties that are not reducible to basic physics. What makes them naturalistic is that their properties have substantive explanatory connections to properties in other sciences.
> (Shea 2013, p. 497)

On an intuitive level, the problem of the naturalization of content is that we lack a clear idea of how a purely naturalistic description of the inner workings of the human mind can give us reasonable explanation of how mental states, including beliefs, can be 'about' any portion of reality. Paradigmatic, purely physical states do not seem to be 'about' anything; movements of celestial bodies and the interactions of subatomic particles do not present themselves as representing anything. But if mental properties, especially beliefs, are to be connected to more fundamental physical properties, then there must be some sort of connection between the natural basis of beliefs and their representational aspect.

This problem becomes especially dramatic with regard to beliefs: they are not only 'about something' in the sense of object-directness, but they possess truth conditions, which means that they are capable of representing possible states of affairs. But explaining in a naturalistically acceptable way how any mental state (or any other state for that matter) can have the property of depicting possible states of affairs is not an easy task.

What makes this problem relevant to the issues discussed in this book is that there is a strong presumption – shared by most of the participants in the naturalization of content debate – that the issue of the naturalization of content and the problem of realism about representational mental states are strictly linked. It is commonly assumed that in order to be a realist about mental representation one must be able to provide a story about how the vocabulary of mental representations can be connected with naturalistic vocabulary. This contention is underscored by both proponents and sceptics of naturalization of content. Shea (2013), for example, is explicit that his defence of naturalization of content is thought to be a defence of realism: for him, to be a representational realist is to say that 'content is a real property of the system' (Shea 2013, p. 498). Miłkowski (2015) also considers the naturalization of content project to be of utmost importance, as for him giving up on the naturalization of content would result in untenable semantic nihilism. Rosenberg (2013, 2015), on the other hand, motivates his eliminativistic approach to the mental by his insistence that providing a naturalistic explanation of content is impossible.

An interesting (especially from the point of view of the conception developed in this book) and mildly anti-realistic approach to mental representations was presented by Egan (2014, 2020). Her approach to mental content is neither realist nor purely eliminativist. She rejects straightforward realism, as she is explicit about the claim that 'no naturalistic relation is likely to pick out a single, determinate content' (Egan 2014, p. 124). On the other hand she is reluctant to embrace a fully eliminativist position as she claims that content attributions might be warranted. For Egan, attributions of content should be seen as a kind of a theoretical gloss which helps us understand the relevant mental phenomena but, at the end of the day, adds little to genuine theoretical explanations.

This proposal is more or less similar to the general idea developed in this book; however it needs to be emphasized that the target of Egan's analysis is different from mine. Egan aims to explain the function of representational talk in the context of the mental states posited by cognitive science. This is a different problem from the issue of whether the content of propositional attitudes can be naturalized. This brings us to another important observation which needs to be made here, namely that theories about naturalizing representations might have different targets: some of these theories are devised to provide naturalization of propositional content of propositional attitudes; others aim to explain the representational properties of the posits of cognitive science. Theories that are devised to solve the problem of naturalizing the content of the sub-personal states that are postulated within cognitive science need not solve the problem of the naturalization of the content of propositional attitudes. What is common to these two issues is, however, the relation of both of them to the problem of realism. In both cases, the success of the project of naturalization seems to be a prerequisite for embracing a strong version of realism.

There are several proposals on how to provide a naturalistically respectable account of representational properties of beliefs. An exposition and critical analysis of them will be presented in Chapter 6, section 3. At this point, let us just note that not all theorists would be willing to accept the premise that securing the reality of beliefs qua representational states requires explaining their representational properties in terms of physical properties. An alternative account of how to link beliefs and their content to more natural/fundamental properties is the view according to which the representational aspect of intentional states such as beliefs should be explained not in naturalistic terms but in relation to the notion of phenomenal consciousness (see Mendelovici & Bourget 2014 for a useful overview of this position). This proposal is as intricate as it is controversial, and for this reason a detailed analysis of it must be postponed.

Phenomenal intentionality theory presents itself as an important alternative to the naturalistic view of content. However, even on this account, the reality of the intentional properties of beliefs seems to hinge on their relation to something which is considered to be more metaphysically fundamental. For purposes of the simplicity of the exposition, in the course of the few next chapters I will assume that realism about beliefs requires an explanation of content in terms of natural (i.e. physical) properties. Still, it is worth keeping in mind that there is an alternative to naturalism, but the detailed analysis of this alternative phenomenal intentionality approach must be postponed until Chapter 8, section 5.

4.2 Describing paradigmatic (anti-)realism

The proposal put forward in this book is that the distinction between realism and moderate anti-realism about beliefs should be read in terms of the distinction between natural and non-natural properties. Having characterized the criteria of naturalness in the previous sections and their connections to the debates on the metaphysics of mind, we are now in a position to describe the paradigmatic realist and minimal non-realist positions in the area of beliefs.

As was stated at the end of Chapter 3, a realist about beliefs is someone who claims that beliefs exist and that attributions of beliefs track natural properties; on the other hand, a minimal non-realist admits that beliefs exist yet denies that their attributions track natural properties. We are now in a position to characterize the positions in the debate in more detail. A paradigmatic proponent of realism about belief is supposed to be someone who is committed to the following claims:

a. Beliefs exist and their attributions are often true.
b. There are objective similarities between states which are described by attributions of the form 'x believes that p'.
c. Beliefs as a category constitute a genuine cognitive natural kind.
d. Attributions of beliefs are causal-explanatory; there is a theory which shows us how we might treat beliefs as possessing genuine causal relevance.
e. There is an interesting story about the naturalization of propositional content which would show how to explain the representational properties of beliefs in terms of physical properties.

The opponent of realism who is a paradigmatic proponent of minimal non-realism about beliefs would be committed to the following claims:

a. Beliefs exist and their attributions are often true.
b. There are no objective similarities between states which are described by attributions of the form 'x believes that p'.

c. Beliefs, as a category, do not constitute a genuine cognitive natural kind; rather, we should see the category of 'belief' as being more or less arbitrary.
d. Beliefs do not have a genuine causal-explanatory role and their attributions lack genuine explanatory power in the context of causal explanations.
e. There is no illuminating story about the naturalization of propositional content; we cannot explain the fact that beliefs have content in terms of more fundamental properties.

As we can see, both positions are 'realist' in the most minimal sense: both realists and minimal non-realists accept the idea that beliefs exist and that our folk attributions of them are truth-apt and often true. Yet, behind this agreement lies a deep metaphysical difference. For realists, beliefs are part and parcel of the objective structure of reality; attributing them reveals deep truths about human cognitive structure and improves our understanding of the world. For a minimal non-realist, this is not the case: although attributions of belief are indeed often true, they are true in a purely minimal sense and appreciation of such truths does not increase our genuine understanding of the world.

Let us take a closer look at how a minimal non-realist sees the truth of belief attributions and try to analyse a stock example of belief attribution in the proposed framework. Consider two persons of whom it is true that they believe that John F. Kennedy went to Harvard. If these attributions are true of these people, then a minimal non-realist would admit that such beliefs exist. The attribution of this belief is justified on the grounds that both persons meet the common-sense criteria of attributing such beliefs: they might have sincerely expressed the statement 'John F. Kennedy went to Harvard'; they might answer in the affirmative when asked; they might exhibit some behavioural dispositions related to this belief and so on.

Moreover, a minimal non-realist would not object to the idea that there is something that makes such attributions true. In each and every case, there is something that makes such an attribution true: this might be some combination of behavioural and verbal dispositions, sub-personal cognitive states, and phenomenal feels. So when a belief can truly be attributed to a person, then there is something that such an attribution aptly describes. Thus, a person who believes that John F. Kennedy went to Harvard probably has certain dispositions related to this belief; moreover, there are some sub-personal cognitive mechanisms that underwrite these dispositions. It might also be the case that there is some phenomenology to this belief: there might be some conscious phenomenal feel related to acceptance of the claim in question.

The minimal non-realist denies, however, that there is any deep similarity between the factors that make such attributions true in different cases. Let us consider two specific persons who believe that John F. Kennedy went to Harvard. One is an academic who studies American presidents in the second half on the twentieth century; she knows a lot about Kennedy's life and background and has been to Harvard on several occasions, etc. The other is a distracted student who is utterly disinterested in the life of past politicians but has read some stuff about Kennedy and somehow remembered the fact that he went to Harvard. The dispositions of these two persons – both behavioural and verbal – would most probably be divergent in this case, and we might suppose that the more basic sub-personal cognitive states would also be very different (probably the content of the long-term memory of the academic is much richer than that of the student). We have also no reason – at least according to a minimal non-realist – to suppose that the phenomenal aspect of belief would be the same (or reasonably similar) in these two cases. The professor might be suspected of having some vivid phenomenology related to her belief, whereas the student cannot be accused of having any such feelings and so on. (This example is somehow similar to Crane's [2017] example of people believing that the Houses of Parliament in London are the British Parliament, and to Curry's [2021] example of three different people believing that coffee in a mug is hot, despite having very different sub-personal states.)

In this way, the minimal non-realist's claim is that although such a belief attribution points to some property which is shared by these two subjects, it does not describe any deep or substantial similarity. Consequently, belief attributions might be true but they add very little to our understanding of what is really, 'on a fundamental level', going on within the subjects; additionally, attributing beliefs adds little to our predictive abilities.

It is important to note that the minimal non-realist's claim is significantly stronger than the commonly accepted thesis of the multiple realizability of higher-level mental states such as beliefs. The thesis of the multiple realizability of mental states is, in most basic terms, the idea that the very same mental state can be realized by different sorts of physical processes: pain in humans is realized by one sort of neuronal firings, by a different sort of neuronal firings in octopuses and by entirely different physical events in the case of Martians. Although the idea that mental states in general are multiply realizable is a source of ongoing controversy, it is more or less plausible in the case of higher-level states such as beliefs (it is difficult to show that we could identify the state of believing that Dublin is south of Glasgow with a particular neural state).

The issue we are dealing with here, however, is not the question of the multiple realizability of beliefs. What is at stake is somewhat more substantial. As Fodor (1974), who was one of the early champions of the multiple realizability claim, rightly notes, the idea that higher-level mental states are multiply realizable might (and for him should) be combined with the view that there is a genuine higher-level natural kind which can be realized by various lower-level natural kinds. So, for Fodor, who is a paradigmatic realist about propositional attitudes, the predicates of psychology refer to genuine natural kinds, but these kinds are multiply realizable by certain distinct lower-level states. According to him, this claim holds for beliefs: a belief is, on this view, a genuine higher-level natural kind that is multiply realizable by more fundamental states. In this way, this multiple realizability might be (and probably would be) accepted by the strong realist about beliefs.

A minimal non-realist would also most probably agree that a belief-property is multiply realizable, as they might be tempted to accept some version of minimal physicalism about the mental and to say that it is true that all contentful mental states are somehow realized by lower-level physical states. A minimal non-realist's difference with Fodor-like views lies elsewhere. The conflict is about the status of higher-level mental kinds such as beliefs: for Fodor, such kinds are natural, and psychology is in the business of describing genuine similarities and explanations; on the other hand, for the non-realist, a higher-level kind of belief is not a natural one but rather a wildly unnatural property in the Lewisian sense.

4.3 The spectrum-like character of the distinction

The positions described in the previous section should be seen as being ideal-type positions. The existing views on the metaphysical status of beliefs need not fit ideally into the positions I have more or less arbitrarily defined. They might be more or less similar to clear-cut realism or non-realism. In this sense, on the proposed account, being a belief anti-realist is a spectrum condition. One might be a theorist who is fully committed to all the negative claims that a prototypical minimal non-realist would make. However, another philosopher might not fully conform to the stereotype, but if they still accept enough of the main indicators of the anti-realistic view, then they should count as being (somehow) non-realist. On the other hand, some thinkers might accept some (but not many) of the claims of paradigmatic non-realism; they should be seen as being somehow anti-realistic or tending towards anti-realism.

The situation is the same on the other end of the spectrum: there could be some specimens of a perfect or near-perfect full-blown realism about belief. Other philosophers, however, could be committed to realism in a more modest fashion, and there could be some that are only slightly but not fully committed to realism.

The fact that the view defended here suggests conceiving of the distinction between belief realism and anti-realism as spectrum-like should be seen, in my opinion, as a theoretical advantage. The binary character of the traditional ontological way of framing the issue puts philosophers in an uncomfortable position: either you are ready to say that beliefs exist and thus you become a realist, or you admit that they do not and you end up being treated as an eliminativist or fictionalist (one example of dissatisfaction with this binary character of the question is Dennett's refusal to unequivocally answer the question of whether beliefs are real in his 'Real Patterns' [Dennett 1991]).

Adopting the approach according to which the distinction is a spectrum allows us to express our commitments regarding the metaphysics of mind a bit more subtly: one might express some reservations about beliefs being fully real without committing oneself to any problematic form of eliminativism or fictionalism. One might also express some reservations about fully fledged realism yet remain a realist up to some point, and so on.

That this distinction is a spectral one stems in a straightforward way from the Lewisian account of the distinction between natural and non-natural properties. First, this distinction is graded: properties might be more or less natural – closer to or further away from the ends of the spectrum. At one end, we have properties which are fully natural (i.e., properties of fully developed basic science); at the other end, we have completely arbitrary collections of modal objects; in between, there is a graded series of properties, some of which are more and some of which are less natural/elite. Second, there are several logically independent criteria for assessing the naturalness of the property in question: there is the criterion of connection with fundamental properties, the criterion of causal efficacy, and the criterion of objective similarity. And although Lewis himself seems to suggest that these criteria go hand in hand, one might be sceptical about this. It seems at least conceivable that there could be certain property, P, which is quite easily explainable in terms of most fundamental properties; still we might be unable to show that P is causally relevant. In short, there seems to be some room for claiming that a certain property would count as being reasonably natural if we used one criterion provided by Lewis, but under another criterion it would count as being slightly less natural.

In this way, the realism/non-realism distinction has a spectrum character in the familiar psychological sense because it is graded and multi-criterial. Nonetheless, as was noted in the previous chapter (section 4), it is possible to provide a tentative demarcation line between realism and anti-realism, as conceptualized within the proposed framework: what is needed here is the notion of a reasonably natural property, i.e., a property which plays at least some genuine causal explanatory role, tracks some objective similarities, and is explainable in a relatively reasonable way. So, to be an anti-realist about beliefs is to deny that beliefs are reasonably natural in this way. Obviously, there will be some murky areas around here: some positions will be hard to classify as their view on the nature of belief properties will be such that it would be hard to say whether they conceptualize belief properties as reasonably natural or not. But, in many other cases, the classification would work, and a vague criterion is better than none.

In the next chapter, I will try to show how several positions developed in the metaphysics of belief can be situated within the proposed spectrum. First, however, let us look at the general advantages of the proposed conceptualization.

4.4 Advantages of the proposed account

The definition of realism and non-realism I propose here, i.e., in terms of Lewis's conception of natural properties, is certainly a non-standard one. However, I believe that it has three important theoretical advantages: first, it allows the anti-realist position to be formulated in a coherent manner and, in this way, it makes the debate non-trivial; second, it makes the debate about the reality of beliefs tractable; third, it introduces theoretical unity into various debates in the metaphysics of beliefs.

Minimal non-realism, defined as a position according to which beliefs exist but attributions of beliefs track non-natural properties, is coherent. At least, this is true in the sense that it does not lead to an obvious contradiction, as the simple form of error theory about beliefs was supposed to. As we remember from Chapter 2, section 3.1, the popular way of disproving the classic version of eliminative materialism was to say that one cannot consistently maintain the claim that 'there are no beliefs'. By adopting this claim, eliminativists were accused of being guilty of a sort of implicit contradiction: if there are no beliefs, then how can one believe that there are no beliefs? But, if it is impossible to believe that there are no beliefs, then it is impossible to sincerely profess that there are no beliefs – or so the popular argument went.

However, such simple arguments to the effect that belief anti-realism is inconsistent are not so convincing when the anti-realist backs down from the claim that there are no beliefs and rejects simple-minded irrealism about belief discourse. Minimal non-realists have no problem in admitting that they believe that beliefs exist and that their attributions can be true. The truth of belief attributions is licensed by the application criteria of the belief predicates in folk discourse. In this way, proponents of minimal non-realism about beliefs have no problem admitting that they believe their own theory: if they, for example, argue for this position in print or by making conference presentations, then they certainly meet the folksy criteria for believing in an obscure metaphysical position about belief properties being non-natural.

Minimal non-realism thus avoids the simple argument against the consistency of belief anti-realism. It does so just because it does not embrace irrealism about belief ascriptions. There are truths about beliefs, and they include truths about beliefs that the proponent of minimal anti-realism holds. Transferring the debate from the level of the question about the existence of beliefs and the truth of belief ascriptions to the level of the question of the reality of belief properties allows the anti-realist position to be formulated in a prima facie coherent manner.

There are more arcane arguments to the effect that belief anti-realism is an inconsistent position: the most popular come from Boghossian (1990) and Wright (2002), who aim to show that anti-realism about beliefs undermines the ability to make the distinction between realism and anti-realism. I will have more to say about this way of arguing in Chapter 8, section 2.1. At this point, let me just note that the way of arguing against the coherence of belief anti-realism that Boghossian and Wright propose is far from trivial and rests on substantial theoretical assumptions. Many philosophical positions have been accused of being inconsistent in that sense, but this is not a reason to reject such theories out of hand.

It is important to note that minimal non-realism is not an obviously incoherent position: it is a prima facie consistent option that one might accept without risking making an evident fool of oneself. Consequently, the debate between realism and anti-realism about beliefs becomes non-trivial, as both positions in this debate are at least prima facie acceptable. This should be good news not only for non-realists but also for self-professed realists, as it makes their position non-trivial. Arguing against a patently absurd position is too easy a victory.

The conclusion that anti-realism about beliefs is not an obvious theoretical non-starter is important for another reason: there is a strong presumption towards realism in the debate. Traditional ways of expressing anti-realist intuitions about the metaphysical status of beliefs are commonly rejected as they are treated as self-defeating. However, once we reformulate the anti-realist intuition in a more coherent way, we see that it might be an open theoretical option. In this way, we might overcome the unreflective presumption of belief realism that seems to somehow dominate contemporary analytic philosophy and see that there are more theoretical options available than many are willing to admit.

The second main advantage of the proposed way of conceptualizing the distinction between realism and anti-realism about beliefs is that it makes the distinction in question tractable. As was noted in the previous section, voices in the debate have expressed exasperation with the traditional way of framing it. Not only are the questions 'Are beliefs real?' or 'Do beliefs exist?' uncomfortably binary, thus forcing theorists into one of two ill-defined boxes, they also do not come with clear criteria for deciding whether one should accept realism or anti-realism. Stich, who changed his position from being an eliminativist to being a vocal critic of this view, expressed (in both phases of his philosophy) the contention that it is actually extremely hard to say what it would mean, precisely, to claim that beliefs exist or that they do not (Stich 1996).

The aim of the account I propose here is to show how we might proceed with the metaphysical discussion about beliefs: there are substantial questions in the metaphysics of beliefs that need to be solved; by doing so and by summarizing the answer in a single position, one should be able to locate one's place on the realism/non-realism spectrum. Needless to say, none of the questions that we need to answer in order to do so are particularly easy: in each case, it is necessary to engage in substantial inquiry. Moreover, there is no guarantee that any of these questions can be given a definite answer. Still, adopting this way of theorizing shows us how to proceed: if we want to know what the metaphysical status of beliefs is, we should engage in inquiries about particular questions regarding the metaphysics of beliefs.

The third advantage of my proposed way of characterizing the debate is that it introduces a kind of theoretical unity into debates about the metaphysics of beliefs. The issues of whether we should treat belief as a natural kind, of the causal efficacy of beliefs, and of the naturalization of content are often explicitly said to bear on the problem of the reality of beliefs. However, prima facie, these issues seem to be distinct and unrelated to both one another and to the general question of whether there really are beliefs. The conceptualization I propose here helps us, I hope, to see how these questions are related on a deeper level: in each case, what is at stake seems to be the question of whether belief talk depicts some substantial aspect of reality or not. Possible solutions to all these seemingly distinct debates should point us to a unified view of the proper metaphysics of beliefs.

5

Inspirations

In the last chapter, I defined realism and minimal non-realism in terms of the distinction between natural and non-natural properties in Lewis's sense. According to the proposed definition, to be a realist about beliefs is to see belief properties as being natural in a Lewisian sense, whereas to be an anti-realist is to deny this. This definition of the realism/anti-realism divide is largely stipulative, as no one who has participated in the debate has defined their position in this way.

However, I think that many views on the nature of beliefs which have been developed within analytic metaphysics of mind can be made to fit within the proposed analysis. The minimal non-realist position, although it might seem to be established by pure conceptual fiat, is, nonetheless, modelled on some of the existing positions. In what follows, I will present the views that served as inspiration for the formulation of this proposal.

As this book aims to justify the non-realist position, this extremely selective overview will focus on the positions which might be seen as underpinning the non-realist view. However, in the last section I will also introduce an example of the realist view as it might be useful to see how the contrast actually looks.

5.1 Dispositionalism and neo-dispositionalism

One position which is an important example of a broadly understood mild anti-realism about beliefs is dispositionalism: both in its historical form presented by Ryle and in the more contemporary version presented by Schwitzgebel.

Ryle's main aim was to banish the spectre of dualism from the philosophy of mind; this was to be achieved by means of providing an analysis of mental state attributions in terms of dispositions (Ryle 1949/2009). On Ryle's account, mental terms should not be seen as denoting a mysterious non-physical mental quality which resides in the metaphorical ghost in the machine. Rather, we should treat these terms as denoting behavioural dispositions – capacities to act in certain ways in certain circumstances. Regarding beliefs, Ryle writes:

> [T]hey [epistemologists] postulate that, for example, a man who believes that the earth is round must from time to time be going through some unique proceeding of cognising, 'judging', or internally re-asserting, with a feeling of confidence, 'The earth is round'. In fact, of course, people do not harp on statements in this way, and even if they did do so and even if we knew that they did, we still should not be satisfied that they believed that the earth was round, unless we also found them inferring, imagining, saying and doing a great number of other things as well. If we found them inferring, imagining, saying and doing these other things, we should be satisfied that they believed the earth to be round, even if we had the best reasons for thinking that they never internally harped on the original statement at all. However often and stoutly a skater avers to us or to himself, that the ice will bear, he shows that he has his qualms, if he keeps to the edge of the pond, calls his children away from the middle, keeps his eye on the life-belts or continually speculates what would happen, if the ice broke.
>
> (Ryle 1949/2009, p. 32–3)

As this quote shows, at the core of dispositionalism about beliefs lies the conviction that believing something is not a hidden internal state but rather something that lies in plain sight – a combination of dispositions to verbal and non-verbal behaviour.

Let us note that being committed to such a dispositional analysis does not in itself necessarily mean that Ryle is a full-fledged anti-realist about beliefs. However, there is one aspect of Ryle's theory which makes it anti-realistic in at least one dimension: his dispositionalist analysis leads to the consequence that there are no unitary kinds denoted by mental terms such as 'belief'. As Ryle puts it:

> Dispositional words like 'know', 'believe', 'aspire', 'clever' and 'humorous' are determinable dispositional words. They signify abilities, tendencies or pronenesses to do not things of one unique kind, but things of lots of different kinds. Theorists who recognise that 'know' and 'believe' are commonly used as dispositional verbs are apt not to notice this point, but to assume that there must be corresponding acts of knowing or apprehending and states of believing.
>
> (Ryle 1949/2009, p. 102–3)

Ryle might plausibly be read as claiming in the above passage that because there are no 'states of believing' that are understood as single internal states, the attribution of beliefs cannot be taken as denoting 'things of one unique kind'. According to Ryle, there is no unitary kind that can serve as a referent of the word 'belief'. Instead this word denotes a disparate bundle of phenomena belonging to different kinds. As the claim that there is no unitary kind denoted by the term 'belief' is one of the central claims of non-realism (as I defined it), Ryle might be counted as being a moderate anti-realist (with some qualifications that will be added soon).

This denial of there being a unitary kind denoted by 'belief' is even more pronounced in the more contemporary version of dispositionalism, namely in neo-dispositionalism, which was developed by Schwitzgebel in a series of papers (Schwitzgebel 2002, 2010, 2013). The guiding idea of Schwitzgebel's theory is to retain the central insights of the original dispositionalism, while making this conception more palatable and rejecting the common reasons for scepticism about it. The main improvement that Schwitzgebel makes to the original dispositionalism is that he accepts that the dispositions that define mental concepts could also include phenomenal and cognitive dispositions. Thus, to believe is not only to be disposed to act in a certain way but also to feel in a certain way and to possess certain cognitive capacities.

Central to Schwitzgebel's account is the following claim: 'To believe that P (…) is nothing more than to match to an appropriate degree and in appropriate respects the dispositional stereotype for believing that P. What respects and degrees of match are to count as "appropriate" will vary contextually and so must be left to the ascriber's judgment' (Schwitzgebel 2002, p. 253).

There are several aspects of this view that are relevant from the point of view of the project developed here. Schwitzgebel explicitly accepts the claim that the category of belief does not have clear boundaries; consequently, there are cases in which there is no definite answer to the question of whether the subject in question has the belief that p, or whether the attitude that a subject has is that of belief or some other category. According to Schwitzgebel, in cases of discrepancy between professed opinions and behaviour (like in the famous skywalk case, where the subject is supposed to believe that the skywalk is safe but is hesitant to walk it), the correct thing to say is that we are dealing with in-between beliefs: states which are to be classified neither as cases of believing that p, nor as cases of not believing that p.

As Schwitzgebel (2013) notes, this commitment to the indeterminacy of belief is a direct consequence of the fact that his account is a superficial one in the sense that it does not postulate any deep structures to match our folk-psychological stereotypes. There are no deep facts about our cognitive structure that our folk attributions track and which could provide us with definite answers to questions about the classification of mental states into beliefs and other mental states. Moreover, it is clear that this superficial definition entails that beliefs do not play an important causal-explanatory role.

Matthews, another prominent proponent of neo-dispositionalism, explicitly notes this affinity between neo-dispositionalism and a weak version of realism about belief. According to Matthews:

> We should (…) think of this common-sense psychology not as a proto-scientific cognitive psychology, but primarily as a useful tool for conceptualizing and dealing with ourselves and others. We can still be realists about the attitudes, but the realism here is of a theoretically rather shallow sort, of a piece with a realism about tables, chairs, and other middle-sized physical objects. Our individuation of such objects reflects our particular pragmatic interests, consistent with and constrained by our inherent abilities to distinguish, recognize, etc. such objects. And so too with propositional attitudes: There are such states, but they are aggregations of dispositions whose type-individuation reflects our particular pragmatic interest.
>
> (Matthews 2013, p. 119)

Thus, the neo-dispositionalist account aligns, in a broad sense, with the minimal non-realist position I have proposed: in both cases, it is assumed that beliefs exist in a shallow sense of existence but talk about beliefs is not taken to track any deep truths about human cognitive architecture.

It is important to note here, however, that proponents of (neo-)dispositionalism do not necessarily think of themselves as anti-realists about belief. Rather, they give the impression that they conceive of themselves as providing an analysis of the folk concept of belief and a correct alternative to the more strongly realist, representationalist approach. The issue of the relation between dispositionalism and common sense and the consequences of this relation for the question of realism about beliefs is a complex one; a more detailed analysis of this problem will be presented in Chapter 7, section 1.

5.2 Interpretivism

Interpretivism is another position in the metaphysics of beliefs which might be seen as being broadly similar to the minimal non-realist position I have defined. It was originally proposed by Davidson (1970, 1974) and Dennett (1989);

recently, it has been defended by, among others, Slors (2007), Mölder (2010), Tollefsen (2015), Eronen (2020), and Curry (2020).

The guiding idea of interpretivism is that propositional attitudes (including beliefs) should be seen as being (in some sense) constituted by the process of interpreting certain systems as being intentional. As Slors characterizes it, central to interpretivism is 'the idea that systems really are intentional or "minded" systems, if their behaviour can fruitfully be interpreted as issuing from beliefs and desires or in short: folk-psychological states' (Slors 2007, p. 322).

This position might be, in a way, treated as some version of anti-realism: for the interpretivist, beliefs are not something that pre-exist in human minds and are ready to be discovered by outside interpreters. Rather, the process of interpretation is – in some way or other – constitutive of attitudes such as beliefs. According to interpretivists, it is not the case that we can interpret people (and other systems) as having beliefs because they have beliefs; rather, they can be said to have beliefs because they can be interpreted as having them. In this way, interpretivists reverse the traditional order of explanation, according to which the epistemology of mental states should follow from the metaphysics of them: on most accounts, beliefs are thought to exist before they are cognized. On the interpretivist account, however, the epistemology comes first.

Let us first focus on Davidson's views. On his account (see Davidson 1970, 1974), the basic constituents of reality are events. All events can be said to be physical events because they can be truly described using the predicates of physics, and they fall under physical laws. Some of these events, however, can also be said to be mental events as they can be truly described using psychological predicates and they fall under mental descriptions. Thus, a particular event, e.g., Jones's believing that his pencil is on the table, is at the same time a mental event (as it can be described in a psychological idiom) and a physical event (as it, qua being a brain event, can be described using physical vocabulary).

The main advantage of Davidson's position is that it allows us to retain broadly understood metaphysical monism (there are only physical events) combined with a non-reductivist approach to psychology. The mental sphere is not reducible to the physical because the predicates of mentalistic language cannot, as a matter of principle, be reduced to physical language.

This non-reductivist aspect of Davidson is a consequence of the fact that the language of physics is concerned with providing laws; thus, given the fact that causes require laws, it is physical language that describes causal relations. However, according to Davidson, psychology is essentially anomalous, which means there can be no strict psychological laws. There can only be law-like generalizations in the domain of psychology, but no strict deterministic laws. This is due to the fact that the language of psychology is dependent on the idea of the constitutive ideal of rationality: when we are describing actions in psychological language, we are interested in rationalizing the action in question, not in providing a law-based causal explanation. Thus, mental and physical languages cannot be identified: there is no possibility of providing a translation of mental predicates into the language of physics, as one set of predicates describes causal relations, while the other depicts the relations of rational explanations.

There are two aspects of Davidson's view that make it similar to the minimal non-realist position developed in this book. The first is his insistence on the fact that having mental characteristics is a matter of falling under an appropriate psychological description. To be a mental event amounts to nothing more than being describable by a mentalistic predicate. As Davidson puts it, 'Let me first make clear that in my view the mental is not an ontological but a conceptual category. Mental objects and events are at the same time also physical, physiological, biological, and chemical objects and events. To say of an event, for example an intentional action, that it is mental is simply to say that we can describe it in a certain vocabulary – and the mark of that vocabulary is semantic intentionality' (Davidson 2004, p. 114).

This view is certainly in accord with the general spirit of minimal non-realism; as I have defined it, beliefs can be said to exist, but this obtains not in virtue of some deep metaphysical facts. Rather the truth of belief attributions is a result of the way our mentalist discourse operates.

The other way in which Davidson's theory might be considered anti-realistic is that it is quite explicit about the fact that psychological predicates do not provide us with causal explanations. It is the role of physical predicates to provide us with descriptions of the laws which in turn describe causal relations. For this reason, many philosophers (including Kim 1998) accused Davidson of being a covert epiphenomenalist. From our perspective, this scepticism about belief causation might be considered to be a virtue rather than a vice: minimal non-realism claims that belief properties do not play a causal role.

However, these similarities should not be overstated. Davidson would certainly not accept the idea that some properties are 'more natural' than others because they play a role in causal relations. He was a staunch proponent of predicate nominalism and vehemently rejected the idea that events enter causal relations 'in virtue of' possessing some property or other. For Davidson, all properties are just descriptions, and causal relations between events should be taken as primitive (this is most clearly stated in Davidson 1993). For this reason, the Davidsonian framework should be treated as significantly different from the one proposed here.

Another version of interpretivism which needs to be considered here is the one developed by Dennett. On his account, the truth of belief attributions should be seen as a result of successful adoption of what he calls the intentional stance. When we are confronted with a system, we might adopt one of three stances to interpret and predict its behaviour (Dennett 1989). The first is 'the physical stance', by which we treat the system as a purely physical object governed by physical laws. Sometimes, however, it is more practical to adopt 'the design stance', by which we treat a certain system as being designed to perform a specific function: it might be more effective, for example, to explain the operations of the heart by claiming that its purpose is to pump blood rather than by trying to describe the physical interactions of the particles of which the heart is composed.

The third option is the intentional stance. When we adopt it, we explain the behaviour of a system by means of its mental states, especially beliefs, desires, intentions and so on. For example, the best way to understand the behaviour of a chess-playing automaton might be by means of trying to understand its beliefs about what is happening on the chessboard. In the general interpretivist spirit, Dennett claims that to have states like belief is to be interpretable by means of the intentional stance (Dennett 1989) (it is worth noting that in his later writings Dennett somewhat qualified his view – see the end of the section).

There is a certain instrumentalist air to the way Dennett presented his theory in his early writings. One could get the impression that according to Dennett there was nothing more to having a mind than being interpretable through the lens of the intentional stance. As he wrote, 'What it is to be a true believer is to be an intentional system, a system whose behaviour is reliably and voluminously predictable via the intentional strategy' (Dennett 1989, p. 15). This strongly instrumentalist pronouncement caused several theorists, including McCulloch (1990), Braddon-Mitchell and Jackson (2007), and Hutto (2013), to express suspicion that Dennett is a covert fictionalist about intentional categories, including beliefs.

However, I believe that this label is unjustified: Dennett and other interpretivists should instead be seen as adopting a version of minimalism about beliefs and other intentional states (see Poslajko 2020 for an elaboration of this reading). As I see it, Davidson, Dennett and other interpretivists want to adopt a view according to which there is no need to postulate any deep facts about human cognitive architecture in order to justify the claim that beliefs exist. According to interpretivists, what is needed to retain the minimal form of realism about belief discourse is to adopt the idea that believers are truly describable from the point of view of intentional states. They also want to express their scepticism regarding extreme forms of realism: they deny that we are in possession of discrete, internal, representational states that are referents of belief attributions.

In this way, interpretivist theory might be treated as somewhat similar to the position I develop here. As was noted in Chapter 3, section 2, Mölder (2010), who is one of the leading contemporary interpretivists, explicitly embraces Schiffer's view on pleonastic properties and analyses mental properties in such terms. In this way, he paves the way for the merging of interpretivism and the deflationary approach to the existence of mental properties, including beliefs. Such a position is obviously close in some aspects to the one I propose here. Minimal non-realism, similarly to interpretivism seen through a deflationary lens, rejects both irrealism and strong realism about beliefs. Instead, both minimalism and deflationary interpretivism propose that we see belief properties as existing in the minimal sense.

However, there are important differences between deflationary interpretivism and minimal non-realism. The main point of difference is the issue of how to conceptualize scepticism about the strong version of realism. Interpretivists express this scepticism towards realism regarding beliefs by claiming that beliefs (and other intentional mental states) are constitutively dependent on the process of interpretation. (Mölder 2010 strongly emphasizes this aspect of interpretivism.) It is not entirely clear how we should understand this claim of constitutive dependence. Still, most interpretivists, as we have seen, embrace the idea that the process of interpretation plays a constitutive role with regard to attitudes. In this way, they want to reject the idea that attitudes are simply out there waiting to be discovered.

However, this thesis about beliefs being constituted by interpretation might reasonably be taken to lead to serious theoretical troubles. Some (see, e.g., Kriegel 2010) have claimed that it leads to a vicious regress, whereas others have tried to show that it has unacceptable consequences in the area of epistemology of attitudes (see, e.g., Byrne 1998). These arguments, if successful, would be fatal for interpretivism. A more detailed analysis of these arguments might be found in my other work (Poslajko 2020), where I try to defend the claim that interpretivism either leads to implausible epistemological consequences or loses its distinct character.

I will not elaborate on these issues here due to the limitations of space. However, what is important to note in the present context is that minimal non-realism does not entail the claim of constitution. As was noted before, minimal non-realism is not committed to any claims that beliefs depend on the process of ascription and interpretation. In my view, such constitutive claims lead to problematic consequences, so it is best not to espouse such views. Conceptualizing the distinction between realism and minimal non-realism in terms of the distinction between natural and non-natural properties is, in my view, a better way to understand the issue of the reality of beliefs.

On a final note, it is important to remember that the interpretivist theory, at least in some versions, is not a fully anti-realist one. As Dennett claims in his 'Real Patterns' (1991), looking at humans (and other systems) through the lenses of the intentional stance is not a matter of caprice: the intentional interpretation reveals important behavioural patterns to us. According to Dennett, giving up on this way of explanation would be a genuine epistemic loss; therefore the rejection of realism on his part is not wholesale. Dennett should be seen as being somewhat close to but not at the very end of the non-realist end of the spectrum of possible positions in the metaphysics of belief, as for him attributions of beliefs seem to capture some important objective similarities.

5.3 Mild eliminativism

Some authors who have traditionally been classified as eliminativists might also be treated as espousing a position that is close in spirit to the minimal non-realist theory I defined in the previous chapter. In the present section, I will focus on two such philosophers, namely Stich and Chomsky.

Although Stich later distanced himself (see Stich 1996) from his early views, his 'From Folk Psychology to Cognitive Science' (Stich 1983) remains one of the classic expositions of eliminative materialism. As is often noted, Stich's way of arguing for eliminativism is remarkably different from that of Churchland, who focused on the conflict between the folk-psychological description of the mental sphere and (future) cognitive science (Churchland 1981). Stich – although also interested in the conflict between the folk-psychological and the scientific outlook on the human mind – seems to be more focused on the internal problems of folk psychology. For him, the main reason to embrace eliminativism is that it is often impossible to arrive at definite answers to questions about the sameness of content (this issue was presented in Chapter 4, section 1.1).

Although it is customary nowadays to present Stich (in his early phase) as an unqualified eliminativist, his actual conclusions were presented in a more qualified way. As a possible alternative to eliminativism, he entertains the possibility of adopting what he calls the 'Panglossian paradigm'. The core idea of the Panglossian paradigm is that we might retain folk-psychological discourse (together with the possibility of explaining human behaviour in folk-psychological terms in areas such as history) by treating the generalizations of folk psychology as vague and 'rough-and-ready, rule-of-thumb' generalizations that can be viewed as true even if they do not correspond to the laws of mature cognitive science (Stich 1983, p. 228).

However, Stich finally contends that such a Panglossian solution is not viable. This is because, as he sees it, folk psychology makes certain empirical assumptions about the internal organization of the human cognitive system. Should these assumptions turn out to be false, Stich argues, the category of belief would be worthy of elimination, and we would be forced to subscribe to the claim that beliefs do not exist. For the same reason, Stich rejects the interpretivist account of belief that was presented in the previous section: for him, such a way of defending the mildly realistic position disregards the empirical assumptions that folk psychology is forced to make. (Stich makes important critical remarks about Dennett also in Stich 1981, but I will leave the issues raised there aside.)

In my view, Stich is only partly right here: it is correct to say that the falsity of the empirical presuppositions of folk psychology should be seen as a reason to reject realism about beliefs (and other related categories). However, I disagree with Stich's contention that such a rejection of realism must lead us to the claim that beliefs do not exist and the category of beliefs should be eliminated. In my view the anti-realist conclusion might be, in some reasonable way, combined with elements of what Stich calls the Panglossian paradigm. The guiding principle of the view I propose is that we might appreciate the arguments against the reality of beliefs and retain belief discourse.

An example of a view that is close to minimal non-realism, at least in this respect, is the position of Chomsky, who is sometimes classified as being an eliminativist of sorts (see Collins 2007). Although Chomsky does not present a unified metaphysical account of beliefs (at least, this is not his primary aim), he presents several insightful remarks on this topic in his 'New horizons in the study of language and mind'.

Chomsky presents his views in the following way:

> Such notions as desk or book or house, let alone more 'abstract' ones, are not appropriate for naturalistic inquiry. Whether something is properly described as a desk, rather than a table or a hard bed, depends on its designer's intentions and the ways we and others (intend to) use it, among other factors. (...) The term house is used to refer to concrete objects, but from the standpoint of special

human interests and goals and with curious properties. A house can be destroyed and rebuilt, like a city; London could be completely destroyed and rebuilt up the Thames in 1,000 years and still be London, under some circumstances. It is hard to imagine how these could be fit concepts for theoretical study of things, events, and processes in the natural world. Uncontroversially, the same is true of matter, motion, energy, work, liquid, and other common-sense notions that are abandoned as naturalistic inquiry proceeds (...).

It is only reasonable to expect that the same will be true of belief, desire, meaning, and sound of words, intent, etc., insofar as aspects of human thought and action can be addressed within naturalistic inquiry. To be an Intentional Realist, it would seem, is about as reasonable as being a Desk – or Sound-of-Language – or Cat – or Matter-Realist; not that there are no such things as desks, etc., but that in the domain where questions of realism arise in a serious way, in the context of the search for laws of nature, objects are not conceived from the peculiar perspectives provided by concepts of common-sense.

(Chomsky 2000, p. 21)

Elsewhere, Chomsky reiterates this point: 'Beliefs, desires, perceptions, rocks rolling towards the ground, storms brewing, etc. are not subject to scientific laws, nor are there bridge laws connecting them to the sciences. Uncontroversially, science does not try to capture the content of ordinary discourse, let alone more creative acts of imagination' (Chomsky 2000, p. 89).

The above quotes show several important aspects of Chomsky's views on the status of beliefs (and similar categories). First, Chomsky clearly thinks that beliefs can be said to exist, but the way this thesis is framed suggests that it can be considered to be fairly trivial and unimportant. According to Chomsky, beliefs do exist, but they exist in the same way as books or cities, namely as entities that are postulated within our folk framework and whose identity criteria are determined by our interests.

This idea is important from the perspective of the project developed in the present book. As we remember from Chapter 3, section 4, Stoljar (2014) proposed that we should interpret Chomsky's views on the metaphysical status of things like cities as a claim that such things exist yet are not natural in Lewis's sense. Thus, if, according to Chomsky, beliefs are on a metaphysical par with cities, then we should treat Chomsky as claiming that belief attributions do not track natural properties in Lewis's sense.

The second important aspect of Chomsky's views is that beliefs, along with other postulates of the folk worldview, should not be treated as serious targets of 'naturalistic inquiry', i.e., mature sciences. This is an important postulate in the context of cognitive science and scientific linguistics: according to Chomsky, the aim of linguistics is not to provide us with an account of 'semantic meaning', and the aim of cognitive science is not to explain what 'belief' and 'intentionality' are. These sciences, if they are to become mature and successful, should dispose of notions taken from folk discourse and forge a new conceptual repertoire which can be used to explain human behaviour adequately.

This idea has a certain eliminativist air to it: as Chomsky takes folk categories to be of no use in the context of serious scientific inquiry, they should be eliminated from the conceptual repertoire of the sciences. For this reason, Chomsky might rightly be seen as espousing meta-scientific eliminativism (see Collins 2007). On the other hand, there is a certain anti-eliminativist streak in the position he sketches: although intentional language, including the concept of belief, should be eliminated from science, this postulate has no bearing on the functioning of our folk discourse. Chomsky neither postulates nor predicts that intentional vocabulary will be eliminated from folk discourse. Desks are not a useful scientific category, yet this fact gives us no reason to eliminate this category from our everyday speech nor to say that desks do not exist. In this way, the Chomskyan proposal is somewhat irenic as it seems to propose that we use one set of concepts within the area of serious naturalistic inquiry and another within folk discourse.

It might be useful to compare Stich's and Chomsky's approaches at this point. For Stich, in his eliminativist phase, an important aspect of folk psychology was that it has substantial empirical presuppositions. The possible failure of these presuppositions heralds bad news for the concept of belief: if folk psychology is fundamentally mistaken, then beliefs should be treated as non-existent and this category is likely to be eliminated from our general worldview. For Chomsky, however, the category of belief – although essentially useless in serious cognitive science – might well function in folk discourse, and beliefs can be seen as existent on a par with other entities postulated within folk discourses.

These might be considered two paradigmatic reactions to the claim that a certain folk category cannot be squared with the deliverances of contemporary science and the empirical presuppositions of applying a certain category are false. One possible reaction is to say that in such a case the thing in question does not exist and the category might eventually be banished from our everyday discourse. This is the approach of Stich. Another reaction is to adopt the view according to which folk discourse and science might exist peacefully alongside each other if one does not try to import folk categories into science: this seems to be the approach that Chomsky prefers.

The view that I am promoting in this book is much closer to Chomsky's. I contend that the putative fact that the empirical presuppositions of folk psychology are false is not a strong enough reason to say that beliefs simply do not exist. Moreover, I think that the chances that we will substantially reform our folk framework in the foreseeable future are scant. Beliefs, qua posits of folk discourse, might be said to exist in the same way as desks and cities. However, I also think that there is a grain of truth in Stich's diagnosis. The fact that the empirical presuppositions of the folk-psychological notion of belief are not met should have some consequences for the metaphysics of belief and should lead to rejection of the strong realistic view. But, as the main idea of the book goes, this anti-realistic impulse is better expressed in non-eliminativistic terms.

5.4 Representationalist theories of beliefs

So far, I have focused on the theories which serve as inspirations for my interpretation of the anti-realist approach to beliefs. However, to make the map of the conceptual space complete, it will also be useful to present the position which serves as the inspiration for the way I conceptualized the opposition to minimal non-realism. In my view, the position that can be said to relate to the strong realist view most closely, as I have defined it, is the position of representationalism about beliefs. The core idea of representationalism is that 'to have a belief is to stand in a particular relation to a mental representation' (Quilty-Dunn & Mandelbaum 2018, p. 2354).

Classically, the representationalist theory of belief was associated with the language of thought hypothesis, endorsed by Fodor (1975). According to the original Fodorian position, to have a propositional attitude (and belief was thought to be a paradigmatic example here) was to stand in the appropriate relation to a certain mental representation. On Fodor's take, such mental representations were postulated to have both syntactic structure and semantic properties that made them similar to sentences of natural language. These syntactic and semantic properties of mental representations were thought to be required for the successful individuation of attitudes. In this way, beliefs were considered to be real and, as it were, 'concrete' entities: even though the language of thought theory was compatible with the multiple realization claim, there is a certain sense in which beliefs might be said to be 'located' in the metaphorical 'belief box'.

The popularity of the original language of thought theory has definitely waned in recent decades: few theorists would nowadays subscribe to the idea that human cognition literally consists in processes operating over mental representations with language-like syntax. Even Fodor distanced himself from some of his original claims (see Fodor & Pylyshyn 2015); notably, in his later writings he denied that concepts, which for him were the building blocks of the language of thought, have semantic (as opposed to purely denotational) properties.

This lack of enthusiasm for the language of thought hypothesis does not mean that the general spirit of representationalism is gone: quite the contrary, representationalist views of the nature of belief, broadly understood, are still very popular.

There are three main claims of contemporary representationalism. First and foremost, the most important idea is that beliefs, understood as states with semantic content, are somehow stored. This means that there is some sort of representational content 'in the head' that might be thought of as the belief we have. As Quilty-Dunn and Mandelbaum (2018) rightly note, the general idea of representationalism does not commit anyone to any particular claims about how and in what format beliefs are stored: it might well be the case that the storage is fragmented – that there is no separate 'module' for beliefs, and so on. What is important for representationalists, however, is that there is some cognitive architecture – no matter how dispersed – that is responsible for the storage of beliefs.

This thesis is importantly linked with the second claim of representationalism: that beliefs are causally responsible for our actions. According to Quilty-Dunn and Mandelbaum, the only way that we could appreciate the truth of causal claims involving beliefs is by identifying beliefs not with behavioural and verbal dispositions but with the 'categorical base' of these dispositions. This causally active categorical base of belief-related dispositions is, according to the proponents of representationalism, best understood as being identical to internal, deep, psychological states: namely beliefs. For some, this claim might seem obvious: if we are to understand claims about beliefs causing actions as literally true, then we'd better analyse such claims as being about some sort of causal relation between actions and some sort of internal psychological states.

The third aspect of contemporary representationalism is the idea that beliefs should be defined psycho-functionally. The general idea of functionalism about beliefs is that beliefs (like other mental states) should be defined by appeal to their role in the functional organization of the mind, i.e., their role as mediators between psychological 'inputs' or 'outputs'. This general functionalist idea might be specified in two ways. The first way (already discussed in Chapter 2, section 3.3) is the common-sense functionalism of Jackson and Pettit. According to this position, the 'laws' which define the functional role of belief (and other psychological categories) should be taken from folk psychology. The other (and more pertinent here) way of detailing the general idea of functionalism is psychofunctionalism, championed in its classic form by Block (1978). The core idea of psychofunctionalism is that 'laws' which specify the functional role of belief (and of other mental categories) are provided by empirical psychology and not by common sense.

The main difference between those two versions of functionalism is the level of granularity of functional descriptions. Common-sense functionalism offers coarse-grained definitions of mental states, i.e., definitions which allow a wide range of states to count as beliefs and a wide range of subjects to counts as believers (Martians, octopuses and AIs are the common examples here). Psycho-functionalist definitions are more fine-grained: fewer states would be classified as beliefs, and only those subjects which satisfy the laws of empirical psychology would qualify as true believers. Representationalists naturally opt for the psycho-functional option. According to representationalists, there are genuine, non-trivial, empirical generalizations that describe the causal role of beliefs and that are discovered by contemporary empirical psychology (see Porot & Mandelbaum 2020).

We are now in a position to verify the claim that representationalism meets the criteria of strong realism as it is defined in this book. First, beliefs, as representationalists see them, are certainly causally relevant. Second, the idea that the category of belief should be defined via laws of empirical psychology corresponds in an important manner to the idea that beliefs constitute a natural kind. The claim that there is such a natural kind as belief might plausibly be spelled out as the idea that there is a set of laws governing causal relations in which beliefs play important roles (see section Chapter 6, section 1 for elaboration on the connection between the notion of natural kinds and empirical generalizations). Thus, proponents of representationalism can be said to be implicitly committed to the idea that beliefs constitute a genuine cognitive natural kind. This is because they believe that there are important, non-trivial generalizations of empirical psychology that govern beliefs. Consequently, they assert that the category of belief possesses objective, non-arbitrary boundaries. Quilty-Dunn and Mandelbaum suggest that, in problematic cases of a discrepancy between a professed belief and actions, there is an objective answer to the question of whether certain mental states qualify as beliefs, and this answer might only be established from the point of view of empirical psychology (even though folksy criteria might not lead to clear decisions in this matter).

As we can see, the realist commitments of representationalism are much more substantial than is sometimes assumed. Realists not only think that beliefs are somehow 'in the heads' in the sense that they are stored. The more realist aspect of the representationalist theory is the claim that such stored beliefs are genuine causes of action and that there are important, non-trivial empirical generalizations that define belief as a genuine cognitive natural kind. In this way, representationalists see beliefs not only as existing but as very real things which are genuine causes and are subject to scientific discovery.

I would risk a conjecture that representationalism, when understood in this way, is far more often implicitly assumed than explicitly defended. In many areas of philosophy, it seems to be taken for granted that people actually do have internal, stored, causally active states like beliefs. This presumption seems to be quite widespread in philosophy of language (think of the debate around the notion of singular/de re beliefs), epistemology, philosophy of perception and philosophy of action.

A representative exposition of such a representationalist presupposition can be found in Burge:

> I assume that talk of perception, belief, desire, and intention has a place in scientific as well as in common-sense descriptions of the world. I assume that these types of psychological states are representational in the sense they are about something, indicate a subject matter as being a certain way, and (constitutively and non-trivially) have veridicality conditions on being accurate or true. These assumptions have been richly supported in empirical psychology and philosophical work. I believe that they are sufficiently well entrenched, not only in common sense but in serious scientific theory, not to require extensive support. What they need is explication, sharpening, delineation. I think that explanation in terms of distinctively psychological representational notions is, as far as we now know, basic and ineliminable. That is, we have no reason to believe that psychological explanation in terms of representation can be reduced to some other type of explanation.
>
> (Burge 2010, p. 27–8)

As we can see, there are several aspects of realism that Burge accepts here: for him, beliefs (along with other mental states) possess representational content. Additionally, he claims that postulating such representational states is necessary to adequately explain human mental life. What is characteristic about Burge's approach is that he treats these claims as his starting point: he assumes representationalism about beliefs (and other mental categories) in order to make progress with relation to other philosophical issues. This is hardly an unusual approach: Burge is just laudably explicit about his commitments.

To sum up, the representationalist position is rightly treated as the main specimen of the strong realist view on the nature of beliefs. The representationalists' commitment to realism is deeper than is usually thought as it is not only the idea that beliefs are stored that makes this view realistic: it is the adherence to the view that beliefs are genuine causes of behaviour, that there are robust empirical generalizations about beliefs, and that beliefs are ineliminable in explanations. When taken together, all these claims paint a picture that is remarkably distinct from the anti-realist proposals described in the previous sections of this chapter. Even though some of the thinkers I have characterized as anti-realists would agree with representationalists on the basic claim that there are beliefs, the underlying metaphysics couldn't be more different.

6

Reasons for non-realism

The stage has been set: I believe I have managed to define the realist and non-realist positions in sufficient detail, and I have shown how the definitions I proposed are rooted in the historical debate. Now the time has come to try to argue for the preferred position, namely that of minimal non-realism. As we remember from Chapter 4, section 1, there are three main criteria of realism in the proposed framework: objective similarity, of causal relevance, and of relation to more natural properties. Now I will try to argue that in each case there are important reasons to prefer the anti-realist hypothesis.

6.1 Problems with belief as a natural kind

The first question that needs to be answered is that of whether belief properties describe objective similarities. As was noticed in Chapter 4, section 1.1, this problem can be divided into two issues: the first is whether attributions of specific beliefs track objective similarities; the second is whether the category of belief denotes a natural kind.

The first issue, namely whether attributions of the same specific belief to two subjects (or to the same subject at different times) track objective similarities, might be considered as central to the debate between representational realists and mild anti-realists about beliefs. For representationalists, the answer is clearly positive: there is something that makes such subjects objectively similar, namely the fact that both subjects have beliefs with the same content. These beliefs are thought to be stored in some way in their cognitive systems. The minimal non-realist would obviously deny this. For the proponent of such a view, people sharing the same belief that p might be extremely different with regard to their sub-personal cognitive organization, dispositions and phenomenal states.

Although this issue is indeed central, there is no easy way to answer it. There is no direct way in which we can empirically check the hypothesis that beliefs are stored. This hypothesis resists any form of straightforward empirical confirmation or dis-confirmation. We cannot, as it were, look into people's heads to ascertain whether their specific beliefs are similar. The only arguments that we seem to possess can best be interpreted as being of an indirect nature. Representationalists argue that they can justify their insistence on the idea of the objective similarity of specific beliefs by some sort of inference to best explanation: they are convicted that the truth of certain psychological claims lends credence to the idea of the storage of beliefs. Opponents of representationalism are unconvinced by these arguments; in their view, there is no need to postulate belief-related deep structures to explain human psychology.

In my opinion, given the uneasy status of this issue, the best way to proceed is to focus on the other criteria for realism in order to see if the general result would favour the anti-realist side. If this is so, then we will be in possession of an indirect reason to reject representationalist explanations.

I will now turn to the issue of whether beliefs as a category constitute a natural kind. In order to answer this question, we must first establish which notion of natural kinds would potentially be applicable in this domain. It is often acknowledged that the traditional model of natural kinds, namely the one proposed by Putnam (1975) and Kripke (1980), is not well suited to the area of psychology. In the Putnam-Kripke model, natural kinds are understood as sharing some hidden essence: biological kinds are, for example, constituted by shared DNA, whereas chemical elements, such as gold, are thought to be constituted by their atomic structure. It is the putative fact of sharing such micro-essences that was thought to constitute the objective boundaries of the kinds in question. Many philosophers (including Cooper [2013], Beebee & Sabbarton-Leary [2010]) have noticed that this model cannot be extended to psychological kinds as there is little sense in claiming that they might be seen as possessing hidden micro-essences. If psychological kinds are defined functionally, then we cannot postulate a hidden structure common to all instances of such a kind.

A better way to conceptualize natural kinds in the context of psychology is to adopt a more liberal conception of natural kindness. As was noted in Chapter 4, section 1.2, the main component of the liberal, 'naturalistic' approaches to natural kindness was their focus on the idea that what is characteristic of categories that deserve to be treated as natural is that they are projectible, i.e., they function in successful and robust inductive generalizations. This was ingrained in the 'homeostatic property cluster' approach (Boyd 1991). However, for our present purposes it would be best to focus on the even more liberal view proposed by Khalidi (2013) and (to an extent) endorsed by Cooper (2013). On this approach, if we want to delineate between psychological categories which are arbitrary ('choleric personality' might serve as an example here) and those which are, in a sense, objective, the criterion of projectibility might be the one which does the trick. If there are some robust surprising generalizations about a certain category, then we might suspect that there is some joint in nature that we managed to discover using this category.

Proponents of strong realism, quite unsurprisingly, claim that there are robust empirical generalizations about the notion of belief. Porot and Mandelbaum (2020) point to several instances in which it is used to formulate generalizations in empirical psychology. Let us focus on one such example, namely the well-known phenomenon of cognitive dissonance, discussed by Quilty-Dunn and Mandelbaum (2018). Cognitive dissonance, i.e., the situation in which a subject has two dissonant cognitions that lead to discomfort, is widely confirmed in contemporary psychology (see, e.g., Harmon-Jones & Mills 1999). For representationalists, the fact that there are laws of cognitive dissonance which make use of the concept of belief provides strong reason to think that the category of beliefs is projectible (Quilty-Dunn & Mandelbaum 2018).

If this were the right appraisal of the situation, then we would have important evidence for the claim that beliefs can be treated as constituting natural kinds (as we would have some genuine inductive generalizations). However, there are some strong reasons to be sceptical about such a rosy picture.

First, it is not clear that we are presently in a position to say that we are in possession of 'the laws of cognitive dissonance'. Whilst the phenomenon itself is fairly well established, there are several competing theories regarding how to explain it (see again Harmon-Jones & Mills 1999 for an overview). This sheds some doubt on the claim that we have discovered 'the laws' of cognitive dissonance. This worry might not necessarily be decisive: it is common in science (especially outside the areas of physics and chemistry) to be dealing with several competing theories regarding one phenomenon, and there might be some robust empirical generalizations to be discovered in such areas. Nonetheless, until we can indicate specific generalizations about beliefs, there is some room for scepticism about the claim that this category is a projectible one. The same worry holds for other putative generalizations concerning beliefs: it might be that we are not yet in the position to say we have discovered the laws that make essential use of the notion of belief. What we have is something more modest: useful, pro tanto generalizations, and a model which explains certain psychological effects but still lacks enough support to be called laws.

The other more principled worry about the idea that there are genuine empirical generalizations about the notion of belief was presented by Jenson (2016). According to him, we should treat 'belief' as a fragile theoretical entity (the distinction between robust and fragile theoretical entities is taken from Wimsatt [1981]). As Jenson summarizes this distinction:

> A theoretical entity is fragile if the results of multiple, independent, putatively reliable measures of that entity turn out to radically vary and this variation cannot be adequately explained away. If our theories posit an entity or process as real, then we should expect the detection of that entity, ceteris paribus, to be fairly robust. That is to say, one would expect the results of various methods of measurement or detection of the entity to produce invariant results.
>
> (Jenson 2016, p. 970)

As we can see from the above quote, there is a strong link, according to Jenson, between the issue of robustness and the question of realism. Only entities that are robust deserve to be treated as real, whereas the fact that some postulated entity is fragile gives us a good reason to eliminate it from the scientific discourse.

According to Jenson, there is strong evidence that we should treat the category of belief as being fragile in this sense. One of the main reasons for this is the problems we face with interpreting implicit association tests (IATs). As is well known, studies on IATs reveal that (in many subjects) there is a startling gap between their professed opinions about, say, the equality of races and the subtle behavioural cues which suggest that they are in fact prejudiced. For Jenson, the important lesson from studies on IATs is that we have two independent procedures for establishing subjects' beliefs: on the one hand, we have their verbal self-reports; on the other hand, there are behavioural cues. These two methods, as it turns out, provide us with systematically distinct results. Thus, as Jenson concludes, the category of belief is fragile as distinct methods of measuring beliefs do not converge.

In my opinion, this observation gives us an important reason for scepticism about the claim that the category of belief is projectible. If there are distinct ways of measuring belief that give incompatible results, then putative generalizations about belief are questionable. What is, the worry goes, the inductive basis of such generalizations? Are we really discovering generalizations about belief, or maybe the laws in question are about some other psychological category? The idea of discovering laws about a certain category seems to presuppose that we can independently establish whether the examples on which we are conducting our studies really belong to the category in question: so, if we want to discover a genuine generalization about beliefs, we must be sure to have a reliable way of measuring them. But if beliefs are indeed fragile, then it could be doubted that we have such a reliable measure. The main problem that seems to arise here is that the category of belief might not be, on a deep level, a unitary one. It is this lack of unity that casts doubt on the status of beliefs as natural kinds.

This lack of unity of the category of beliefs is something of which cognitive psychologists seem to be well aware. In their overview of the state of research on beliefs in cognitive science, Connors and Halligan state that '(…) complexity of beliefs poses challenges for empirical investigation (…). In practical terms, it makes it difficult to isolate beliefs from other cognitive processes and operationalise their investigation. Perhaps as a result, and despite their considerable importance for a complete description of a cognitive neuroscience, the cognitive nature of beliefs has attracted little formal investigation' (Connors & Halligan 2015, p. 3).

Elaborating on the complex nature of belief in contemporary psychological inquiry, Connors and Halligan write:

> Beliefs are best considered as being multidimensional. Beliefs share a number of common properties but can vary across dimensions within these properties. These include the following:

(1) Beliefs have different origins. Beliefs, for example, can be formed through direct experience or by accepting information from a trusted or authoritative source (…).
(2) Beliefs vary in terms of the level of evidence and support they command. Some beliefs have high levels of evidence, while others appear to be accepted without requiring much evidential support (…).
(3) Beliefs can be said to be 'held' at different levels of awareness. Whereas some beliefs may involve considerable conscious preoccupation and rumination (…), other beliefs may appear implicit, unconscious, and only evident by inference from behaviour (…).
(4) Beliefs vary considerably in generality and scope. Beliefs may refer, for example, to specific objects or individuals, groups of objects and people, or whole classes of objects and people (…).
(5) Beliefs vary in their degree of personal reference (…).
(6) Beliefs can be held with different levels of conviction or degrees of confidence. This can range from firmly held (…) to relative uncertainty (…).

(7) Beliefs vary in their resistance to change in response to counter-evidence and social pressure. While related to conviction, people can also vary in how open they are to disconfirming evidence towards their belief and to considering alternative points of view.

(8) Beliefs can vary in their impact on cognition and behaviour. This may likewise be influenced by degree of conviction. Whereas people may act on some beliefs, they may fail to act on other beliefs that they verbally endorse (…).

(9) Beliefs can produce different emotional consequences. Whereas some beliefs may be relatively innocuous or even self-serving, other beliefs may cause considerable distress (…).

It remains to be seen how these different properties are cognitively and neutrally instantiated. It is possible, for example, that some properties reflect qualitatively distinct subtypes of beliefs. It is also possible that some properties instead simply reflect variation along a continuum within a single type of belief.

(Connors & Halligan 2015, p. 3–4)

As this quote shows, beliefs are indeed a subject of psychological inquiry, but the most important message here is that there is important evidence for the claim that what we call beliefs might be generated by different mechanisms, and the effects of belief possession might be distinct in different cases.

Two conclusions can be drawn at this point. First, it might be granted to representationalists that beliefs are used in contemporary psychology to formulate explanatory theories; moreover, there are some psychological results that might suggest that this category is indeed projectible. Nonetheless, there are also important reasons to be sceptical about the claim that beliefs are projectible as there seems to be insufficient evidence that this category is robust and unitary. Importantly, there seems to be no convergence in the criteria for detecting beliefs, and the category of belief (as defined in cognitive psychology) seems to play many distinct theoretical roles. This last fact might reasonably lead to the conclusion that we are dealing with several distinct mechanisms and processes that we label 'beliefs', and the mechanisms and processes in question belong in fact to different cognitive kinds. The label 'belief' can then reasonably be seen as used to describe a variety of phenomena which would be best considered as constituting more than one natural kind.

Another reason to be sceptical about the claim that beliefs constitute a natural kind is that there is significant evidence that folk-psychological categories vary cross-culturally, and that the category of belief is not a universal one (see

Strijbos & de Bruin 2013 for a useful overview and discussion of the results). For example, in some cultures the distinction between beliefs seen as cognitive states and emotions/desires seen as conative states might not be so straightforward as in our 'Euro-American' conceptual framework.

Obviously, the fact that some category is not a cultural universal does not in itself prove that there is no natural kind denoted by this category. It might be that our notion of belief denotes a cognitive natural kind which other cultures somehow missed. Still, for anti-realistically inclined theorists the more plausible explanation of this cross-cultural variation is that our folk-psychological conceptual scheme, in which the notion of belief plays a central role, is one of the many possible ways of classifying the underlying psychological phenomena, but it is not necessarily the only correct one. If, as the anti-realist suggests, there are many distinct complex mechanisms which we lump together using the label of 'belief', then it should come as no surprise that in other cultures the same domain of complex mental processes might be categorized in a significantly different manner.

Arguments from cross-cultural variation are notoriously controversial: both on the evidential side (there is always a problem of correctly interpreting the empirical data about other cultures) and on the interpretational side. So, we cannot treat the argument from cross-cultural variation as the decisive reason to adopt anti-realism. However, a more modest conclusion seems justified: the observation that there is some (perhaps modest) variation in the way different cultures carve out the mental sphere fits nicely with the general anti-realistic outlook. In this way, we gain some reason to be in favour of minimal non-realism.

To sum up, the reasons to claim that the category of belief is a cognitive natural kind seem to be outweighed by arguments to the effect that it is not. The best interpretation of the evidence we have in this respect is to consider this category as just one of the many possible ways of categorizing the human mental sphere and that we should have no presumption that by using it we are referring to any joint in cognitive nature. The preferred alternative to the idea that beliefs constitute a natural kind seems to be the view that they constitute a human kind. This claim has been recently put forward by, for example, Dewhurst (2017), according to whom the 'belief' kind should be treated as, in a way, socially constructed and not necessarily matching the deep cognitive ontology. In my opinion, such a view corresponds nicely with the idea that belief properties are non-natural, in Lewis's sense, which is the central claim of the minimal non-realist view I develop in this book (but see Chapter 8, section 6 for an important objection to the idea that construction goes hand in hand with rejection of realism).

6.2 Causal exclusion and beliefs

The criterion of causal relevance is the second criterion for deciding whether belief properties should count as natural ones, and, as a consequence, whether we should adopt realism or minimal non-realism about beliefs. As was shown in Chapter 4, section 1.2, there is a general problem with maintaining that mental states, including beliefs, qua being higher-level states, can be genuine causes of behaviour. The causal exclusion argument threatens us with the conclusion that only physical properties/events can be truly causally relevant in explanations of our actions.

The debate surrounding Kim's argument is extremely complex: there have been numerous proposals on how to solve it and probably as many attempts to show that these solutions fail. Giving a full account of these debates is a near-impossible task that would divert us from the main theme of this book.

My proposal of how to proceed with the issue of the causal relevance of beliefs is to focus on one popular way of responding to the challenge of causal exclusion. The hope is that showing that this specific attempt fails would allow us to draw some more general conclusions about the problems generated by the idea that beliefs are causally responsible for our behaviour. I will focus on one of the most prominent and perhaps most interesting attempts to solve the problem of causal exclusion both in general and in the specific context of beliefs: the attempted solution is based on the idea of the difference-making account of causation.

The basis of the difference-making account is the observation (which has already been referred to in Chapter 4, section 1.2) that the causal exclusion argument conflates two distinct notions (see, e.g., List & Menzies 2017): the notion of 'productive causation' and the looser notion of causal relevance/non-fundamental causation. Proponents of the productive account of causation tend to think that only events which are somehow nomologically necessary for their effects are genuine causes of events. List and Menzies characterize this view in the following way: 'Causation here involves a causal "oomph", i.e., the production of an outcome through some causal force or power, on the model of a billiard ball's causing the motion of another by transmitting a force on impact' (List & Menzies 2017, p. 278).

This productive notion of causation aligns well with the causal exclusion argument. If we understand causation along the lines of the productive account, then it seems convincing that there can be only one cause of a given event and that physical events have only physical causes. Proponents of the difference-making account, however, note that a productive notion of causation is applicable only to fundamental physical causation (if there is such a thing). This leads to the conclusion that most of our ordinary causal claims, such as 'smoking causes cancer' and 'money-printing leads to inflation', would turn out to be automatically not true as they try to describe causal relations between higher-level events/properties. This is an obviously unwelcome consequence: first, it makes the causal exclusion argument trivial (if the only genuine causes are located on the physical level, then mental events cannot be causes); second, it is utterly counter-intuitive as in both empirical science and ordinary speech we do treat higher-level phenomena as being causally relevant.

To avoid these consequences, many theorists have claimed that we need to offer a less stringent notion of causation/causal relevance to deal with higher-level phenomena, and proponents of the notion of causation as difference-making (see, e.g., List & Menzies 2017, Menzies 2008, Woodward 2008) offer exactly that. For them, the proper way of conceptualizing causal claims in special sciences (such as medicine and economics) is as follows: when we say that property A causes property B, it means that making a difference in the value of property A would result in a change of value in property B.

The important feature of this account is that it allows higher-level properties to play a role in causal relations. The phenomenon of difference-making can happen when either only A or both A and B are higher-level properties. In making claims about causation understood as difference-making that involve higher-level properties, we abstract away from the details of the fundamental properties which serve as realizers of these higher-level properties. Let us take a stock example: when we say that a certain drug causes drowsiness, we are, in effect, saying that by changing the value of the intake of the drug (say from 0 to 1 mg) we are making a difference in the level of drowsiness that the patient feels. This might be true irrespective of the details of the biochemical story behind the mechanism of this drug. In this way, the notion of causation as difference-making might be treated as an example of the general notion of causal relevance, which was introduced in Chapter 4, section 1.2.

This general idea of difference-making might seem to be easily applicable to the issue of the causal relevance of beliefs. Mental states (such as beliefs) might be taken as causes if it is true that making a difference to such states makes a difference in other states, such as our behaviour. For Woodward (2008), once we buy into the interventionist framework of causation (i.e. the version of the difference-making account that he offers), the issue of the causal status of beliefs becomes easily solvable. For him, there is ample evidence for the claim that manipulating beliefs leads to changes in behaviour. As he writes:

> Many experiments in psychology and the social sciences are naturally regarded as involving, among other things, successful attempts by the experimenters to manipulate subject's beliefs by giving them verbal instructions (about e.g., what the experimental task is, what they will be rewarded for doing, etc.), where the goal of the experiment is to discover how these changes are systematically associated with changes in subjects' behaviour. Similarly, it is very natural to interpret many experiments (in, e.g., social psychology and experimental economics) involving interactions between people as investigations of, among other things, how changes in subject's beliefs about one another's beliefs and desires cause changes in behaviour. For example, changes in my beliefs about how likely you are to cooperate in an iterated prisoner's dilemma or trust game will cause changes in my behavior toward you, changes in responder's beliefs about the alternatives available to the proposer in an ultimatum game will cause changes in the probability of responder rejecting the proposer's offer and so on.
>
> (Woodward 2008, p. 231)

This passage strongly suggests that the solution to the problem of causal exclusion is a straightforward one. There is ample empirical evidence which shows that making a difference in beliefs leads to difference in actions. This, according to proponents of the difference-making account, is all that we need to secure the claim that beliefs are causally relevant. If matters were indeed so simple and we could defend the idea of the causal role of beliefs by appealing to the notion of difference-making, then it would be a serious argument for realism about beliefs. On this account, the status of beliefs as causes would be as secure as that of medicines, which should be enough to placate concerns about the causal relevance of beliefs.

Still, there are some important reasons to be sceptical about this solution. First, the ability of the difference-making account of causation to defend the idea of higher-level causation might be debated: according to some philosophers (see Baumgartner 2009), the causal exclusion worries might be restated even in the interventionist framework. In what follows, however, I will ignore this problem and will assume, for the purposes of the discussion, that the difference-making account is successful in the general case. Instead, I will focus on the second worry that arises in this context: whether it is actually as easy to apply this framework to the specific case of beliefs as is suggested. I will presently offer an argument why this application should be considered problematic (this argument is an adapted version of the reasoning I offered in a different context in Poslajko

2017; a somewhat similar line of thought – although applied to all functional properties, not only to beliefs – has recently been presented by Rellihan 2020).

The argument, in most general terms, goes as follows: the starting point is the basic fact that beliefs are states which possess content. This claim will be shown to have important consequences for the questions of the supervenience base of beliefs. Specifically, the claim will be that the base of beliefs is wider than the occurrent psychofunctional state of a believer. This conclusion about the supervenience base of beliefs will, in turn, be used to show that the difference account of causation does not vindicate the idea that beliefs are causes.

Let us first introduce the notion of the supervenience base of beliefs and its relation to the concept of content. The issue of the supervenience base of beliefs boils down to one question: what are the lower-level facts that constitute the base of beliefs? If we consider beliefs to be higher-level states, then there should be some lower-level states which beliefs supervene upon. The idea is that beliefs are somehow metaphysically dependent on some more basic (preferably natural) properties. The notion of supervenience is used here as the most generic notion of metaphysical dependence (it might well turn out that some other notion of metaphysical dependence would be more appropriate here, but I will leave this issue aside).

As has already been noticed, one of the central features of beliefs is that they are individuated by their content: beliefs that differ in content are distinct beliefs, even if this difference in content is miniscule. And as higher-level properties differ only if their supervenience base differs, the difference in content must be accompanied by a difference in the base properties. In other words: the same combination of lower-level properties cannot serve as the supervenience base for beliefs with different content.

These remarks might seem to be trivial, but they have important consequences. They lead to the conclusion that content-determination theories should have a bearing on our views about the supervenience base of beliefs. In what follows I will argue that the supervenience base of a contentful mental state should be considered as containing more than the occurrent internal mental states of the subjects. In order to show this, I will consider two main competing theories about mental content and show that they both lead to the same conclusion. Then, I will point to the consequences of this conclusion in relation to the issue of the causal relevance of beliefs.

There are two main contenders in the debate on what determines the content of mental states such as beliefs: externalist and internalist. On the externalist account of content, popularized by Putnam (1975), Kripke (1980) and Burge

(1979), the content of our mental states is, at least partly, determined by factors that are external to the occurrent internal states of the possessors of the mental state. These factors are either objectively existing natural kinds, as in Putnam's theory, or the social environment, as in Burge's account. In either case, externalism leads to the conclusion that the supervenience base of the content of beliefs is wider than the occurrent state of mind of believers.

To show this, let us consider Burge's arthritis example: it describes two subjects who are identical with regard to their internal mental states, but one of them inhabits a possible world where 'arthritis' means 'any pain in the legs', whereas the other lives in our world. On the externalist view, if these two persons believe that they have arthritis in their thighs, their beliefs should count as having different content because the socially accepted definitions of the concepts used in these beliefs are different. Thus, the facts in virtue of which these two beliefs obtain are distinct, but the difference lies 'outside the heads of the speakers'.

Things are less obvious in the case of internalism. The central idea of internalist views is that the content of beliefs is determined by factors internal to the subject (see, e.g., Lau & Deutsch 2019 for an overview). This idea can be spelled out in two ways: either these internal factors are to be understood as being internal physical properties (see, e.g., Segal 2000), or they should include phenomenal properties (such a view, with qualifications, might be attributed to Farkas 2003).

My claim is that both versions of internalism are committed to the claim that whatever constitutes content must, as it were, be temporally external to the occurrent mental states of the believer (a somewhat similar conclusion is put forward by Block 1995). In my view, no matter what this internal factor is, it must be located in my past. This is because whatever constitutes the content of my concept must be responsible for it having the application criteria it has. Such application criteria must be relatively stable. I cannot be said to possess a belief with specific content if it is not the case that something that happened in my past determined the content of the constituents of this belief. If beliefs are standing states and have determinate content, then they must have somehow acquired this content in the past. Some theorists claim that this content determination is achieved by way of conscious meaning-intentions; according to several other philosophers, this is done by way of some naturalistic process of 'concept acquisition'; however, both these theories assume that these events happen before the concept is applied. On the conscious meaning-intention view, the necessary condition of using any concept is that one first formulates an intention to use a token of mental vocabulary before this token is applied. According to the naturalistic view, there is some process of content acquisition that happens on the neuronal level; only after this process is completed might we use this concept in belief formation.

This fact has important consequences with regard to the issue of the supervenience base of beliefs. As it turns out, the supervenience base of my current belief contains at least two states: the first is the past event that is partly constitutive of my concept, which is part of my belief; the second is my current psychofunctional state related to this belief. Both are necessary to obtain in order for me to have the belief in question.

Thus, it turns out that both internalism and externalism about content lead to the conclusion that the supervenience base of beliefs is wider than the occurrent state of mind of the believer (this assumption is explicitly questioned by some proponents of causal role theories of beliefs; more on this below). Now, it is time to show how this conclusion bears on the issue of the causal relevance of beliefs when considered in an interventionist framework.

The basic idea is as follows: imagine a situation in which I am the subject of an intervention which aims to manipulate my belief in order to change my behaviour (to use an example of the sort used in the difference-making account of mental causation); for example, I am presented with fake scientific evidence which makes me to drop my belief $B1$ and change it to $B2$. As a result I perform action A. On the face of it, this situation proves that beliefs are causally active in the interventionist sense, as the intervention on my beliefs caused the change in my action. But closer examination could cast doubts on this claim. Let us assume that it so happens that there is a possible world nearby in which there is my doppelganger, who has nearly the same belief $B1^*$. His occurrent psychofunctional state is the same as mine, but he differs in his history: his way of acquiring the concept which partly constitutes the content of his belief was different than mine. He is subject to very same intervention as I and ends up having a very similar belief to the one I had after the experiment, namely $B2^*$. As a result, he performs the very same action A as I because the minor difference in the content of his beliefs does not impinge on the course of his action.

So, the question which arises now is whether it is actually a change in my belief that was the interventionist cause of the action. It is true that the intervention changed my belief and that the same intervention was indirectly responsible for a change in behaviour, but does this suffice to say that beliefs are causally active?

If we adopt the view that events prior to my current psychofunctional state are part of the supervenience base of my beliefs, then it is obvious that any current intervention cannot change these events. So, what is changed by the intervention is my (and my doppelganger's) current psychofunctional state. Obviously, as my current psychofunctional state is part of the supervenience base of my beliefs, then the change in the former results in the change in latter. Thus, there obtains a counterfactual dependence of actions on beliefs: If beliefs change, then actions also change.

In my view, however, it's the change in the occurrent psychofunctional state that is the cause of the action in question. Let us remember that the feature of the interventionist notion of causation is its contrastive character. As Woodward put it: 'one should think of a causal claim of overt form "C causes E" as having something like the underlying structure: C rather than C* causes E rather than E*' (Woodward 2015, p. 3,597). So, my claim is that psychofunctional states are causes, and beliefs are not causes, and this is because what can be changed by interventions are things that are here and now, but not past, content-determining events. Beliefs and actions covary, and actions counterfactually depend on beliefs, but this is because interventions on occurrent psychofunctional states change beliefs in a non-causal manner.

To sum up, this argument shows that if we assume the interventionist account of causation and the internalist notion of content, we still have a problem with showing that beliefs are causally responsible for changes in behaviour. The more plausible explanation of situations which seem to show that an intervention on beliefs leads to a change in behaviour is as follows: the actual cause (in the interventionist sense) of the change in behaviour is an occurrent mental state which is part of this belief's supervenience base. Beliefs, on the proposed picture, are not genuine interventionist causes.

The argument presented above is a variant of the well-known arguments which aim to show that broad content, i.e., content which includes factors external to the subject, is causally inert. A clear exposition of the claim that broad content states are causally inert might be found in Kim:

> [W]hat semantical properties are instantiated by the internal states of an organism is a relational fact, a fact that essentially involves the organism's relationship to various environmental and historical factors. This makes semantical properties relational, or extrinsic, whereas we expect causative properties involved in behavior production to be nonrelational, or intrinsic, properties of the organism. If inner states are implicated in behavior causation, it seems that all the causal work is done by their "syntactic" properties, leaving their semantic properties causally idle. The problem of mental causation generated by syntacticalism, therefore, is to answer the following question: How can extrinsic, relational properties be causally efficacious in behavior production?.
>
> (Kim 1993, p. 289–300)

So, the problem of how beliefs, qua content-bearing states, might be causally relevant is not a new one. My argument is meant to add two things to this issue. First, that this problem is relevant not only for the externalist but also if we adopt an internalist approach to content. This is because all content, even that which might be called 'narrow' in the standard technical sense, is 'wide' in a looser sense: even if we buy into the idea that all the factors which determine content are localized 'inside our heads', it is rather implausible to say that they are present in a given moment. So, if all content is wide in this temporal sense, then the problem of causal relevance arises for all content-bearing states, regardless of how we wish to conceptualize content.

My second addition to the issue of content causation regards the plausibility of the interventionist account of causation as the solution to the issue of the causal relevance of beliefs. We might agree, for the sake of argument, that the difference-making account of mental causation resolves the issue of higher-level causation; however, even then, the problem persists of how content might be causally relevant. This is because what turns out to be genuinely causally relevant in explanations of actions, even in the interventionist framework, are not beliefs qua content-bearing states but psychofunctional occurrent states.

It is important to note that these psychofunctional states, which we should, as I see it, take to be genuine causes of behaviour, might be considered to be higher-level psychological states, albeit of the sub-personal variety. In this way, the causal role of psychology might indeed be saved by the interventionist framework; we do not have to accept the counter-intuitive view that mental causation works only on the purely neural level. But this does not show that we might treat personal-level content-bearing states such as beliefs as causally relevant (the issue of the relation between subpersonal mental states and folk-psychological states such as beliefs will be discussed in more detail in Chapter 9, section 2). The problem of causal exclusion for beliefs is not that causal powers drain away and that only the most basic physical level is causally active: the problem is that beliefs lose their status as genuine causally relevant factors for sub-personal psychological states which are individuated purely psychofunctionally.

Some proponents of the causal role theory of beliefs (see, e.g., Carruthers 1996) explicitly reject the main assumption of the argument I put forward here, namely the claim that the content of my currently held beliefs must be determined by something prior to my current psychofunctional state. In the strong version of the causal functionalist view, the content of my belief is determined fully by my current state, namely by the network of causal dispositional relations between the belief in question and other mental states. No reference to prior concept acquisition or meaning-intentions is required. If such a theory of the individuation of the content of beliefs were indeed feasible, then the argument I have presented above would be a non-starter. However, the idea that the content of beliefs might be determined purely by reference to a network of causal dispositional relations between mental states is highly dubious, and currently such proposals are virtually invisible in the debate on the naturalization of content (see next section). The reasons why such proposals do not seem to get off the ground are twofold. First, it seems that the network of such relations is not rich enough to generate content that is specific enough. Secondly and more importantly, the idea of content seems to presuppose that there are some standards of correctness for applications of concepts. However, if the content of concepts is determined solely by the occurrent causal states of the mind, there seems to be nothing that can play the role of a correctness-determining factor.

To sum up the main idea of this section, most of the proposed solutions to the problem of mental causation tacitly assume that the 'lower-level' supervenience base of a given belief state is identical to the internal states that are causally relevant for behaviour. But if this assumption is false, then the problem remains unsolved. Even if we found an answer to the question of how to account for higher-level, non-reductive causation, this would not necessarily mean that we are able to provide an account of how contentful mental states might be seen as being genuinely causally active. I focused on the difference-making framework because this seems to be the most promising one to deal with the problem of higher-level causation on a general level. Still, it is not able to show how beliefs can be causally relevant.

6.3 Natural origins of content problems

The last criterion of realism which we need to look at is the issue of the connection between belief properties and more fundamental ones. As was indicated in Chapter 4, section 1.3, this problem is nowadays discussed under the heading of naturalization of content. In this section I will try to show why we should consider this project unsuccessful. My arguments here have no claim to originality: rather, I wish to summarize the existing arguments against the naturalization of content project.

It is important to remember that the idea of the naturalization of content does not imply any commitment to the idea of a strictly reductionist account of content; even more so, it does not rely on the notion that we could define content properties in terms of natural properties. Quite the contrary, many prominent proponents of the idea of the naturalization of content are also committed to some version of non-reductive physicalism; as such, they reject the project of the straightforward identification of content with more basic properties. In this way, the framing of the debate proposed here might differ from Lewis's original idea that less-elite properties should be linked by definitional chains with the most-elite ones. Still, I think that a negative conclusion regarding the issue of the naturalization of content would count as a strong argument for the claim that belief-properties are not natural properties.

Although there have been many proposals regarding how to solve the naturalization of content issue, two main ideas might be considered the most prominent: the first is that we should try to naturalize content by invoking causal relations between cognitive systems and their environment; the other is that the best way of naturalizing content is by reference to evolutionary notions.

According to the causal-representational paradigm (classical expositions of which might be found in Dretkse 1981 and Fodor 1990), the representational features of mental states should be analysed in terms of their causal connections to elements in the environment. Of course, not just any causal relation between mental states and their surroundings would be appropriate: my concept of tiger is causally connected to many things, including children's books about animals, but no one would claim that my concept of tiger is 'about' books. The task of causal-representational theories is to specify what kind of causal connections do the trick.

The general idea of how to think of representational relations in this framework is the following (the following reconstruction heavily draws on Adams and Aizawa 2017): suppose we have a mental vehicle of content (X) which is supposed to represent dogs. Thus, there should be a certain causal relation between X and dogs: this might be the relation of co-variance, or the relation such that the thing that X represents is the cause of the formation of X, etc. The idea is that it is possible to specify a special sort of causal relation which would determine that the referent of the vehicle is dogs.

There are two main problems with this approach. The first is the question of how to account for systematic/reliable misrepresentations in this paradigm (see, e.g., Mendelovici 2013). The problem is that it is perfectly possible that a certain representational device would be systematically tracking something different than the intended subject of the representation. For example, someone might reliably use the word 'centaur' when seeing certain weird-looking horses from afar, but his concept of centaur is still intended to represent 'half human, half horse', and, as such, it should be considered empty. But if the simple version of the causal theory of content were true, then it could turn out that the concept of centaur would represent 'certain weird-looking horses located afar'. This would be inconsistent with our intuitions about the content of such a concept.

To solve the problem of misrepresentation, proponents of causal-representational theories need to draw a distinction between two kinds of causal relations between mental representations and items in the environment. Causal relations of the 'right' kind are those which are constitutive of representational relations, whereas causal relations of the 'wrong' kind are not relevant for determination of content. In the example above, proponents of the causal theory, if they wanted to avoid the counter-intuitive conclusion that the concept of 'centaur' refers to weird-looking horses from afar, would have to claim that the causal relation between the concept in question and these weird horses is of the wrong kind. The problem with such a solution is that this distinction between 'right' and 'wrong' kinds of causal relations is either circular (we would have to presuppose the notion of representation in order to draw this distinction) or lacks independent naturalistic credentials.

The other and, in my opinion, more powerful kind of worry about causal-representational theories is that they cannot do justice to the fact that the contents of our thoughts should be distinguished from their referents (this is what caused Fodor to become sceptical of the ability of his own theory to explain the content of thoughts, see Fodor & Pylyshyn 2015). Let us consider the classic example: one may simultaneously believe that Paderewski was a famous pianist and that Paderewski was a politician. However, one might not be aware that Paderewski the pianist and Paderewski the politician are the same person; still my concept of 'Paderewski the pianist' and of 'Paderewski the politician' might be connected via the same causal links to the historical figure in question.

The central 'Fregean' idea, as Fodor and Pylyshyn observe, is that our thoughts, or elements of them, represent reality under a mode of presentation: the same element of external reality might be represented by two distinct concepts that might, as it were, include different information about the subject. And, as Fodor and Pylyshyn admit, the causal theory of mental content does not have enough resources to distinguish between these modes of presentation. For this reason, Fodor adopts the view according to which we should see concepts as having only referential properties and as lacking 'meaning' understood as the mode of presentation. In my opinion, however, such a claim amounts to an admission of defeat: the causal-representational theories cannot provide a naturalistic account of the content of mental states. The purely referentialist account of the concepts that Fodor and Pylyshyn propose might, at best, be considered to be an ersatz notion.

In the light of the failure of the causal-representational theory, the other strategy for naturalizing content, namely the one which appeals to evolutionary notions, might seem to be a more promising idea. According to some philosophers, this approach is the only viable one. The following Rosenberg quote might be characteristic here: 'Darwinian processes are the only way in which adaptation, the appearance of goals, ends, purpose, etc. is created in a purely physical world' (Rosenberg 2015, p. 539).

The central idea of the teleosemantic accounts of mental content (see, e.g., Millikan 2000 for a clear exposition) is that the proper naturalistic account of the mind–world representational relation should be provided in terms of the notion of proper function. Millikan characterizes this notion in the following way:

> A thing's proper functions are effects which, in the past, have accounted for selection of its ancestors for reproduction, or accounted for selection of things from which it has been copied, or for selection of ancestors of the mechanisms that produced it according to their own relational proper functions, it being their function to be guided by certain variable aspects of the environment in this production. Whatever has proper functions must have had predecessors that historically effected such functions, thus helping to account for its existence or presence.
>
> (Millikan 2000)

The general idea of proper function is quite convincing: we might say, in a completely naturalistically acceptable way, that the function of the heart is to pump blood because it is the blood-pumping function that is responsible for the evolutionary selection of the heart. Proponents of teleosemantics want to extend this idea of proper functioning to representational systems. They claim that certain biological systems have the proper function of representing. This is supposed to justify the idea of representation being a naturalistically acceptable notion. The famous example of bee dances is illustrative here: it might be said that the proper function of bee dances is to represent the location of nectar; this is because the mechanism of bee dances was historically selected for representations of nectar.

An important advantage of employing the notion of proper function is that it allows us to make room for the notion of malfunction in the naturalistic framework: a thing malfunctions if it does not fulfil its proper function. Thus, we can easily get a respectable naturalistic notion of misrepresentation into our vocabulary: if a proper function of a system is to represent certain Xs, and this system does not fulfil this function and indicates something different that it is supposed to represent, then we might say the system misrepresents.

So far so good: we seem to be in possession of a naturalistically respectable concept of misrepresentation that is crucial for the notion of content. However, does this mean that teleosemantics can explain our folk-psychological notion of the content of beliefs? There are at least three familiar reasons for scepticism: first, the teleosemantic account provides us with counter-intuitive content ascriptions; second, it is unable to distinguish between the different possible contents that we attribute to mental states; third, it does not account for the fact that truth is the satisfaction condition of beliefs.

The first problem is that there is no guarantee that the content we attribute to a given mental state from the intuitive perspective would be the same as the one attributed from the perspective of teleosemantics. The classic argument for this conclusion was presented by Pietroski (1992): in his thought experiment, he imagines creatures ('kimus') that have acquired the ability to see red, but this ability proved evolutionarily useful because it allowed them to avoid predators ('snorts'); in the story, kimus are attracted to red-looking areas, like the top of a hill at sunset; fortunately for them, these are areas that snorts avoid.

The moral of this story is that although, from the intuitive perspective, kimus can detect red-looking areas, from the point of view of the teleological theory of content, the content of their mental state is 'this is a snort-free area'. This is because, as the story assumes, the evolutionary gain from detecting red was that it helped kimus to avoid snorts. The moral of this story can be easily generalized: if the content of mental states is derived from evolutionary gains, then attributions of content would not necessarily be intuitively plausible. Evolutionary explanations might be counter-intuitive, and this also applies to evolutionary explanations of mental abilities to represent.

The second problem that the teleosemantic theory faces is more specific to propositional attitudes. The issue is that once we agree that our attitudes, including beliefs, are individuated by their propositional content, then we must agree that there are extremely fine-grained ways of distinguishing between distinct contents. To use a well-known example, my belief that Paderewski was a famous pianist is a different belief than the belief that the prime minister of Poland in 1919 was a famous pianist (because I might hold these two beliefs even if I forgot that Paderewski was the prime minister of Poland in 1919).

Evolutionary approaches to content seem unable to make room for such fine-grained distinctions. Content of beliefs, as specified by our folk theories, is intensional, i.e., there might be a difference in content between two representations with the same referential properties. But such fine-grained distinctions might not be adequately captured by the teleosemantic theory because evolutionary explanations do not care about such detailed descriptions (this worry has been raised many times, e.g., by Fodor 2008, Hutto & Myin 2012). There seems to be no evolutionary advantage in my ability to refer to the same fact (that Paderewski was a famous pianist) in two different ways. Whatever the evolutionary advantages of having representational systems are, they cannot account for the subtle distinctions we are able to draw in the contents of our beliefs.

The third worry is that the teleosemantic approach cannot account for the intuition that truth is, in a way, a satisfaction condition of beliefs. Although there have been numerous debates over how to spell out the idea that 'truth is the aim of belief' (see Chan 2013 for an overview), it might be said that central to our folk understanding of the concept of belief is the claim that the contents of our beliefs aim to represent the world as being a certain way.

However, this platitude about beliefs cannot be adequately rendered by the teleological theory of content. In the evolutionary framework, success must be always understood in evolutionary terms: a certain biological entity is deemed to perform its proper function if it performs the function for which it was selected. But there is little reason to suspect that there is a biological mechanism that was selected for its ability to track down the truth about the external world (again, this argument has been put forward many times; for a nice exposition, see Rosenberg 2015). Knowing the truth is not any evolutionary advantage in itself: not all truths are of evolutionary use, and sometimes the evolutionary advantage might lie in not getting things right.

All these three arguments show a similar point: there is an important conceptual lacuna between the content of beliefs as they are understood in the folk-psychological framework and the representational properties of mental states as described by the teleofunctional approach. In the folk-psychological framework, we see beliefs as states which possess determinate fine-grained content and which aim to be true. In the teleological framework, representations are natural devices which serve evolutionary functions.

These sceptical considerations do not particularly aim to show that a teleofunctional account cannot secure the naturalistic credentials of any notion of representation or content whatsoever. The conclusion is more modest: the above arguments show that whatever the merits of the teleosemantic approach are, it cannot provide a naturalistic explication of the intuitive content of beliefs, as defined by folk psychology. There might be some representational features that some cognitive states might be reasonably said to possess, and the teleological account might provide us with an explanation of the naturalistic credentials of a representationalist psychological theory. The aim of this section is not to argue for an austere psychological anti-representationalism; rather, the aim is to show that the currently existing theories of naturalization of content cannot offer a naturalistic explanation of the notion of the propositional contents of beliefs, as we see this notion in our folk-psychological framework.

This modest conclusion is, however, of utmost theoretical importance. If beliefs are individuated by their content, and there is no good naturalistic explanation of the notion of content of beliefs, then we might say that there are no interesting explanatory links connecting belief properties with more fundamental/natural ones. This conclusion lends support to the main claim of this chapter, namely that belief properties are not natural in Lewis's sense.

6.4 Status of the arguments

Some readers might feel somewhat underwhelmed by the arguments that have been offered in the previous sections. These arguments do not constitute anything that could be plausibly considered to be a 'master argument' against strong belief realism; I have not presented any reasoning that would prove beyond any reasonable doubt that the representationalist-realist position is patently false. Instead, what I have tried to do is show that whenever we consider a criterion which I propose to use to distinguish between strong realism and minimal non-realism, there are strong reasons to be sceptical about the realist proposals. The arguments I have presented are mostly negative in nature as their main aim is to show that realist claims lack adequate support. We do not have enough evidence to secure the claim that beliefs constitute natural kinds, that they are genuine causes of behaviour and that there is a way of linking beliefs with more fundamental vocabulary.

I genuinely consider the question of belief realism to be an epistemically open issue: there is still not enough evidence to say that either realism or minimal non-realism is certainly true. Specifically, I do not think that realism is an internally incoherent or conceptually misguided option which can be debunked by a simple *a priori* argument. I think belief realism is a bold and interesting hypothesis, but its problem is that it does not have adequate empirical support. It is possible – both logically and empirically – that the realist account of beliefs is the right one. However, to my mind – the way things stand at the moment – betting on the negative option is the safer option.

The consequence of the view according to which the distinction between the real and the unreal should be spelled out in terms of the distinction between natural and non-natural properties is that being a realist about a certain category might not be treated as a default option. Natural properties are sparse: it is only sensible to think that the number of truly natural properties that capture the genuine joints in reality would be quite low. Obviously, the 'reasonably natural' properties that are studied by special sciences, including psychology, would be more numerous. Still their number would be quite small.

We might reasonably suppose that many of the categories that we postulate in our folk framework would not track any categories which would be postulated within mature science. This observation has been made many times: Dupré (1995), for example, makes this point in the context of philosophy of biology. In contrast to the optimistic assumptions that are often made by proponents of natural-kind term theories, Dupré claims that, more often than not, our folk-biological classifications denote categories which we have created with our parochial interests in mind, but they do not track 'objective' biological categories. Contemporary biological classification has no use for categories like 'fish' or 'shrub', yet these categories seem to be central to our current folk-biological classificatory practices. Dupré insists that such a mismatch should not lead us to the conclusion that such human categories do not exist, and I feel that this is the right conclusion.

It is important to note, however, that my approach is distinct from that of Dupré. In his view, the fact that folk categories do not match scientific ones does not support denial of realism about folk categories. In my view, however, at least in the specific case of beliefs, the conclusion that belief properties are not natural gives credence to the mildly anti-realist view on beliefs. A more detailed analysis of the relation between the issue of the non-naturalness of beliefs and anti-realism will be presented in the next chapter.

Framing the debate about the reality of beliefs in terms of the question about the naturalness of belief properties has important consequences with respect to the issue of *onus probandi* in this debate. When we are confronted with the question of whether a given property which we use in our folk discourse is natural, we cannot just assume that the answer is positive. Some positive corroboration is needed because there is always a possibility that the categories we ordinarily use do not successfully denote natural properties. In the case of the category of belief, there is some evidence that this category could be treated as denoting reasonably natural properties; however, in my view, the reasons for scepticism outweigh the reasons for optimism.

The modest claim I put forward here is as follows: the issue of belief realism is epistemically open and there are important reasons to prefer the minimal non-realist view. This conclusion is important because, as I see it, there is a certain presumption towards realism in the philosophical literature that partly stems from the fact that the traditional anti-realist paradigms have been considered failures. In such a dialectical situation, it seems important that we start to treat the anti-realist account of beliefs, at least in its modest version, as a viable theoretical alternative.

7

Minimal non-realism and common sense

7.1 Moderate (anti-)realism as an analysis

The last chapter was devoted to arguments which support the idea that belief properties are not natural. One worry might arise at this point: in what sense might this conclusion be seen as expressing an anti-realist view about beliefs? Even if we agree with the conclusion of the previous chapter and admit that the reasons to prefer the view that beliefs aren't natural properties outweigh the reasons for the strongly realist view, this is not enough to claim that we have reasons to adopt anti-realism. One could argue that what I have managed to show is that the strongly realist conception of beliefs is (most probably) mistaken. But to show that one particular theoretical view on the nature of a certain category is mistaken is not the same as proving the truth of anti-realism about this category. It might be the case that we just need to adopt a different theory, but according to this new theory the phenomena we are trying to describe would count as real.

In the case of beliefs, one might suggest that once we show that there is not enough evidence for the strong realist approach, we might simply conclude that some other less metaphysically loaded conception of belief is the right one. Changing a mistaken philosophical theory of beliefs for a better one does not necessarily point us in an anti-realist direction. This observation is important, as some of the theories that were discussed in Chapter 5 and presented as being inspirations for the non-realist proposal can (and should) be seen as being in the businesses of trying to offer a proper analysis of what beliefs are. These theorists, moreover, did not present themselves as providing arguments for anti-realism. Two important examples of such approaches are (neo-)dispositionalism and interpretivism. It seems that in both these cases the aim is to provide us with a proper analysis of beliefs rather than to prove that they are not real.

Let us first consider Schwitzgebel's neo-dispositionalism. On this view, beliefs should be seen as superficial, and this excludes the view that they are natural 'deep' properties. But what is important is how Schwitzgebel justifies this approach. His argument for the superficial approach to beliefs relies on his reconstruction of our intuitions regarding mental categories. What Schwitzgebel claims is that our folk notion of beliefs and other similar mental states supports the superficial view.

A good illustration of this approach is one of the arguments that Schwitzgebel offers for the claim that we should prefer the superficial analysis of attitudes over the substantial one, namely the case of 'BetaHydrian valuing'. In this example, he invites us to imagine a race of alien creatures that 'show all signs of valuing molybdenum over gold' (Schwitzgebel 2013, p. 83). BetaHydrians are willing to trade gold for molybdenum; they have all the appropriate phenomenal processes and verbal dispositions of subjects who exhibit such valuations, and so on. According to Schwitzgebel, we might say that it is true that BetaHydrians value molybdenum over gold even though we know nothing of their internal cognitive organization. More importantly, Schwitzgebel claims that such an appearances-based approach to attribution of this attitude is something that is justified by the proper analysis of our folk view. As he writes, 'Ordinary opinion would, I think, favor saying the BetaHydrians value molybdenum over gold' (Schwitzgebel 2013, p. 84). For Schwitzgebel, this analysis is true across the board: the superficial analysis correctly captures all of our attitudes' concepts, including the concept of belief (it is important to note that Schwitzgebel does not extend his dispositionalism to all mental states, e.g., he does not say that phenomenal states can be analysed dispositionally).

This claim has important consequences. If Schwitzgebel is right that belief properties are superficial and our concept of belief is superficial, then there seems to be little reason to adopt belief anti-realism. If the folk consider beliefs (and other attitudes) to be superficial, and beliefs are in fact superficial, then the correct appraisal of the situation is that the folk have the correct concept of beliefs. There is, as it were, a certain correspondence between the folk concept and mental reality. The only people who got things wrong were some philosophers, but this is hardly surprising as philosophers can often be accused of reading too much into folk notions. Nonetheless, if the folk consider the notion 'X' to denote a superficial/insubstantial category, and the property X that is denoted by this notion turned out to be a non-natural one, then the only thing we should conclude is that the folk concept adequately renders reality. This looks very much like realism.

A similar strand of thinking can be found in Dennett's writings. For him, the purpose of intentional systems theory is twofold: the first aim is to provide us with a proper metaphysics of propositional attitudes; the second is to explain the practice of attribution of these attitudes. The conception of the intentional stance aims to show that our practice of attributing beliefs (and other intentional states) is guided by external superficial criteria. Dennett puts it in the following way:

> The central epistemological claim of intentional-systems theory is that when we treat each other as intentional systems, using attributions of beliefs and desires to govern our interactions and generate our anticipations, we are similarly finessing our ignorance of the details of the processes going on in each other's skulls (and in our own!) and relying, unconsciously, on the fact that to a remarkably good first approximation people are rational.
> (Dennett 2009, p. 341–2)

As this quotation shows, it is important for Dennett that in adopting the intentional stance we do not care about any putative deep cognitive structures: we only care that the behaviour of a certain system can be productively explained by using the assumption that the system is guided by rationality (understood in a folk-psychological way). Again, this assumption directly leads to the claim that our concept of belief (and of other psychological attitudes) is, at least in a certain respect, superficial. Dennett's final position is, however, a bit more complex than the one presented here: he admits that there is some conflict between some aspect of the folk concept and reality, and that the concept of belief requires some regimentation. This aspect of Dennett's thought will be discussed below, in section 3.

To sum up, in both neo-dispositionalism and certain versions of interpretivism, the superficial character of our concept of belief is somehow mirrored by the fact that belief properties are superficial (non-natural, as I would put it). But this means that both these theories do not aim to provide us with an anti-realist theory of beliefs. The aim of both these theories is not to deny their reality but to provide a correct account of what beliefs are.

Minimal non-realism, in opposition to neo-behaviourism and interpretivism, is intended to be a version of anti-realism about belief. But, as the considerations presented above show, adherence to the claim that belief properties are not natural in Lewis's sense is not in itself enough to classify a position as being a specimen of belief anti-realism. What is also needed is some sort of commitment to the idea that the folk notion of belief is in the wrong with respect to mental reality.

7.2 Where is the conflict?

The conclusion from the previous chapters of the book was that we have good prima facie evidence for the claim that beliefs are non-natural properties in Lewis's sense. But the fact that, all things considered, the minimal non-realist option is the most reasonable one does not mean that the folk concept of belief is such that it is in agreement with the notion that belief properties are non-natural. In this section I will argue that the proposal that beliefs are non-natural properties indeed comes into conflict with our folk conception of belief.

In order to achieve this aim, it is necessary to show that our folk notion of belief includes some theoretical commitments that are impossible to square with minimal non-realism. In other words, we need to provide an analysis of the folk concept of belief that would show that this concept has important realist aspects.

It has to be admitted that the notion of 'folk' used in the present context is a parochial one: the common sense I am trying to reconstruct is the common sense of the contemporary, educated, western person. This is important to note, given the fact that there is strong evidence for cross-cultural variation in the way mental states' attributions function in different conceptual schemes, as was described in Chapter 6, section 1. I also admit that I bracket, for the sake of the argument, any worries about the viability of the project of armchair conceptual analysis. Although there are some serious reasons for scepticism about the ability of philosophers to reconstruct folk notions, I think that there is some version of the project of philosophical analysis of concepts that can be defended; however, a proper defence of this project must be left for another occasion.

So, my claim is that the folk notion of belief is substantial, at least in the respect that, according to our folk notion, beliefs should be seen as concrete causes of behaviour. Moreover, I contend that, at least in this aspect, there is a deep-seated conflict between superficial theories of beliefs and the folk understanding of this concept. This is because the consequence of the superficial theories of beliefs is that they do not see beliefs as being genuinely causally relevant. This might seem like a genuine problem for my proposal, and the ways to solve this problem will be discussed below, but for now let's focus on the justification for the claim that there is indeed such a conflict.

There are two main sources of evidence for the claim that the folk see beliefs as being literally causally active: the first is the observation of ordinary language; the other is the mindreading literature in experimental psychology. Egan observes that reflection on both ordinary use and scientific psychology supports the view that beliefs as understood by the folk are causally active:

> Neo-Ryleanism is revisionary about our shared explanatory practices. It certainly seems as if we take beliefs to be effects of perception and inference, and causes (in conjunction with desires) of action. We often say things such as 'He believed he was about to be fired because he saw a confidential memo that criticized his job performance' and 'She quit smoking because she believed

it was affecting her health'. There is no reason to suppose that 'because' here functions any differently here than in locutions which are clearly causal, such as 'The fire started because the electrical system was overloaded'. In claiming that common sense explanations of belief fixation and action are not causal, despite appearances, the neo-Rylean assumes a rather heavy burden of proof.

The case for a causal construal of belief-desire attributions does not rest solely on linguistic intuitions. (…) Of present relevance is the fact that a large and influential body of research in empirical psychology is predicated on the claim that beliefs, desires, and more permanent conditions such as character traits are implicated in causal explanations of behavior.

(Egan 1995, p. 187–8)

I contend that Egan is right on both counts. First, it seems correct to claim that we should take the practice of attributing causality to propositional attitudes in the folk idiom at face value and that attempts to paraphrase these claims lead to substantial difficulties. Second, it is right to say that contemporary psychology offers substantial evidence for the thesis that we normally treat attributions of attitudes as providing us with knowledge of the causes of other people's behaviour.

The first way of arguing, namely the one that rests on the claim that our folk idiom treats belief explanations as causal, has been subject to some debate. It is uncontroversial that in our everyday speech we use belief attributions to make causal claims, and these causal claims have the same surface structure as causal claims involved in explanations that resort to perfectly natural causes. However, some theorists have suggested that behind this superficial similarity lies a deep difference: according to them, we mean something utterly distinct by 'because' when we say, first, that his house caught fire because there was a short-circuit, and second, when we say that someone went the wrong way because he believed that this was the right way. An example of such an approach might be found in Curry (2018), who attributes such a view to Ryle. According to Curry (and to Ryle in Curry's reading), the explanation in folk psychology is different from the explanations used outside the psychological domain as in the psychological case we are providing reasons instead of causes. This account is hardly unique. There have been numerous theoretical proposals which suggested that folk-psychological explanations are somehow special and that they cannot be treated on a par with normal explanations (see, e.g., Knowles 2002 for an overview and criticism of such approaches).

In my view, such theories might be interesting in their own right, but they do not constitute a proper analysis of the meaning of ordinary attributions of causality in folk psychology. No matter how we spin it, it seems that there is no deep difference in the way causal vocabulary functions in the context of psychological explanations and other types of explanations. The proponents of the idea that psychology is in some sense special might be right in claiming that there are some aspects of folk psychology that are specific to it (like the fact that there is some normativity involved in the ascription of attitudes). However, this putative special character of folk psychology does not provide us with enough evidence for the claim that the word 'because' functions differently in the context of explanations in which we use beliefs than it does in other forms of causal explanation. There is no point in denying that folk-psychological attributions often serve purposes other than providing causal explanations. However, this does not change the claim that in many contexts we do ascribe beliefs in order to provide causal explanations of behaviour; or, at the very least, this is what the superficial reading of our practice suggests, and we do seem to lack a credible alternative to this reading.

Contemporary empirical psychology research seems to offer even more decisive evidence for the claim that ordinary people treat propositional attitudes such as beliefs as being genuine causes of behaviour. The sub-field of psychology which seems to provide the most relevant evidence in this respect is studies on the phenomenon of mindreading. Although there are several competing theories on how to best account for our ability to attribute attitudes to other subjects (which offer different answers to issues such as whether, for example, this ability is innate), there is a strong consensus among psychologists that the attribution of beliefs to other subjects is used for behaviour prediction (see, e.g., Kovács, Téglás, & Endress [2010]).

A striking outcome of studies on mindreading is the effortless character of the propositional attitudes-based ability to attribute intentional agency: if the proposed interpretation of developmental psychology studies is credible, children can easily interpret the behaviour of just about anything (e.g. cartoon blobs) in the framework of intentional agency, and they can attribute beliefs to such entities if the object in question behaves in an appropriate manner (see Arico et al. 2011). Some theorists remain sceptical about the tendency to (over-)attribute the full-fledged capacity to attribute full-blown attitudes to young children and non-human animals; but even they seem to retain the position that grown humans do attribute attitudes in a 'realistic' way. An example of such an approach can be found in Zawidzki:

> The social cognition of nonhuman animals, human infants, and human adults engaged in unreflective, quotidian interactions is often guided by tacit

knowledge of behavioral patterns, sometimes highly abstract ones, involving categories like 'goal', 'efficient means', 'information access', and 'teleological rationality'. The most sophisticated examples of such low-level mindreading plausibly involve adopting something like Dennett's intentional stance. As Dennett (...) himself makes clear, this is better characterized as an unreflective, tacitly encoded 'craft' than an explicit theory (...).

In addition, some adult human social cognition is guided by the representation of propositional attitudes as such. We can predict each other's behavior based on attributions of concrete, unobservable mental causes, which represent situations under individually variable modes of presentation and must combine with indefinitely broad networks of other mental states to yield behavior. This is more than a tacit theory of observable behavior; it is a theory of the underlying mental causes of observable behavior.

(Zawidzki 2013, p. 17–18)

As this quote shows, Zawidzki, despite his sympathy for Dennett's 'superficial' approach, considers interpretivism to be an inadequate theory, at least as a comprehensive analysis of the folk understanding of beliefs. The superficial approach might shed some light on the capacities of non-human animals and infants, but it does not do full justice to at least some elements of the practice in which we, human adults, are involved. In this practice, we do, according to Zawidzki, treat beliefs as being 'underlying mental causes' and 'concrete' states that possess semantic properties (although this is only a partial function and is by no means the earliest or primary function of belief attribution).

Many researchers in the debate about mindreading claim that it is wrong to interpret every episode of mindreading in terms of attributing causally active beliefs (and other propositional attitudes). It is common to postulate mechanisms like 'minimal mindreading' (Butterfill & Apperly 2013; see also Zawidzki 2018): these mechanisms (to put matters in the simplest terms) explain the automatic processes of attributing goal-oriented behaviour. Proponents of minimal mindreading postulate that many situations which were traditionally interpreted as involving attributions of causally active propositional attitudes can be explained by using this minimal process. Still, advocates of minimal mindreading do not deny the existence of a 'full-blown' form of mindreading which indeed involves attributing causally understood propositional attitudes. It is important to note that a commitment to the idea that our folk notion of belief involves the idea of the causal import of beliefs does not have to claim that every social cognition act involves a full-fledged attribution of beliefs: what is needed is the claim that we often interpret others by resorting to the idea of beliefs as causes.

Curry (2018) complains that this consensus among mindreading researchers, namely that beliefs are conceptualized by the folk as being genuinely causally active, stems not from empirical data but from the fact that psychologists have internalized philosophical dogma. This is a fair point, but this concern seems to be general: any philosophical interpretations of psychological claims might be seen as underdetermined by actual empirical evidence. Still, the fact that there is a near-consensus in the field might be taken as indicating that such an interpretation provides the most efficient interpretation of the data.

Neither the argument from the folk idiom nor the argument from empirical studies on mindreading is foolproof. It is possible to try to reinterpret the data so as to make folk practice seem compatible with the neo-behaviourist reading of it. However, in my opinion, if we weighed the evidence for and against both the realistic and the neo-behaviourist vision of the folk concept of belief, the realistic reading would come out as more justified. This is because the realistic reading seems to offer a simple and comprehensive account of the data from the observation of the folk practice and from empirical psychology. On the other hand, although the behaviouristic reading is in principle capable of explaining all the data, it is less plausible than the realist reading because the behaviourist reading is more complicated and postulates a convoluted reinterpretation of practice and empirical evidence.

If my appraisal of this situation is right, then superficial theories of beliefs, including neo-behaviourism and certain versions of interpretivism, should be treated as at least partially failing to deliver a proper analysis of the folk notion of belief. There is a significant theoretical conflict between the way the superficial theories conceptualize beliefs and the way we conceive of this category in our folk schema. This conflict stems primarily from the fact that in our folk approach we treat beliefs as being concrete causes of behaviour, whereas the superficial approaches cannot make room for the claim that beliefs are causes in the most literal sense of the word.

The typical response to this problem that is offered by proponents of the superficial approaches is to either downplay the evidence for the claims that the folk treat beliefs as genuine causes, or to offer some paraphrases of sentences in which we attribute causation to beliefs (and similar states). In my opinion, both strategies are, at best, theoretically risky: the downplaying strategy might be considered to be a sign of unhealthy dogmatism, while the paraphrase approach might seem to be an *ad hoc* solution. Although there is no guarantee that the aforementioned strategies cannot work, there is considerable room for scepticism about the superficial theories' ability to adequately render folk intuitions.

This conclusion is important, as it might be said that the issue of mental causation is a central crux that differentiates between the strong realist and minimalist approaches to beliefs. If beliefs really are to be understood as internal causes of behaviour, then it is natural to suppose they must be some concrete internal states. In other words, the idea that beliefs can be internal causes of behaviour seems to correspond naturally with the claim that beliefs are somehow stored (unsurprisingly, Quilty-Dunn & Mandelbaum [2018] treat the issue of mental causation as one of the main reasons for adopting a strong, realist, representationalist view). It is hard to see how else beliefs could be seen as entering genuine causal relations if they are not stored internal states. Behavioural dispositions are not something that can be located in space in any meaningful sense, thus they cannot be treated as causes in the 'productive' sense of causation. This in turn suggests that the folk treat beliefs as if they were concrete entities, and that the folk notion of belief is the one captured by the representationalist approach. In this way, we show that the superficial minimal accounts of beliefs fail to capture the content of the folk concept.

The proponent of the superficial analysis might try to argue (as, for example, Eronen [2020] does) that it is possible to salvage some sort of interventionist vision of mental causation from within the broadly superficial framework. Such a strategy might lead to two kinds of concerns. First, it might be said that such an approach does not solve the conflict because the folk conceptualize belief causation in a way which is similar to the productive notion of causation (see, e.g., Hutto 2011). Another more serious worry is that once we embrace the view that belief properties are not natural, then beliefs would turn out to be not causally relevant, even on the interventionist account (this was argued for in Chapter 6, section 2). If this is true, and beliefs, on the minimalist take, cannot be seen as causally relevant in any sense, then there is a deep conflict between minimalism and the folk view on beliefs.

7.3 Application criteria and metaphysical commitments

The main conclusion of the previous section is that there is a serious error in the way some of the minimalist approaches (including neo-behaviourism and certain versions of interpretivism) reconstruct the folk understanding of the notion of belief. What needs to be stressed at this point, however, is that these theories should be seen as being only partly wrong in their reconstruction. There are also some important correct insights into the way these positions reconstruct the folk notion.

What the minimal approaches to beliefs seem to get right about beliefs is the fact that in our practice of attributing beliefs we are guided by superficial criteria: we only look at behavioural and verbal cues in order to decide whether we can attribute beliefs to a certain system. We do not require any information about the internal goings-on of this system in order to be able to successfully describe it using the language of beliefs; this is simply because we do not have any epistemic access to the internal organization of other subjects in typical situations when we attribute beliefs.

The conclusion that we might draw at this point is that there is a significant tension in the way the folk conceptualize belief. On the one hand, it might be said that the folk use a thin, superficial notion of belief as a guide to the attribution process. On the other hand, the folk seem to suppose that by way of attributing beliefs we are describing genuine, internal, causally active states to the subjects in question. These two claims are incompatible: it is difficult to see how states which have only superficial characteristics can be seen as being genuine internal causes of behaviour. Conversely, it seems hard to see how one can justifiably ascribe internal, causally active states when these ascriptions are based on superficial characteristics.

The tension just described is substantially different from the one we encounter in the case of natural-kind terms: in these cases, as is suggested by, for example, Putnam (1975), we use a term while being guided by superficial criteria, yet we trust that there is an essence of the kind to which we refer and that this essence determines the proper extension of the term. In the case of beliefs, however, we are implicitly presupposing a non-substantial, non-essential notion to guide our extension-determining process, but we semi-explicitly claim that the elements of the kind 'belief' share some deep characteristics that make them causally relevant.

This tension makes it challenging to provide an adequate philosophical exposition of the folk concept of belief. The folk seem, on the one hand, to endorse the idea that beliefs are 'substantial' states; on the other hand, the important aspect of the folk concept of belief is the fact that we attribute beliefs in accordance with insubstantial criteria. This issue has already been noted: a clear exposition of the problem can be found in Dennett (1998) and Hutto (2011). According to Dennett, when describing folk psychology we should distinguish between 'folk craft' and 'folk theory'. The folk-psychological craft is our ability to do what we do when we interpret other people (and ourselves) as possessing beliefs (and other attitudes). Folk theory (or folk ideology, as Dennett sometimes calls it) is the set of our quasi-theoretical presuppositions which we embrace as an 'explanation' of why the application of folk craft is successful. As Dennett is quick to point out, these two are distinct. Folk craft might be considered to be perfectly acceptable in practice, even if we find folk theory to be erroneous and in need of serious revision.

There are two important aspects of Dennett's view. First, he contends that the error involved in folk-psychological theory does not need to lead to the elimination of folk-psychological practice. Second, he admits that folk-psychological theory might be open to revision. What is missing in his view, however, is a detailed view of how to conceptualize this distinction between craft and ideology, and how it bears on the content of the concept of 'belief'. In his reply to Zawidzki, who critically evaluated the ability of the intentional stance theory to adequately analyse our mental concepts (Zawidzki 2018), Dennett (2018) explicitly admits that his theory does not capture all aspects of folk-psychological concepts: it captures only those that are worth saving for cognitive science. Not clarified, however, is the relation between this new concept and the old one, nor the issue of how this change bears on the question of realism.

Hutto (2011) raises a point which is even more pertinent to our purposes. He notices that there is a tension between the way we use folk-psychological vocabulary and the presumption, endorsed by the folk, that mental states such as beliefs productively cause our actions. Hutto's insight is valuable, as he points to the fact that the problematic aspect of the folk theory of beliefs lies in the folk commitment to the strong notion of mental causation. However, in my view, Hutto is wrong in quickly dismissing this folk commitment to the productive causal character of beliefs; for him, it just stems from the folk commitment to a mechanical picture of the world. In my view, we have good evidence that the idea that beliefs are causally relevant is ingrained in the concept of beliefs, and the proper analysis of this concept should include this fact.

In what follows, I will try to present my account of the concept of belief, which will treat this tension between the superficial character of folk practice and the commitment to belief causation as real but will at the same time provide us with a way of somehow managing this tension. In my opinion, the best way to achieve this is by distinguishing two aspects of the folk notion of belief: the application criteria and the metaphysical inferential commitments. I will presently argue that the former aspect is captured by the 'superficial' theories of belief, whereas the latter is captured by the strongly realist representationalist approach.

In order to clarify the distinction between these two aspects of the concept of belief, it will be useful to adopt, at least provisionally, one of the many possible theories of concepts. I have no ambition to provide a definitive explanation of this notoriously difficult philosophical notion here; instead, I will try to adopt some plausible theory of concepts and use it to shed some light on the issue at hand. Given the fact that the central theme of this book is the defence of psychological anti-realism, I will not adopt any of the psychological theories of concepts. Instead, I will tentatively espouse a simplified version of the inferentialist theory of concepts that is loosely based on the inferentialist theory of meaning, developed classically by Brandom (2008); however, for the purposes of this section, I will adopt the version developed by Williams (2010, 2013). This is obviously a heterodox approach to meaning and concepts, but I think using this theory could be of use when we want to see different aspects of how the concept of belief functions in ordinary discourse.

The general idea of the inferentialist approach to meaning (and concepts) is that we should conceptualize the meaning of a given term as being determined by the set of normatively acceptable/prescribed inferences in which the term in question functions. To use a well-worn example, the meaning of the term 'east' is partly determined by the fact that once we accept the statement 'x is east of y' we are licensed to infer the statement 'y is west of x'. In general, according to inferentialists, each term is equipped with a set of normatively permissible inferences which determine the concept in question. There are two main features of such an understanding of meanings/concepts. First, this is an anti-representationalist account in the sense that the meaning of a given term is not determined by what the term purports to refer to. Second, this is an anti-psychological theory of meanings/concepts: they are constituted not by anything mental but by the social practices which determine the permissible inferences.

It should be stressed that Williams's theory is mainly intended to serve as a theory of the meaning of expressions, not as a theory of psychologically real concepts. However, in the present context such a theory might be of use as the phrase 'the folk concept of belief' is used in this chapter to refer to what is meant by the folk when they use the world 'belief' in ordinary discourse. I do not make any claims about what is internally represented by users of language when I talk about the concept of belief.

Williams's development of the general inferentialist idea consists mainly in his proposal to distinguish several components in the characterization of the meaning of a given term. For our purposes here, the most important aspect of his theory is the distinction between the epistemological component and the inferential component. The epistemological component of the meaning of a given term tells us in what circumstances we are justified in using the term in question. The inferential component, on the other hand, specifies the licensed inferences in which the term in question stands.

Let us take colour terms as an example (Williams 2010). The meaning of the term 'green' is characterized, among other things, by two factors. First, by the fact that we are licensed to use this term if we have a reliable discriminating reaction to green things (this is the epistemological component of the concept). Second, we are licensed to infer statements such as 'x is not yellow' from the statement 'x is green' (this is the inferential component).

This is an obviously simplified characterization of Williams's proposal, but this rough-and-ready idea might be helpful in seeing the sources of the tension in the concept of belief. As I see it, this tension might be explained in the following fashion: the epistemological component of the folk concept is adequately captured by the superficial theories of beliefs, while the substantial theories adequately render the inferential component.

To be more precise, the epistemological component of our folk concept of belief specifies that we are justified to ascribe beliefs to a given subject if the subject in question satisfies fairly weak behavioural criteria. This means that 'x has a belief that p' is a justified claim if x fits the behavioural stereotype of a subject who believes p, or when the subject can be described as someone who believes p from the point of view of the intentional stance. Thus, the justification that is needed to attribute beliefs is modest: we only need to know publicly observable facts about behaviour and the verbal pronouncements of the subject in question in order to be justified in the claim that x believes that p.

However, once we make this attribution, we are licensed by the inferential norms guiding the folk concept of belief to infer from the claim 'x believes that p' to the claim that 'x is in some definite internal state which is causally responsible for x's behaviour'. Although most people would probably not be able to formulate this claim in such a specific way, they could be seen as implicitly treating such inferential moves as justified. Thus, the inferential component of the folk concept of belief should be seen as supporting the representationalist analysis.

In my opinion, this inferential component of the folk notion of belief is what constitutes the potentially problematic metaphysical commitments of this concept. While we are perfectly justified in using this concept because the common-sense epistemic criteria of applying it are empirically met, by doing so we are also acquiring a metaphysical debt of sorts. When we attribute beliefs, we implicitly commit ourselves to attributing internal, causally active states to subjects of beliefs. This is because the inferential component of the folk concept licenses the transition from the ascription to the claim that the subject to whom the attitude is ascribed is in a causally relevant internal state. This inference is licensed by communal, normative standards, and as such the fact that it is correct does not depend on individual inferential propensities.

It is important to note that even though these two components (epistemic and inferential) are indeed constitutive for our present folk notion of meaning, they are in principle separable. It is imaginable that some linguistic community could use a concept somewhat similar to our concept of belief, but such a concept would only include the epistemological component of our actual concept. Consequently, this alternative concept of belief would not support the inferential transition from the claim 'x believes that p' to the claim 'x is some concrete internal state that causally explains her/his behaviour'. Users of this concept would not incur any metaphysical debts by using this concept, and the content of it would be adequately rendered by some of the superficial theories of belief.

This alternative belief-concept is, arguably, not the one we are using now, but perhaps it is the one we should be using. The metaphysical commitments that are incurred by the inferential aspect of our actual concept of belief are erroneous because there are no causally active internal states that we refer to when we use belief attributions. The metaphysical picture that is associated with our current concept is misleading, and for this reason we might see this concept as deficient. But this deficiency does not have to be a reason to eliminate this concept; it might be more advisable to perform a conceptual revision.

This is then the main claim of the present book: as the available evidence strongly suggests that we cannot treat the folk concept of belief as denoting a natural property, then we must contend that there is some error involved in this concept. The best way to do away with this error is by changing the concept in question in order to get rid of its problematic and unjustified metaphysical commitments.

7.4 Analogies with free will and gender

The last section ended with the postulate that we should somehow revise the concept of belief so as to free it from the problematic metaphysical commitments that are incurred by the concept we presently use. Such a revisionary proposal has not, to my knowledge, been put forward with regard to the concept of belief. However, in other areas of philosophy, revisionary postulates along similar lines are not unknown. Currently, analytic philosophy is witnessing a renewed interest in the idea that the aim of philosophy is not only to deliver analyses of the concepts we use but also to revise these concepts if they turn out to be deficient. This project is sometimes put under the general heading of 'conceptual engineering' (although not all philosophers involved in the project of revision embrace this label). Many track this project back to Carnap (1950), and its more contemporary proponents include Cappelen (2018), Eklund (2017), Machery (2017), Plunkett (2015), Scharp (2021) and Chalmers (2011).

I will not discuss conceptual engineering in general. Instead, I will focus on some specific examples of broadly understood conceptual engineering that are most relevant for the project developed in this book. So, in this section I will present two proposed revisions of philosophically important concepts: the revisionary approach to free will championed by Vargas, and the ameliorative analysis of the gender concepts proposed by Haslanger. My aim here is not to endorse any of these proposals but to highlight certain important methodological aspects of them in order to show how these cases can shed light on the revision of the concept of belief.

Vargas introduces his position in the following way: 'Revisionism about free will is the view that an adequate philosophical account of free will requires us to jettison some aspects of our commonsense thinking about it' (Vargas 2009, p. 45). Vargas builds his approach on two main premises: first, that commonsense thinking about freedom is, for the most part, committed to libertarianism. We do think that, in order for our decisions to be free, these decisions must genuinely not be pre-determined and that real alternative possibilities must be available to us before we decide on the course of action.

The second premise of Vargas's account is that this libertarian view of free will is false. We do not have free will in the strong sense in which libertarians wish we had. As Vargas puts it:

> [A]n adequate picture of human agency should be one that is plausible, given a broadly scientific view of the world. Unfortunately, our common-sense understanding of ourselves as free and responsible agents is not plausible in this way. I think that many libertarians (…) have done an excellent job of describing what must be true of our agency for us to make good on a widespread set of convictions about free will. The trouble is there is no principled reason to think that our agency, and in particular, the physical systems underpinning our agency, are indeed built in the way described by (…) libertarians. Speculative metaphysics has an unimpressive track record, and wishing our agency had indeterminism located in just the right places and none of the wrong places

provides us with no reason for thinking that we have so fortuitous an alignment between phenomenology, the moments of moral concern, our causal powers, and the conditions of their collective realizers.

(Vargas 2009, p. 51)

Thus, according to Vargas there is a deep-seated conflict between the folk conception of belief and the objective reality of our agency. There is an important analogy with the case of beliefs here: the concept of free will, similarly to the concept of belief, is, as it were, too metaphysically demanding. In our folk approach, we imagine that reality contains certain facts which would correspond to our mental vocabulary. These facts are, in a sense, metaphysical. In the case of beliefs, we imagine that our mental sphere contains concrete, internal, content-bearing, causally active states; in the case of free will, we imagine our actions to take place in a world in which there are objective alternative possibilities. Yet these metaphysical demands of our folk conception of ourselves are, in both these cases, most probably not fulfilled; our scientifically informed worldview does not give us reasons to think that there are such things.

Vargas also claims that this mismatch between our concept of free will and the reality of agency is not a reason to embrace eliminativism about free will. In his opinion, such an eliminativistic approach is untenable (see especially Vargas 2004, 2005) because the role of the concept of free will in our conceptions of moral responsibility and the like is too central. There is little credibility to the idea that we would stop using the language of moral responsibility altogether, and this would seem to be a natural consequence of adopting a straightforward eliminativism about free will.

According to Vargas, the best way forward in this situation is to revise our concept of free will. As he puts it:

[P]erhaps (..) free will, strictly speaking, does not exist, it does not follow that some very close analog, free will*, also fails to obtain. Indeed, on this account, we have an excellent candidate for free will*: namely moral consideration-sensitive capacities. Now here's clincher: (1) if free will* does everything we want of free will (...), and (2) it has the virtue of existing, then (3) it seems like we would do well to abandon any concern for free will and move on to the theoretically and existentially superior business of keeping track of free will*.

(Vargas 2009, p. 61)

In this way, what Vargas is proposing is that we should, in a way, switch concepts: instead of clinging to an unrealistic idea of free will, we should start to use an alternative notion which would not contain false presuppositions. This alternative notion of free will is closer to compatibilist intuitions and does not require any unsavoury metaphysical commitments.

Again, the analogy with the case of beliefs is clear. The solution I am proposing is that we should switch concepts of belief: from the metaphysically demanding yet unrealistic representationalist notion to the less demanding superficial one. The latter might not preserve all our intuitions, but it is consistent with the application criteria we employ for this concept; more importantly, beliefs understood in this way have the virtue of existing, and for this reason alone such a revision might be advisable.

A similarly revisionary account was proposed by Haslanger (2012) in the context of gender and race. Her starting point is the observation that there are two main theories about the concepts of gender and race: essentialist and social constructionist. According to the essentialist theory, gender/race concepts entail the idea that people belonging to the same gender/racial category share a hidden gender/race essence which, in turn, determines the visible gender – and race-specific properties of individuals. This essentialist analysis is often used to motivate an error-theoretic approach to race and gender. It is often argued that there are no such gender and race essences: no one is 'white' if by 'white' we mean something along the lines of 'possessing the hidden essence of a white person which determines the appearance and mental characteristics which we stereotypically associate with a white person'.

On the social constructionists' account, on the other hand, the categories of race and gender are constructed by our attitudes towards them. People belong to races and genders only because we treat them as possessing features which allow us to racialize and genderize others. Races and genders conceptualized in this way can be uncontroversially said to exist because the practices of attributing genders and races are real. What is important is that these constructivist claims are presented as if they were intended to constitute an analysis of our folk concepts.

According to Haslanger, the essentialist analysis is, in a sense, the correct one, as people seem to harbour essentialist beliefs about gender and race (and for this reason the constructivist account fails as an analysis). But this essentialist account of folk gender/race concepts captures only what Haslanger calls the manifest concepts of gender and race, i.e., the concept we think we are employing, which is available to us by introspection. However, as Haslanger contends, this manifest concept is not something that regulates our linguistic behaviour. What actually guides our practice of applying these terms is our operative concepts.

Haslanger illustrates the distinction between manifest and operative concepts by the example of the concept of 'parent'. The manifest concept of 'parent' is probably the concept of 'immediate progenitor': this is what we think we mean by the word 'parent'. However, as Haslanger notices, in many contexts the concept is used as if we were applying it 'to the primary caregivers (…), whether they be biological parents, step-parents, legal guardians, grandparents, aunts, uncles, older siblings, informal substitute parents, and so on' (Haslanger 2012, p. 389).

In cases of gender and race, the difference between the operative and the manifest concept is obvious. The manifest concept is the essentialist one, as we apparently believe that there are hidden gender and race essences, whereas the operative concept is not: we are not tracking hidden essences when we are attributing races and genders; rather, we are relying on publicly observable criteria, from which we infer (erroneously) the possession of said essences.

This mismatch between the operative and the manifest concepts gives rise to scepticism about error theory concerning race and gender. Even if it is true that nothing in the world satisfies the manifest concept of genders and races, it does not follow that there are no genders and no races: there are operative concepts we use which somehow determine the extensions of the concepts in question. This mismatch between the operative and manifest concepts of race and gender should not be taken as a reason to eliminate these concepts. Rather, it should invite us to rethink which concept of gender and race we want to use. Haslanger here uses the notion of 'target concept': this is the concept we should be employing, taking into account pragmatic and moral considerations.

The proposal about the status of the concept of belief shares important analogies with Haslanger's account of gender and race. It could be said that the manifest concept of belief, similarly to the manifest concepts of gender and race, is a metaphysically demanding one, and there is a strong reason to think that nothing corresponds to it. However, the diagnosis that the manifest concept does not track reality is taken to be a reason to modify the concept in question rather than eliminate it. An important factor that blocks the simple error-theoretic conclusion is that we are able to successfully apply the concept in question. It might be said that the operative concept of belief, i.e., the concept we use when applying the concept to actual subjects, is the 'superficial' one, and this concept definitely has a non-empty extension (which also explains why we have no problem with using this notion in everyday life).

It must be made clear here that I haven't presented Vargas's and Haslanger's views in their full complexity. My aim was not to reconstruct these proposals: rather, I wanted to point out certain important affinities that my project shares with these conceptions. One point of difference between my revisionary account of belief and Vargas's and Haslanger's approaches must, however, be made fully explicit here. Neither Vargas nor Haslanger thinks of their project as being anti-realist in the full sense: although Vargas is ready to admit that there is some grain of truth in anti-realism about free will, he ultimately rejects it (see, e.g., Vargas 2013). In my opinion, this rejection of anti-realism stems from the fact that for Vargas and Haslanger (as for many other contemporary philosophers) the sole form of anti-realism that is worthy of its name is irrealism, i.e., the claim that the concepts in question do not refer to anything. Both Vargas and Haslanger emphatically reject anti-realist views of the irrealist and eliminativist variety. In my opinion, however, there is a way of embracing some of the important insights of anti-realism without fully embracing traditional eliminativism.

It worth noting that a suggestion to the effect that we should change our concept of belief has been recently made, albeit only briefly, by Zawidzki (2021). He claims that our current folk-psychological notions present to us as 'spectatorial' ones that aim to describe the inner world of ourselves and other subjects. However, in fact, the function of our folk-psychological notions is more regulative than cognitive: we use folk-psychological vocabulary to regulate behaviours rather than to describe and to predict. There is a conflict between what we think a function of folk-psychological discourse is and what its actual role is; this conflict should lead us, according to Zawidzki, to changing of our folk-psychological concepts in such a way as to include their regulative character. This proposal shares important affinities with the one I developed in this section, as Zawidzki explicitly puts forward the idea that folk-psychological categories should be seen as some sort of social constructs. There are also, however, important differences. First, central for Zawidzki's project is the idea that the main function of folk-psychological attributions is regulative, whereas my project does not hinge on this idea. More importantly, Zawidzki does not see his view as being anti-realist, whereas in my view revising the concept of belief should be coupled with an anti-realistic approach (Zawidzki's view on the issue of realism will be discussed in some more detail in Chapter 8, section 6).

7.5 Truth in eliminativism

The conclusion alluded to at the end of the last section brings us back to the central question of this chapter: in what sense is minimal non-realism an anti-realist position? This is a vital question in the context of the last section as minimal non-realism turns out to be a preservationist proposal; the practical consequence of this view is that we should retain the notion of 'belief' in our everyday vocabulary. This proposal stems from the fact that, according to minimal non-realism, we can truly say that beliefs exist because the commonsense criteria of application of the term 'belief' are met. What is needed is the precisification of how such a preservationist proposal can be thought of as a bona fide form of anti-realism.

In Chapter 5, section 3, I contrasted two possible ways of reacting to the conclusion that important empirical presuppositions of folk psychology are not fulfilled and the central categories of folk psychology are basically useless in serious science. The first reaction, which can be attributed to early Stich and Churchland, is that in such case we should claim that beliefs (and other categories of folk psychology) do not exist and these categories should be eliminated. The other reaction, which can be attributed to Chomsky, is that even though these categories are scientifically useless there is no point in postulating the elimination of this category from folk discourse. All we should do is to eliminate it from scientific theorizing.

The position of minimal non-realism about belief is closer to Chomsky's than to Stich's and Churchland's in this respect. As was indicated previously, there are two main reasons why the strict eliminativist proposal should, in my opinion, be rejected. First, the idea of eliminating belief (and other central folk-psychological categories) seems to be unworkable in practice. Second, the deflationary analysis of existence supports the idea that beliefs might be taken to exist if the application criteria of belief predicates are adequately fulfilled.

Even though minimal non-realism accepts the preservationist-yet-revisionary approach to beliefs, it does not change the fact that, according to the minimal non-realist, there is a substantial error in the way the folk conceptualize mental reality. This is the central 'anti-realist' element of the proposed view. According to minimal non-realism, the empirical presuppositions of the folk categories are not met. There are important inferences which co-define the concept of belief and which lead to claims that should be deemed false. In other words, there are important metaphysical commitments included in the folk notion of belief that need to be rejected. The mere admission that the category of 'belief' should not be eliminated does not neutralize the claim that there is a serious error in the folk conception of the mental sphere.

It might be objected here that the mere claim that the folk are mistaken about a particular feature of a certain thing does not imply any anti-realist conclusions.

To use a somewhat trivial example, the folk used to think that velociraptors did not have feathers, but it is now widely accepted by science that they did. So, the folk view of velociraptors was wrong to an extent (and perhaps still is). However, the idea that the discovery of this mismatch should lead us to some sort of 'velociraptor anti-realism' would be rather silly.

In response, I want to contend that the case of belief is a substantially different one. The mistake of the folk in the case of beliefs is significantly more serious than in cases of common mistakes. The mistake that the folk are making with regard to beliefs concerns the metaphysical category to which beliefs belong. The folk treat belief as being a substantial part of reality – as a metaphysically real category – whereas in fact this is not so: beliefs exist, but as 'thin', insubstantial properties.

Let me use a crude analogy here: according to certain views on the ontology of fictional objects, literary characters such as Sherlock Holmes exist because they are abstract artifacts that are created by authors of works of fiction (see, e.g., Thomasson 2003a). On this view the claim that Sherlock exists is true, as there is such a literary character. But what to make of someone who would treat Conan Doyle's stories as accounts of the adventures of a real detective? If such a person uttered the statement 'Sherlock existed', it would seem to us that such a person made a mistake, and we would be tempted to deny this claim.

Thomasson (2003a) contends that we should treat intuitively correct claims of the form 'Sherlock does not exist' as meaning 'Sherlock does not exist as a person'. If we agree on this proposal, then perhaps the best way of thinking about the mistake the person in our example made would be by saying that this person mistook a fictional character for an actual person. Thus, when someone wrongly says that Sherlock existed, this claim might be seen as a metaphysical category mistake. The person making this claim could be seen as mistakenly putting a certain object in a wrong category: someone thought that the entity denoted by the name 'Sherlock' belongs to the category of 'real persons', whereas in fact this object is in the category of abstract artifacts (this way of thinking about mistakes about fictional characters is inspired by Voltolini's [2013] treatment of mistakes regarding the existence of Santa Claus).

This proposal about fictional characters might be controversial, but I think it provides us with a useful model of how to think about our mistake that occurs in the case of beliefs. If what I have written so far is correct, then we can say that the folk are mistaken about the metaphysical category to which beliefs belong. In the folk schema, beliefs belong to the category of substantial, explanatory, internal states. In fact, however, they belong to the category of thin, metaphysically inconsequential, 'deflationary' states that are attributed to subjects on the basis of superficial characteristics. Additionally, this model allows us to reinterpret the pronouncements of the traditional eliminativists. Their central claim that 'there are no beliefs' might be re-read as the claim that 'beliefs as not real'. This latter thesis should, in turn, be understood as the claim that beliefs do not fall into the category of real things, even though the folk think so.

If this diagnosis is correct, then it should be said that there was an important correct insight into the original eliminativist theory: there is a serious mistake ingrained in the folk-psychological concept of belief, and this mistake is of a metaphysical character. In our common framework, we are mistaken about the reality of beliefs: we think that they are more real than they actually are. In this sense, the position of minimal non-realism is a version of anti-realism as it postulates a deep and substantial mismatch between the folk view on belief and mental reality.

However, what traditional eliminativists were wrong about was the way they expressed this insight: the attempt to persuade us to embrace irrealism about beliefs was doomed. Still, I believe that the core truth of eliminativism can be maintained even in my framework, which postulates preservation together with revision of the concept in question. The revision that minimal non-realism postulates cuts deeper than the revisions that other philosophers have postulated. It is not only that our folk ideas are empirically false: the metaphysical picture of the mind that is implicitly assumed when we make attributions of beliefs needs to be revamped.

This is the core of my proposal. Because the existing category of belief is based on a grave metaphysical error, we should combine an anti-realist outlook on this category with the revisionary-preservationist proposal about the future use of this concept. Such a combination might seem overly complicated but, in my view, it is the best position we are able to accept given the current state of the evidence.

8

Possible charges

8.1 Is it not just fictionalism?

Minimal non-realism was defined in the first chapter as the combination of three claims: that beliefs do exist in the deflationary sense; that they are not real in the sense that they are not natural properties; and that the folk concept of belief is in need of reform (as it assumes strong realism). After defending the main tenets of this position, it is time to consider some potential objections to it.

The first objection might seem natural in the context of the conclusion of the last chapter: minimal non-realism contends that the folk concept of belief contains an important metaphysical error yet postulates preservation of this notion in our everyday vocabulary. Thus, a question might arise: in what way is this conception distinct from the position of mental fictionalism?

As was noted in Chapter 2, section 4, mental fictionalists, whose number include Toon (2016), Demeter (2013) and Wallace (2016), postulate that we should retain the belief discourse as it is practically useful, although statements that attribute beliefs are uniformly false (or at least untrue). For fictionalists, the best way to deal with belief attributions is to treat them as useful fictions. It might seem as if there were little difference between the minimal non-realist position and the fictionalist account: both positions contend that there is a serious error in the way the folk describe mental reality, yet they consider elimination of this category from our everyday discourse to be unworkable.

A tempting answer to this concern would be to say that there is one crucial difference between the fictionalist and the minimal non-realist outlook on beliefs: while fictionalists deny that beliefs exist and that atomic statements about belief attributions can ever be literally true, the minimal non-realist accepts the claims that there are beliefs and that many of our ordinary attributions of beliefs are perfectly true. However, it might be said that although proponents of minimal non-realism do not want to embrace fictionalism and overtly distance themselves from this position, fictionalism might be still the unintended consequence of their position.

It is worth noting at this point that the fact that minimal non-realism treats the ontological status of beliefs as being somehow on a par with the status of fictional characters (as was indicated, for example, in Chapter 7, section 5) does not in itself mean that minimal non-realism is a form of fictionalism. The crucial element of any fictionalism about beliefs (and the mental in general), as was noted in Chapter 2, section 4, is that mental fictionalists deny that ascriptions of beliefs can be seen as true in a literal sense. Minimal non-realism treats ascriptions of beliefs as true and rejects any form of pretence or prefix treatment of such statements. The aim of the analogies I've drawn between fictional characters and beliefs is to underline my claims about beliefs being non-concrete and not causally active; these analogies do not, however, invite any kind of pretence reading. Thus, if such a fictionalist reading is nonetheless an unintended consequence of minimal non-realism, this would be a serious problem for this view.

As was noted in Chapter 5, section 2, a similar charge was directed by several philosophers (see Braddon-Mitchell & Jackson [2007], McCulloch [1990] and Hutto [2013]) at Dennett's intentional stance theory. One of the central tenets of Dennett's approach to the question of the reality of beliefs is his insistence that the strong realist position is false. This, together with the fact that in his early writings Dennett expressed sympathy for the instrumentalist approach to attribution of attitudes, has been taken as a reason to suspect either that Dennett is sort of a covert fictionalist about attitudes or that fictionalism might be an unintended yet unavoidable consequence of his view.

I have tried to deal with the problem of reading's Dennett's position elsewhere (Poslajko 2020). However, the problem of minimal approaches to the reality of attitudes being implicitly committed to fictionalism pertains not only to Dennett's position. It might be said that all theories which somehow try to avoid the strong commitments of the folk conception of belief while putting forward a preservationist prescription must deal with this concern; minimal non-realism is no exception here. If the proponent of minimal non-realism claims that the idea that beliefs play a causal role is deeply ingrained in the folk conception of this attitude yet beliefs in reality do not have such a causal role, then shouldn't they also say that belief ascriptions are at best fictionally true?

This line of argument has been presented by Wright (2002), who briefly considers and quickly rejects a theoretical proposal broadly similar to minimal non-realism. He offers the following reasoning to show that such a position is untenable:

> The concern is thus that the causality of ordinary psychological explanations requires their hypotheses to carry a content that already puts them out of the running for minimalist construal: that there is an objective and at bottom wholly physical causal order in the world and that once a discourse ventures causal claims, it must be entered into the competition for correct depiction of aspects of this causal order and sink or swim accordingly. If certain of its causal claims do indeed depict such aspects, then it is – at least in that respect – providing for the expression of substantial (not minimal) truths; and if none do, then they are not minimally true but substantially false. Minimalism, the contention is, is not an option for theories of the causes of things. So ordinary psychology, to the extent that causal claims are its stock-in-trade, can no more be excused all substantial representational purport than alchemy – and has to be vulnerable, in principle, to the same fate.
> (Wright 2002, p. 220–1)

In short, Wright claims that if belief attributions carry commitments to claims about the causal structure of the world, yet these claims are not true, then belief attributions must be judged to be 'substantially false'. For Wright, the only viable theoretical option for a theorist committed to such a view is that of eliminativism (hence the analogy with alchemy). However, from the contemporary perspective one might argue that a fictionalist route might be best advised. If we deem folk-psychological attributions as failing in their aim of depicting the causal order of the world, then it might seem that the best we can do is to treat them as being fictional in nature and incapable of being genuinely true.

The challenge is then the following one: how can the proponent of minimal non-realism avoid the conclusion that attributions of beliefs are substantially and literally false? The gist of the answer is the following: on the minimal non-realist view, the notion of truth that is being used in the context of belief attributions should be seen as a minimal one. On the other hand, the fictionalist account of belief attributions presupposes the substantial notion of truth. Thus, the minimal non-realist claims that belief attributions are true in the minimal sense (and, respectively, beliefs can be said to exist in the minimal sense). The mental fictionalist would, on the other hand, see the attributions of beliefs as failing to be true in the substantial sense. Consequently, the mental fictionalist denies that beliefs can be seen as existing in the substantial sense. Such a characterization of the contrast between minimalism and fictionalism is, however, in need of further detail.

This problem might reasonably be seen as a special example of a general issue which is discussed in contemporary meta-metaphysics: the debate on deflationism vs fictionalism. The main issue at stake in this debate is whether we should prefer a deflationary or a fictionalist treatment of the potentially problematic elements of our ontology (see, e.g., Thomasson 2013, Plebani 2018 for an overview). An example of a metaphysical issue where this debate arises is the question of whether numbers exist. According to deflationists, the positive answer to this question is quite obvious given the fact that there are some uncontroversially true statements about numbers from which we can infer the conclusion that they do exist. Fictionalists would not be so easily convinced by this kind of reasoning, as for them there is a difference between saying that, say, the number of dragons is zero and the genuine acceptance of the claim that there is such a thing as the number zero (see Plebani 2018). According to fictionalists, existential claims do not trivially follow from other statements.

Trying to solve this issue in its generality would definitely go beyond the scope of this book. Instead, I will try to show that in the specific context of the debate about beliefs there is a reason to prefer the deflationary approach over the fictionalist one. Still, we should admit that there are some important points on which fictionalism is right. It might be granted to the mental fictionalist that there is certain 'literal sense' of attributions of beliefs in which they can be taken to be not true. It is literally not true that people have causally active, semantically evaluable, inner states 'inside their heads'. Still, I believe this conclusion does not justify adopting a fictionalist approach to belief attributions, simply because the reasons to reject fictionalism outweigh its benefits.

Fictionalism about attitudes is, as was already indicated in Chapter 2, section 4, a pernicious theoretical proposal. This is because the very idea of adopting a fictionalist approach to any theory requires making some substantial psychological assumptions. In order to claim to embrace fictionalism about any area of discourse, one needs to make a distinction between two types of attitudes: the one of believing and the one of fictionally accepting. This is because one of the central claims of fictionalism is that statements which are subject to the fictionalist treatment are not believed but are only fictionally accepted; however, making such a distinction seems to make little sense if one is not ready to admit that it is true that people have beliefs. If no belief attribution is ever true, then the fictionalist cannot make sense of claiming that we believe certain claims but accept others only fictionally. This potentially paradoxical character of fictionalism about attitudes and the fact that deflationism is not potentially self-defeating are, in my opinion, good reasons to prefer the deflationary option. This remains true even if there is a perfectly good sense in which we could potentially conceive belief attributions as being non-true.

What to do, however, about the problem raised by Wright? If belief attributions make false substantial commitments, then how can we deny that they are substantially false? The answer that I propose is that we can see belief attributions as being minimally true once we agree on a revision of the concept in question. Thus, belief attributions can be seen as being minimally true once we see them as using a 'reformed' concept of belief which is devoid of problematic metaphysical presuppositions. Thus, it might indeed be the case that belief attributions might be seen as substantially false if we treat them as employing the substantial notion of belief; however, the same belief attributions might be treated as being minimally true if we saw them as employing the new thinner notion of belief. The whole idea of the revisionary-yet-preservationist approach to concepts such as belief (but also free will and gender) is that there are important reasons to retain the concept in our repertoire but with changed content. In this way, we might treat sentences in which the concept in question functions as being true, even though we could not treat them in this way if we were stuck with the original flawed concept.

To sum up: the concern was that once we admit that there are substantial presuppositions embedded in the concept of belief, we are forced to admit that statements involving this concept must be treated as being substantially false. The solution is as follows: as the fictionalist approach to belief attribution is unworkable, the best theoretical option is to adopt a revisionary approach to the concept of belief and to claim that belief attributions which use the changed concept of belief can be minimally true.

8.2 The problem of semantic nihilism

In the last section, and in several other places, I claimed that the advantage of minimal non-realism over other forms of the broadly anti-realist approach to beliefs is that this position is not susceptible to the standard arguments from self-reference which were commonly brandished at the more traditional forms of anti-realism about beliefs. The argument in its simplest form went as follows: one cannot coherently deny that there are beliefs, as making such a claim implicitly commits us to the claim that there are beliefs. Minimal non-realism is resistant to such a simple counter-argument as it does not deny that beliefs exist and their attributions can be true.

However, there are some more subtle arguments that purport to show that any form of anti-realism about beliefs is incoherent; such arguments might seem to apply to the position developed in the present book. One important argument against the possibility of denying the reality of beliefs is the argument from semantic nihilism. The gist of this argument is that when someone claims that beliefs are not real in a strong sense, one is effectively committing oneself to an unacceptable form of semantic nihilism (such an argument is often raised in informal discussion; Miłkowski [2015] might be seen as proposing such an argument, although the main target of his criticism is the anti-representationalist position in philosophy of cognitive science).

The argument from semantic nihilism is often based on the distinction between original and derived intentionality, developed by Searle (1980). The idea behind this distinction is that only mental states can possess original intentionality; all other things, such as linguistic expressions, cultural artifacts, etc., can only be thought of as being about something because their intentional properties depend on the original intentionality of mental states. Linguistic expressions, for example, are intentional, but this is only because they are, as it were, imbued with intentionality that stems from mental states.

So, the possible argument against minimal mental non-realism goes as follows: if there are no substantial mental states like beliefs, then there is no such thing as substantial original intentionality. If there is no substantial original intentionality, then there is no derived intentionality; specifically we cannot claim that expressions belonging to public languages have any meaning. But this latter claim is an expression of semantic nihilism, which is obviously a self-defeating position. If no expression has meaning, then the very formulation of the claim of semantic nihilism lacks any meaning, therefore it cannot be true. Consequently, anti-realism about original intentionality cannot claim of itself that it is true, thus it falls victim to the classic negative self-reference argument.

Both the first and the last step of the reasoning are correct. Minimal anti-realism is, indeed, committed to the idea that there are no mental states which can be said to possess Searle's original intentionality. In fact, one of the main reasons provided in favour of minimal non-realism was the fact that we are unable to provide a naturalistic explanation of the content of mental states. As was indicated in Chapter 6, section 3, there is no theory which can explain (in naturalistically acceptable terms) how it is possible for internal mental states to possess propositional content. Thus, we must grant to the proponent of the semantic nihilism argument that minimal non-realism denies the primitive intentionality of beliefs. It is also fairly uncontroversial that a brute form of semantic nihilism which simply denies that any lexical item possesses meaning in any form is de facto self-contradictory: no statement can be said to be true if there is no meaning that can be attached to linguistic expressions.

What can be challenged, however, is the second step of the argument: the claim that if we deny that there substantially exist mental states possessing genuine original intentionality, then we must deny that any linguistic expression possesses any meaning whatsoever. There are two controversial assumptions behind this transition. The first one is that the meaning of linguistic expressions must be, as it were, grounded by the intentionality of mental states. The second controversial assumption is that the only form of intentionality is substantial. Both these assumptions can be challenged.

With regard to the first assumption, it might be argued that although many philosophers take it to be obvious that linguistic meaning must be seen as being dependent on intentions, such a 'Gricean' outlook on linguistic meaning is not the only possible view and perhaps not even the best one. There are other alternative accounts of linguistic meaning that can be adopted, one of which is the inferentialist approach to meaning that was briefly presented in Chapter 7, section 3. On the inferentialist account, championed prominently by Brandom (see, e.g., 2008), meaning is constituted by the pattern of normatively acceptable inferences. Warren aptly summarizes this position: inferentialism 'locates meaning in the inferential import of our (...) assertions rather than the attitudes they express' (Warren 2018, p. 468). Thus, on the inferentialist account of meaning, there is no need to rely on mental states in order to explain how words can have meaning. One way of reading the inferentialist account of meaning is to see it as a metasemantic claim, i.e., a claim about what constitutes the meaning of sentences (for a definition of meta-semantics, see Burgess & Sherman 2014). In this way we can see inferentialism as providing an account of the foundations of meaning of public language expressions that does not make any assumptions about there being substantial intentionality belonging to internal mental states. I do not wish here to endorse inferentialism as a necessary precondition of minimal non-realism. Rather, inferentialism here is used as an example of a developed theory of meaning that is compatible with denial of the original intentionality of beliefs, but other options might be available.

The other assumption of the argument from semantic nihilism which can be challenged is that we need substantial semantic properties in order to avoid the threat of semantic nihilism. This thesis is rejected by proponents of meta-semantic deflationism, who claim that we should treat semantic properties as being non-substantial. In the deflationary meta-semantic framework, there is no need to postulate any substantial word–world relations. As Thomasson put it, 'deflationism about reference denies that there is any substantive answer to the question of what the reference relation consists in; deflationism about meaning denies that there is any special (non-semantic) property of meaning F to uncover the nature of, thus enabling us to say in general what meaning F consists in' (Thomasson 2014, p. 189). According to metalinguistic deflationism, we should see truths about meaning and reference as being trivial results of linguistic conventions pertaining to the words 'means' and 'refers'; we should not see them as descriptions of some putative substantial meaning property.

If the deflationary notion of meaning is acceptable (and there seems to be no principled reason to think it is not), it seems to be all that is needed to avoid the threat of semantic nihilism. The simple argument from semantic nihilism rests on the assumption that a mental anti-realist must deny that any linguistic expression is meaningful. But this assumption might be easily challenged if we take into account the fact that it is possible to adopt a deflationary approach to meta-semantics. This is hardly a new proposal: as was noted in Chapter 2, section 3, Taylor (1994) suggested that eliminative materialism should be combined with a deflationary approach to truth in order to avoid the cognitive suicide argument. In a similar fashion, it might be said that a proponent of minimal non-realism might adopt a deflationary approach to meaning in order to avert the charge of semantic nihilism.

8.2.1 The Boghossian-Wright argument

The combination of minimal non-realism about beliefs and a broadly deflationary approach to linguistic meaning might be sufficient to easily deflect the simple form of the semantic nihilism argument. However, there is a more sophisticated argument that aims to show that it is impossible to adopt a non-realist approach to propositional attitudes as well as a deflationary approach to truth and meaning. Such an argument has been formulated by Boghossian and Wright, the gist of which is that once we adopt the deflationary framework, we lose the ability to make a meaningful distinction between the real and the non-real, which undermines the very idea of putting forward an anti-realist position.

The classic version of this argument, devised by Boghossian (1990), targets a putative proponent of irrealism about contentful mental states who would wish to embrace a deflationary conception of truth. According to Boghossian, once we adopt the deflationary theory, we lose the ability to deny that any well-formed declarative sentences are capable of being true. This is because on the deflationary account there is nothing that can stop a well-formed declarative sentence from being apt for truth. As truth is a thin notion, on no grounds can we restrict its applicability. Consequently, even though the only option for an irrealist about beliefs is to employ a deflationary account of truth, this view undercuts their ability to make the distinction that is crucial to formulating their own theory.

This argument has been subject to some critical scrutiny, and there are serious reasons to suppose it fails. Holton (1993), for example, complains that Boghossian wrongly equated the issues of truth and truth-aptitude, which led him to claim that a deflationist about truth must be a minimalist about truth-aptitude. For Holton, this is not valid reasoning: a deflationist about truth might adopt substantial criteria of truth-aptitude. Although I agree with Holton in principle, I will not dwell on more details here as the position I am putting forward is a version not of irrealism about beliefs but of minimalism.

Nonetheless, a variant of the Boghossian argument might be directed towards the position I espouse, namely the one that combines minimal non-realism about beliefs with deflationism about truth and meaning; such reasoning was presented by Wright (2002). Wright correctly observes that the proponent of minimalism about propositional attitudes is forced to adopt a deflationary account of meaning and truth. But, in his opinion, this commitment has disastrous consequences. According to him, a proponent of deflationism about meaning and truth is forced to admit that all claims about a distinction between statements which are capable of being substantially true and those which can be true only in a minimal sense can themselves only be minimally true. As Wright puts it, 'the thesis of psychological minimalism is a commitment to its own non-robustness' (Wright 2002, p. 226).

For Wright, this is an unacceptable result because, according to him, it would mean that the theory of psychological minimalism amounts to nothing more than an opinion which lacks rational justification. This does not mean that minimalism about psychology is internally incoherent, but it certainly makes this position paradoxical: someone putting forward such a proposal would have to admit that it cannot be justified in a rational manner.

The central premise in this step of Wright's argument is the following: 'A philosophical claim about the robustness or otherwise of a discourse is, like any philosophical claim, warranted *a priori*, by philosophical reflection, or by nothing at all' (Wright 2002, p. 227). According to Wright, the only way one can justify the claim that a certain class of sentences belongs to the category of sentences which are only minimally true is by way of *a priori* reflection on the semantic properties of said sentences. But if the semantic properties are purely minimal, then there is no way we can make any substantial discoveries about them. Wright's thought seems to be that if semantics is not substantial, then there is no ground on which we can rest the claim that the minimalist version of anti-realism is preferable to realism. In other words, deflationism leads to the conclusion that there is no objective ground to the claim that any area of discourse, including discourse about beliefs, should be treated as being only minimally true.

This way of arguing would, if successful, put the whole enterprise of the present book into serious doubt. However, Wright's central assumption, namely that the only way we can justify the real vs. minimal distinction is by way of *a priori* reflection, is arguably false given the central tenets of this book. On the account proposed here, the claim that we should treat belief attributions as being only minimally true is justified by the fact that belief properties are most probably non-natural. And this fact is not established purely by *a priori* reflection.

The claim that belief properties are not natural ones is justified by reference to facts that are, at least up to a point, contingent and empirically justified. It is certainly not something that might be discovered by pure *a priori* reflection that beliefs are not causally active, that they do not constitute a natural kind, and that there is no good analysis of content in terms of more fundamental properties. In all these cases, we need to take into account some empirical reasons. It is also important to note that strong realism about beliefs is not a theory which can be deemed conceptually incoherent. A proponent of a theory according to which beliefs are causally active, semantically evaluable, internally stored mental states is, in my opinion, guilty of being mistaken but is innocent of conceptual confusion. Strong realism is, to my mind, a bold hypothesis which turned out to be inadequately justified, but it is not *a priori* impossible. It is perfectly conceivable that there could be creatures similar to humans who would actually possess beliefs as they are imagined by strong realists. Thus, the debate about the reality of beliefs as it is conceptualized in the framework I propose should be seen as being a debate about certain contingent (yet obviously crucial) features of the actual world, not a debate about *a priori* truths about the concept of 'belief'.

Obviously, my proposal is not entirely empirically based, and conceptual considerations play an important role in its justification. For example, I claim that the current concept of belief carries substantial commitments, and this fact might fall prey to the charge of the inability of deflationists to make rational statements about semantics. However, I do not feel convinced that a deflationist is unable to make any rational claims about the content of our concepts (or the meaning of our expressions). Such claims might be seen as being the results of reflection on patterns of linguistic usage and not about any putative world–word substantial relations. As long as we do not presuppose that there are any substantial semantic facts, it seems perfectly reasonable to engage in inquiry into the patterns of language use. It is worth emphasizing that deflationists do not claim that there are no facts about language whatsoever; they only claim that there are no substantial semantic facts, i.e., facts about the putative substantial relation that bridges words and things/properties/states of affairs. For example, it is entirely acceptable for a deflationist to claim that one of the functions of the truth predicate is to serve as a disquotation device: this claim has a semantic character, but it is not based on any putative observation of the relation between the truth predicate and the truth property.

To sum up, the Boghossian-Wright argument might be resisted in two ways. First, it might be said that the central claim of minimal non-realism is not something that is justified solely by *a priori* reflection. Second, it might be said that proponents of semantic deflationism are not barred from making any claims about patterns of linguistic use. These two claims, taken together, constitute an effective answer to the Boghossian-Wright argument. As it turns out, the minimalist about beliefs can consistently maintain their position.

8.3 The success argument

Most of the arguments against any form of belief anti-realism are negative in nature: they aim to show that it is impossible, for some reason or another, to embrace this view. One significant exception to this rule is the famous success argument, which aims to directly show that the strong realist theory is true and to refute any form of anti-realism in this way.

The main thrust of the success argument (a classic exposition of which can be found in Fodor 1987, but also in Lahav 1992) is to show that we should adopt a strongly realist stance towards the posits of folk psychology, including beliefs, due to the fact that folk psychology is a very successful predictive tool. The argument from the success of folk psychology is an example of a more general argumentative strategy: the success argument is mounted in the general philosophy of science (see, e.g., Devitt 2005 for an overview) to show the truth of scientific realism, namely the view that the theoretical terms which we use in science to denote unobservable entities successfully refer to real things. According to the proponent of the success argument, the only way we can reasonably explain the predictive success of the natural sciences is by claiming that the entities that sciences postulate do exist.

Although there are some serious concerns about the feasibility of this kind of argument in the context of the general debate in philosophy of science (see, e.g., Laudan 1981), I will assume that on the general plane it is possible to defend realism in this way. What I will debate, however, is the applicability of this argument to the issue of realism about beliefs.

The success argument for realism about beliefs might be summarized as follows:

1. Folk psychology is extremely predictively successful.
2. Beliefs are posits of folk psychology.
3. Posits of extremely predictively successful theories are real.
   Conclusion:
   Beliefs are real.

This argument is valid in the sense that the conclusion follows from the premises, and we might grant – for the sake of the discussion – that the second and third premises are true (although each of them is patently controversial). What I will focus on here is the status of the first premise, and I will show that it can be problematized.

It is true that humans do remarkably well at predicting the behaviour of and coordinating with their conspecifics. Failures do happen, but they seem to be an exception to the rule. In most mundane cases, the prediction and coordination happen so smoothly that it is something we take for granted. Still, the fact that people do very well at predicting and coordinating does not, by itself, prove that folk psychology is a successful theory. To justify the latter claim, one must show that we are successful at prediction and coordination because we use the theory of folk psychology, which makes an essential reference to states such as beliefs. And it is exactly this explanatory claim that can be problematized.

Consider the example given by Fodor (1987): one person is telling another that she will come to a certain town on Wednesday on the 3pm flight. Thus, the second person shows up at the airport and, voila, the first person arrives. The second person thus managed to successfully predict the behaviour of and coordinate with the first person. For Fodor, such examples of successful prediction and coordination are enough to prove realism about the posits of folk psychology. However, what is needed for such an argument to work is a more detailed explanation of how this predictive success relies on folk psychology understood as a theory.

According to Fodor, in such cases:

> The burden of predicting behavior – of bridging the gap between utterances and actions – is routinely taken up by theory (...) the theory from which we get this extraordinary predictive power is just good old commonsense belief/desire psychology. That's what tells us, for example, how to infer people's intentions from the sounds they make (if someone utters the form of words ('I'll be at your airport on the 3 p.m. flight', then, ceteris paribus, he intends to be at your airport on the 3 p.m. flight) and how to infer people's behavior from their intentions (if someone intends to be at your airport on the 3 p.m. flight, then, ceteris paribus, he will produce behavior of a sort which will eventuate in his arriving at that place at that time (...)).
>
> (Fodor 1987 p. 3)

This reasoning is, to say the least, very far from being obvious. Relying on any theory in order to predict the behaviour of others is not something that we know from everyday experience. This claim is more a philosophical interpretation of everyday practice than something that is evident in practice itself.

This controversial nature of Fodor's reasoning was made evident by Dennett, who (as was indicated in Chapter 7, section 3) distinguished between folk psychology understood as a craft and understood as ideology (Dennett 1998). Folk craft is the practice of using folk psychology and the practice of prediction and coordination of behaviour. Folk psychology understood as ideology is what we think we are doing when we are using folk craft: it is the set of our convictions about why the folk practice of understanding works. These two can turn out to be very different: our ideas about how and why we can successfully predict and coordinate our behaviour might not be correct. In general, our ideas about the way we successfully perform certain actions can easily be wrong. As Dennett notes, 'If you ask the native potters how they make their pots, they may tell you one thing and do another' (Dennett 1998, p. 83). Being able to perform a certain action and being able to produce a theory of why one is able to perform such an action are two different things (a related point is also made by Zawidzki 2018).

Fodor's idea that we predict and coordinate behaviour because we rely on the theoretical apparatus of folk psychology is just one of many possible theoretical explanations of the success of our folk-psychological craft. Further justification would be needed to support the thesis that it is the only viable or the best explanation; however, as long as we do not have such justification, the success argument lacks adequate grounds.

Another way of resisting this argument is by claiming that even if the attribution of beliefs and desires lies at the root of our success in prediction, we should not take this success to imply that folk psychology accurately describes the internal organization of the human mind. One way of resisting this idea was presented by Hochstein (2012), according to whom we should see the folk-psychological model of human behaviour as a phenomenological model. A phenomenological model, on Hochstein's account, is a model which, although useful and predicatively accurate, does not describe the internal structure of the system it is used to depict. In other words, the phenomenological model does not identify the structural features of the system, or it describes them in a very limited way. Thus, if we accept the possibility that folk psychology is a phenomenological model, then we can say that although the folk-psychological model is useful in the process of predicting the behaviour of others, it does not adequately illuminate the internal structure of others' minds (it is important to note here, however, that Hochstein's own view on the status of folk psychology is radically different from the one presented here; see Hochstein 2017).

To sum up, the success argument could, in principle, provide us with a good reason to prefer the strongly realist approach to beliefs over minimal non-realism. However, this way of arguing would require far stronger justification than that presented by the proponents of the success argument. We would have to be provided with good reasons to accept two crucial premises: first, that our practical success in prediction and coordination of behaviour stems from our application of folk-psychological theory; second, that the success of folk-psychological theory is based on the fact that it provides us with an accurate description of the internal structure of the mind. Both these premises can be reasonably doubted. As a result, the success argument cannot yet be taken as giving us sufficient reason to embrace strong realism.

This conclusion brings us back to one of the central claims of the present book: the observation that in the debate between the strong realist position and minimal anti-realism about beliefs, the former position is the one which needs to be provided with stronger justification. It is the strong realist that incurs a substantial metaphysical debt by postulating that we possess certain states with peculiar characteristics. The moderate anti-realist view is the more metaphysically conservative one, and, as long as we are not presented with sufficient reasons to expand our commitments, the minimal non-realist approach remains a safer bet.

8.4 The austere character of folk psychology

One of the issues that arose in the last section was the question of whether folk psychology must be seen as providing us with information about the internal structure of the mind. This issue brings us to another charge that might be levelled against the minimal non-realist conception: the charge that it overstates the strength of the presuppositions of folk psychology. According to this charge, folk psychology is actually austere in its presuppositions, and for this reason the anti-realist claim that the folk have mistaken views about beliefs should be dismissed.

The argument from the austere character of folk psychology has been used to disprove Churchland's classical eliminativist version of anti-realism about propositional attitudes; such arguments were presented by, among others, Bogdan (1993) and Horgan (1993). The structure of this argument is quite simple: according to proponents of the austere view, eliminativists assume that the folk are committed to very strong views about the architecture of human minds when they attribute attitudes. Additionally, eliminativists see these putative architectural commitments as actually being false, so they come to the conclusion that attitudes do not exist. However, according to the proponents of the austere ideology argument, this initial assumption of eliminativism – that of the strong commitments of the folk – is actually false, and consequently the eliminativist conclusion is unwarranted. We should rather see the folk as making only austere commitments when making attributions of attitudes. As these austere commitments are actually met, we can safely say that attitudes exist.

A popular and largely justified criticism of eliminativism is by way of showing that eliminativists seem to assume that folk psychology is committed to some version of the language of thought hypothesis. Eliminativists unwarrantedly assume that the necessary presupposition of the truth of the folk-psychological attribution of attitudes is that said attributions track 'internal mental representations that (i) possess language-like syntactic structure, and (ii) possess the propositional content of putatively attributable FP attitudes' (Horgan 1993, p. 283).

Such strong versions of the language of thought hypothesis are widely thought to be empirically implausible, so if folk-psychological attributions really did require them, we would have reasons to embrace anti-realism about beliefs. But, as the austere theorists claim, folk psychology makes no such strong assumptions, and the assumptions it actually makes are empirically true. Thus, we might safely refute eliminativism and adopt a straightforward realism towards the mental. As

Dennett quipped, 'It's really rather curious to say, "I'm going to show you that folk psychology is false by showing you that Jerry Fodor is mistaken."' (Dennett 1998, p. 85). Indeed, 'proving' that there are no mental states by rebuking a far-fetched philosophical account of the metaphysics that is putatively behind the attribution of attitudes seems to be a false victory.

Now, it seems that a similar concern might arise with regard to the position of minimal non-realism. The anti-realist component of the presented position consists in the claim that certain assumptions of the folk conception of beliefs are actually false. If, however, the folksy presuppositions are weaker than I assumed, then there is no reason to claim that there is any important error in the folk account of belief. In this way, we would be left with the view that the folk concept of belief matches mental reality; consequently, we would embrace a straightforwardly realistic view on beliefs. This is the main idea behind Horgan's 'Southern Fundamentalism'; in his view, mental states truly exist and their attributions are robustly true because the assumptions that are needed for the truth of them are minimal. If such a theory about the status of beliefs were true, then there would be no need to adopt minimal non-realism (or any other version of belief anti-realism).

In response to this concern, it should be said that although the original eliminativists could perhaps be accused of claiming that the folk are guilty of very strong assumptions (although more careful textual exegesis would be needed here), I do not make any such claims. My argument for the claim that the folk substantially err in their conceptualization of belief does not rest on the assumption that they are committed to some sort of language of thought hypothesis. I also do not want to claim that folk actually make the other assumptions that, in Horgan's view, eliminativists attribute to them (like the assumption that folk psychology is reducible to more fundamental science). On the contrary, on my account the assumptions that can be attributed to the folk are more or less the same as those that proponents of the austere view are willing to accept. However, in my view, even these less demanding presuppositions of folk psychology are false.

For example, according to Bogdan (1993), the actual, non-overblown-by-the-eliminativist commitment of folk-psychological attributions of beliefs is the claim that they are functionally discrete, semantically interpretable and causally active states. But this account of the folk view of beliefs is more or less the same as the one I assume in this book. And the arguments I presented in Chapter 6 all aimed to show that we have good reasons to claim that there are no states which would possess such qualities.

It seems that most proponents of the austere view of the folk psychology of beliefs accept the idea that the commitment that folk psychology is indeed making is the assumption that mental states such as beliefs are causally active. Horgan, for example, explicitly claims that 'Southern Fundamentalism, being robustly realist about FP, strongly affirms the integrity of folk-psychological causal explanation, and thus affirms the causal/explanatory relevance of FP state-types' (Horgan 1993, p. 287).

However, as I argued in Chapter 6, section 2, there are good reasons to reject the idea that beliefs are actual causes of behaviour. So, there is a way to defend a version of anti-realism about beliefs even if we grant to the proponents of the austere view that the original eliminativists were wrong in their account of what is assumed in folk psychology. The crux of the difference between Horgan-like realism and my version of anti-realism about beliefs is that, on my view, the core presupposition of folk psychology, namely the claim that beliefs are genuine causes, is false; on the other hand, Horgan maintains that beliefs do cause actions.

However, the consensus on the claim that the folk are committed to the idea of beliefs playing a causal role is not universal among the proponents of the austere view of folk psychology. There are some voices of dissent over this issue that deserve attention, one important example of which is Gauker's position (see Gauker 2003, 2021). Gauker criticizes what he calls 'the widespread dogma', namely the idea:

> In attributing beliefs and desires, we are positing unobservable entities in a person for purposes of explaining and predicting his or her behavior. The widespread dogma is supposed to reflect a kind of realism about beliefs and desires. Beliefs and desires are real things. So we should expect to identify them by locating them in a sequence of causes and effects.
> (Gauker 2021, p. 173–4)

According to Gauker, this widespread dogma lacks credible support as there is no reason to think that we are actually able to successfully predict other people's behaviour using the putative laws of folk psychology. The function of folk-psychological attributions, according to Gauker, is their use in indirect communication: when I attribute a belief to someone, I am making an assertion on their behalf.

A detailed discussion of Gauker's positive proposal is beyond the scope of the present book; what is important for our purposes, however, is how his scepticism about the predictive use of folk-psychological attributions translates into the issue of realism. Gauker's rejection of the idea that belief attributions serve to make predictions about human behaviour does not lead him to irrealism: he does not claim that beliefs do not exist. On the contrary, he adopts the view according to which 'Beliefs are real things. They are real things, like promises, votes and money. Like all of these things, they have the reality of things governed by objective norms' (Gauker 2021, p. 185). As there are objective norms governing attributions of beliefs, we might say that a certain person has a certain belief and, consequently, that beliefs exist.

There are certain important affinities between Gauker's position and the view developed in the present book: there is shared scepticism about the fact that beliefs are genuinely causal-explanatory; also, there is a common view that the existence of beliefs is ensured by the fact that there are some norms which govern the practice of belief attribution. But there are also significant differences. The first is that Gauker does not adopt the metaphysical framework I employ here. Second, and more important in the present context, is that, unlike Gauker, I assume that the folk conception of beliefs includes the conviction that they are causally active (see Chapter 7, section 2). This holds true even if one wants to agree with Gauker that examples of actual successful predictions on the basis of belief attributions are hard to find (and such an assumption might be seen as contestable given the fact that, according to many proponents of the standard view of how such predictions work, we are routinely making them on a sub-personal level). Still, the question is not whether our predictions are successful but whether we assume, in our folk framework, that beliefs are causally relevant for our behaviour. In my view, the answer to the second question is positive: we do see beliefs as causes.

This is a significant difference. On my account, there is a significant mismatch between the folk concept of belief and the 'metaphysical reality' of beliefs. Gauker seems to implicate that it is the philosophers who went astray in their interpretation of the folk discourse; this makes his view akin to other versions of the austere view. This difference regarding the role of beliefs leads to distinct views on the issue of belief realism: my approach results in a mildly anti-realist account, whereas Gauker retains a broadly realist position. However, as I see it, Gauker's defence of realism is possible only because he underestimates the strength of the folk commitment to the idea that beliefs cause action.

Let us take stock. The proponents of the austere view on folk psychology might have been right that traditional eliminativism erred in claiming that folk attributions of belief rely on strong and implausible assumptions; however, their defence of straightforward realism should be rejected. Most austere theorists claim that the folk embrace the idea that beliefs are causally active; but if the folk do indeed think so, and if we can show that they are wrong, then we have a good reason to embrace some version of anti-realism. If, however, the proponents of the austere view deny that the idea of mental causation is involved in our folk conception of belief, they might be accused of underestimating the strength of the folk commitments. In either case, the austere view offers no easy way to defend straightforward realism.

8.5 Non-naturalism

The whole theoretical project of this book is based on a major philosophical assumption, namely that of physicalism. I assume that the proper metaphysical account of beliefs should include the claim that beliefs are, at least in some basic sense, part of the natural world. Beliefs are not some extra states which are genuinely non-physical. In other words, I am committed to the position of 'minimal physicalism', i.e., the view that the mental (in this particular case – beliefs) supervenes in some weak sense on the physical (see Kim 2006). I am also committed to the idea that Polger dubbed the 'No ghost rule', namely the view that 'there is no need to appeal to immaterial stuff in order to explain mental phenomena' (Polger 2004, p. xviii). This naturalistic assumption played an important role in the arguments developed in Chapter 6, section 3, which aimed to show that we should adopt a mildly anti-realist view on beliefs because we are not able to provide a naturalistic explanation of propositional content.

It might be said that assuming even the most unspecific form of physicalism is unwarranted as there is no consensus about physicalism in the general philosophy of mind. The non-naturalist option, which calls for broadening our ontology in order to accommodate mental phenomena, is still a live option. It might then seem that the problems for belief realism that I raised might be avoided if we adopt a non-physicalist ontology of mind. However, such a retort might be seen as too hasty as most of the proponents of non-naturalist theories of mind are focused on the problem of phenomenal consciousness. It is the problem of providing a physicalist account of qualia that motivated many theorists to abandon the physicalist position and to postulate a non-naturalist theory of mind. Many of those who reject physicalism explicitly claim that their position is applicable only to qualitative mental states and not to propositional attitudes.

One example of such an approach might be found in Chalmers (1996), who distinguished between 'easy' and 'hard' problems of consciousness; the easy problems are those which can be explained in a naturalistically acceptable way, whereas the hard problems are those which force us to go beyond our physical ontology. Beliefs belong to the category of easy problems, at least when we assume that they are not necessarily entangled with phenomenal consciousness. As Chalmers put it, 'there is at least a deflationary concept of belief that is purely psychological, not involving conscious experience' (Chalmers 1996, p. 18). In this context, 'purely psychological' means analysable in functional terms and susceptible to reductive analysis. So, at least some of the non-physicalist approaches to mind are compatible with a physicalist approach to the particular issue of beliefs.

However, as was already indicated in Chapter 4, section 1.3, some theorists reject the view that the notion of belief is functional and it is therefore possible to reductively analyse it. Under the banner of 'phenomenal intentionality', there is a growing tendency to try to analyse the basis of content in terms of conscious states. The idea of phenomenal intentionality is that the source of original intentionality lies in phenomenal conscious states (an early formulation of this idea might be attributed to Searle [1991]). The thrust of this view is that the phenomenal character of conscious states fixes the content of these conscious mental states. So, if I have a perceptual experience, the intentional properties of this experience are determined by its phenomenal character.

Some of the proponents of the phenomenal intentionality approach explicitly restrict the scope of their approach to occurrent, phenomenal mental states – to occurrent thoughts, for example. They do not think that this approach applies to dispositional states such as beliefs. An important example of this approach can be found in Crane (2017). As he claims, 'unconscious states of mind do not have content in the way that conscious states do' (Crane 2017, p. 3). For Crane, beliefs belong to the category of unconscious states, and as such they do not possess determinate content (as was noted in Chapter 4, section 2, Crane's view of the nature of beliefs is broadly congenial to the view which is presented in this book; still, this does not mean I want to subscribe to his ideas about occurrent states). On Crane's view, only occurrent, conscious mental states can be said to possess determinate, intentional content that is determined by their phenomenal character.

However, some phenomenal intentionality theorists claim that the content of beliefs might be seen as being determined by the content of conscious mental states: such a view might be attributed to, for example, Searle (1991), Kriegel (2003, 2011) and Bourget (2010). According to this approach, the content of beliefs is in some way determined by conscious mental states, which are the original source of genuine intentionality, whereas beliefs (as dispositional states) can be said to possess intentional properties only in a derived sense. If the intentionality of beliefs really hinged on intentional properties of conscious mental states, then the issue of the possibility of providing a naturalized account of consciousness would have a direct bearing on the issue of naturalizing intentionality. As Bourget observed, 'someone who holds that consciousness is irreducible could use this thesis to argue that all forms of intentionality are irreducible, thereby consolidating the anti-reductionist position' (Bourget 2010, p. 54). Bourget himself might be seen as advancing this view, as in his later writings he opts for a non-reductionist account of consciousness (see Bourget 2019).

Thus, it is possible to adopt a view which combines (1) the claim that the intentionality of beliefs stems in some way from the intentionality of conscious phenomenal states with (2) the idea that conscious phenomenal states are fundamental elements of reality which cannot be explained by a naturalistic, physicalist approach. This view might be described as 'non-physicalist phenomenal intentionality theory'. A proponent of such a view would treat intentional properties as being somehow fundamental – or close to being fundamental – and not naturalizable in any meaningful sense. For the proponent of the phenomenal theory, the conclusion that intentional properties of beliefs cannot be naturalized would not be a reason to adopt an anti-realist view on beliefs. In their view, when confronted with the failure of the naturalization of the intentionality project, we should reject naturalism and retain realism about intentional states.

It should be admitted that the non-physicalist phenomenal intentionality theory constitutes a substantial alternative to minimal non-realism as it offers a way to defend realism about beliefs, even if we accept the impossibility of the naturalization of intentionality. Thus, in order to defend minimal non-realism one needs to provide some reasons which show why this view is preferable to the non-physicalist phenomenal intentionality theory. In what follows, I will present some reasons against adopting the non-physicalist alternative.

The first reason to be sceptical about non-physicalist phenomenal intentionality is the issue of mental causation. As was indicated in Chapter 1, section 2, and in Chapter 4, section 1.2, realism about beliefs assumes that they have two features: they are bearers of semantic properties and they are internal causes of behaviour. In the realist framework, beliefs are seen as causally active in virtue of their semantic properties. Now, if one wished to combine this idea with the view according to which the semantic properties of beliefs are based on non-naturalizable phenomenal states, then the natural consequence would be the claim that the non-physical phenomenal properties of mental states would play a genuine causal role.

If this is correct, then the non-physicalist phenomenal intentionality theory would be committed to a version of the strongly dualist view on mental causation, according to which non-physical, conscious mental properties play a genuine role in producing behaviour. This view strikes me as very hard to maintain. In order to accept it, one would have to reject the causal closure principle (see, e.g., Kim 1998), i.e., the idea according to which every physical event which has a sufficient cause has a sufficient physical cause. The causal closure principle is a claim according to which our physical world is, as it were, causally self-sufficient: nothing from outside the causal realm is able to affect the train of events in this realm.

Rejecting the causal closure principle in order to rescue strong realism about beliefs seems to me to be an exorbitant theoretical price. The non-physicalist phenomenal intentionality theory allows us to retain the strong version of belief realism, but it potentially forces us to change the fundamentals of our worldview. For me, this is a strong reason to reject this approach. In my opinion, the price that we have to pay when we adopt minimal non-realism is more acceptable. Minimal non-realism lets us retain the fundamentals of our worldview but requires revision of a certain notion. This sounds reasonable: we have successfully reconstructed many notions in the past, and this change in the folk-psychological notion of belief might not be something overly dramatic. On the other hand, accepting non-physical causation would be a complete overhaul of our theory of the world; in my opinion, such an overhaul would require much stronger justification than the proponents of the non-physicalist phenomenal intentionality theory provide.

The other concern about the non-physicalist phenomenal intentionality theory is that it might somewhat paradoxically be considered to be too good a theory. Let me elaborate on why this might be considered a drawback. In their study comparing 'tracking theories' of intentionality and phenomenal intentionality theories, Bourget and Mendelovici (2014) claim that phenomenal intentionality theories are superior to tracking theories as the latter do not produce empirically adequate results. The content that tracking theories attribute to a particular belief might be different than the content we would intuitively ascribe to this belief. It is indeed true that tracking theories lead to some counter-intuitive results: there are cases of mismatches between what these theories predict a certain item will represent and what we intuitively take this item to represent (this was discussed in detail in Chapter 6, section 3).

According to Bourget and Mendelovici, the phenomenal theory avoids this problem: this means that its predictions about the intentional properties of mental states match our pre-theoretical intuitions. But exactly this fact might raise serious suspicions of a methodological nature. It might be objected that a strategy which solves a serious theoretical problem by way of postulating an irreducible, non-naturalizable element that provides just the right theoretical goods is bogus. The concern is that proposing such a solution is like involving magic to avoid a persistent theoretical obstacle. In the worst case, this could result in postulating something akin to the infamous 'noetic rays' that were criticized by Putnam (1981): a magical element that provides a basis for the intentional relation between mental items and their external elements. Obviously, the fact that the non-physicalist phenomenal intentionality theory postulates a non-naturalizable element does not necessarily make it magical in this sense. Still, the proponents of such a view seem to owe us an explanation of how their theory is capable of providing us with a non-magical solution to the problem of the determination of content.

I am perfectly aware that these two arguments might not be considered fatal by advocates of the non-physicalist phenomenal intentionality theory. Some of them might already be convinced by the non-naturalistic outlook; some others might consider the potential drawbacks of the phenomenal approach to be a reasonable price for solving the problem of content. Still, for those who – like the present author – take considerations of ontological simplicity and methodological caution to play an important role, a more modest theory of minimal non-realism will represent a safer bet.

8.6 Socially constructed real kinds

The characterization of minimal non-realism provided in this book might be seen as relying on a certain tacit assumption regarding the notion of natural/real kinds. The assumption is that a given kind might be either a real/natural one or a socially constructed one. In other words, it might be said that it is assumed in this book that treating beliefs as being somehow socially constructed precludes treating them as constituting a natural kind, or, more generally speaking, being real.

One could object to this assumption by pointing to the idea that it is possible that there are examples of kinds which are both socially constructed and real/natural. In the specific case of beliefs, the objection would be that although the category of beliefs might be reasonably seen as being a somehow socially constructed one, it also denotes a natural kind, and thus beliefs should be considered real.

In the general case, the idea that a socially constructed kind might nonetheless be natural has become much discussed in the context of the debate about social kinds. Recent proposals regarding how to combine the idea that a certain kind is socially constructed yet is a real kind can be found in Mallon (2016) and Khalidi (2015). Although these proposals are very different in detail, the guiding idea is somewhat similar. In general, according to them, even when we agree that a kind is socially constructed, the very same kind might meet criteria for naturalness. The kind in question might, for example, fit the description of being a homeostatic property cluster in Boyd's (1991) sense, or it might be the basis of genuinely surprising generalizations.

According to Khalidi (2015), there are three kinds of social kinds, of which two are of interest for our purposes. The first category includes kinds which are social in the sense that the kind as a whole is socially constructed. The second category includes kinds that are even more strongly socially constructed: not only the whole kind is constructed, but also all facts about particular objects belonging to the kind in question are dependent on social opinions. The 'money' kind belongs to the first category, while the category of 'permanent resident' belongs to the second. The difference is that even though money in general is a social construct in a general sense, there might be examples of objects falling under the category of money that are not recognized as such. In the 'permanent resident' category, this is different as each and every person who has this status has it only because it has been collectively recognized. This feature of kinds of social kinds like money allows Khalidi to argue that such kinds can be understood as natural kinds in the sense that there can be many surprising empirical generalizations about these kinds. This might be, for example, due to the fact that the kind in question might be constructed to perform certain functions (like money is, among other things, a medium of exchange), and the performance of these functions relies on empirical facts.

In Mallon's view (Mallon 2016), the idea that makes it possible to claim that some social kinds are natural is the idea of entrenched social roles. For Mallon, such social roles, even though they are created conventionally and people have these roles because they are ascribed to them, can be seen as constituting natural kinds because they can be seen as homeostatic property clusters in Boyd's (1991) sense. The idea is that the social mechanism that creates a certain category might produce a 'range of effects that further differentiate putative members of the role'

(Mallon 2016, p. 93), thus the category itself becomes a projectible and natural one. So, even though category X is socially created in the sense that being an X is a socially ascribed social role, it might then turn out that all Xs share important properties.

There might be substantial principal reasons to doubt the very cogency of the notion of socially constructed natural kinds (see, e.g., Thomasson 2003b for an account of human kinds which seems to preclude the possibility of them being natural). For the sake of the discussion, however, I will assume that there is, in principle, a possibility that some kinds might be both socially constructed and natural. But the key question from the perspective of the present book is whether we have any reason to suppose that beliefs fall into this category. Such a proposal has never, to my knowledge, been developed in full detail, but there have been some ideas that might be interpreted as pointing in that direction.

One important conception that might lead to the view that beliefs are socially constructed yet natural kind is Fenici and Zawidzki's conception of mindreading and mindshaping (Fenici & Zawidzki 2021). According to these authors, we should see the processes of mindreading and mindshaping as not aiming to track pre-existing, naturally occurring properties or states. Rather, mental states, including beliefs, are socio-culturally created by the processes of their attribution; however, these processes are not arbitrary and their aim is to track the practical commitments of the members of a community (the notion of commitment here is inspired by Brandom's [1994] theory). The whole process has a strong evolutionary underpinning: we engage in the construction of mental states, including beliefs, because this process has a strong evolutionary rationale as it was crucial in developing the human socio-cognitive syndrome.

The consequence of Fenici and Zawidzki's view is that beliefs are socio-culturally constructed, but this construction is, in a certain important sense, a non-arbitrary one. But the question remains whether such a vision justifies the claim that beliefs constitute a natural kind. Although I am not committed to any theory regarding mindreading or the evolution of this capacity, let us assume that the story that Fenici and Zawidzki tell is largely correct and there indeed are strong evolutionary reasons for how folk-psychological concepts have actually developed, and that the socio-cultural construction of beliefs is, in a sense, non-arbitrary. However, as I will try to argue, this is not enough to show that the constructed category can be seen as being a natural kind in the sense defined above.

In order to justify the idea that a certain social kind X is a natural one, we must show some proof of the claim that the people/objects to which the category

X is ascribed share important projectible properties and are a good target for inductive generalizations. It is not enough to show that the people who do the process of ascription share important properties and that the process of ascription itself can be naturalistically explained. To use a somewhat risky example: if one wanted to claim that races are socially constructed natural kinds, one would have to provide positive reasons that the people being racialized share important properties and that we can make surprising empirical generalizations about them. It would simply not do if we tried to show this by pointing to the fact that people who racialize others share some important properties and that there is an important naturalistic story about the origins of the racialization process.

In our case, what would be needed is a story about what properties are shared by beliefs as a general category, and by people to whom we ascribe a belief with a specific content. Only by providing such a story could we claim to have positive reasons to think that beliefs are socially constructed natural kinds. However, this kind of evidence is precisely what we are lacking, and this claim was argued for in Chapter 6, section 1. It is not that we know that there are no generalizations about beliefs; instead, we lack evidence to think that there are any, and this lack of evidence might be taken to support the view that beliefs should not, at the present moment, be conceptualized as being natural kinds. Obviously, this need not be true about mindreading, mindshaping, mindreaders and mindshapers: there might be important empirical discoveries about these processes and people who attribute mental states. In my view, there is no direct connection between the various theories of mindreading and mindshaping and the debates on the metaphysics of beliefs. The evolutionary stories about theories of attribution might, in principle, go hand in hand with various degrees of realism about beliefs.

The worry that that we are dealing with here is that minimal non-realism has conflated two, in principle, different claims: the claim that beliefs do not constitute a natural kind, and the claim that the category of belief is somehow a socially constructed one. The answer to this worry is that the claims in question are indeed separable, and the idea of the social construction of beliefs cannot be taken as providing justification for the thesis that beliefs do not constitute a natural kind. The latter claim, which is central for minimal non-realism, is instead justified in a negative fashion, namely by pointing to the lack of good evidence for there being surprising empirical generalizations about the concept of beliefs (and, to lesser extent, by the claim that there exists a significant cross-cultural variation in folk-psychological categories, see Chapter 6, section 1). The claim of social construction is something that seems to naturally go together with this negative claim, but it has to be admitted that, given certain assumptions, this link might be severed.

The position that would treat the category of beliefs as being at the same time socio-culturally constructed and constituting a natural kind is, as things stand now, a mostly hypothetical one. And even if we put aside any potential misgivings about the very possibility of there being socially constructed natural kinds in general, defending such a position would be an uphill struggle as it would involve showing that belief-properties, as socio-culturally ascribed, could give rise to substantial, surprising empirical generalizations about their holders. Such a conclusion does not seem to have much in the way of justification, even if we take into account the massive developments in the mindreading and mindshaping debates in recent decades. Consequently, the possibility of constructing a view of the kind described in this section cannot be taken as a serious reason against minimal non-realism.

9

Consequences

9.1 Does minimal non-realism generalize?

After dealing with some of the possible challenges to the proposed position, it is now time to consider some consequences of the minimal non-realist view. The first issue that deserves to be discussed here is the question of whether minimal non-realism generalizes. This position has been presented as if it solely applied to the category of beliefs; however, there is a strong suspicion that if this approach can be applied to beliefs, it could also extend to other folk-psychological notions which are related to the notion of belief, such as the notions of desire, imagination, etc.

It has to be admitted that the generality of minimal non-realism is a vexed issue. The arguments presented in the previous chapters which aimed to support the position of minimal non-realism might reasonably be seen as being somewhat specific to the issue of beliefs. The argumentation I developed had two main pillars: first, it was argued that belief properties are not natural ones (in Lewis's sense); second, it was shown that our folk concept of belief is the concept of a natural property. From these two premises, we arrived at the anti-realist conclusion that our folk-psychological notion of belief does not match mental reality.

Both premises need not be easily transferable to other folk-psychological notions. First, the claim that the folk consider beliefs to be substantial relies largely on the observation that they take beliefs to be genuine causes of behaviour; however, in other cases of folk-psychological notions, this assumption need not be so strongly accepted or universally shared. It might, for example, be assumed that desires would be on equal footing with beliefs in this regard as they are most probably also considered to be internal causes of behaviour. This is because desires are paired with beliefs in the intentional explanation of action. Personality traits might also be seen as playing an important role in explaining actions (this is underscored by, e.g., Andrews 2015), but whether other folk-psychological states are taken by the folk to be causally active is not so obvious. It might be hard, for example, to produce any strong argument for the claim that the folk treat imaginations as being causally active in the production of behaviour.

The other important premise in the arguments for minimal non-realism was the claim that beliefs have propositional content, and propositional content is not susceptible to naturalization. Additionally, it is hard to see how states with propositional content can be causally active. It might be doubted, however, whether all the other states which folk psychology postulates also are conceived as having propositional content. The case of beliefs is somehow special in this respect as the notion of propositional, intensional content is obviously central to the notion of belief (mainly due to the fact that beliefs are psychological states that are thought to represent possible states of affairs).

In the case of other folk-psychological mental states, this is not so obvious. It is often said that desires (and similar states) have satisfaction conditions which are in a way similar to the truth conditions that beliefs possess. Still, it is not entirely clear that the satisfaction conditions of desires should be seen as perfectly analogous to the truth conditions of beliefs (see, e.g., Lycan 2012). Further still, personality traits, which we also use in our folk-psychological practice to causally explain behaviour, do not seem to possess anything like satisfaction conditions. There are also cases, such as visual memories, in which it is unclear whether such states have something like 'content', much less propositional content. Thus, as the possibility of applying the key premise of minimal non-realists' reasoning to other categories is questionable, we should be wary of hastily transferring conclusions which pertain to the notion of belief to other folk-psychological notions.

Still, the idea that there are some important folk-psychological notions which sink or swim with the notion of belief is also tempting. The main reason for this is the centrality of the concept of belief in the folk-psychological schema of explaining intentional actions. Admittedly, belief cannot be said to be the single most important explanatory category of our folk-psychological discourse because, as was noted in Chapter 1, section 2, folk-psychological explanations involve many different psychological notions, not only beliefs. Still, the category of belief plays an important and perhaps even indispensable role in the idea of intentional agency and explanations of intentional actions.

On the standard account of intentional action (see, e.g., Davidson 1963), beliefs are essential in the explanation of intentional action as, together with desires, they (at least partially) constitute intentions which are thought to be reasons for actions (and causes of them). Although there have been several attempts to provide an alternative account of agency to the standard causal story (see, e.g., Paprzycka 2014, Sehon 2016, Wilson 1980), none of these accounts has garnered widespread approval. The idea that intentional action requires some sort of causal influence of an agent's mental states on their doings is widely accepted in contemporary theories of agency (see, e.g., Schlosser 2010). Minimal non-realism, if correct, forces us to question this standard causal account of action. However, if the broadly Davidsonian view rightly represents the folk notion of agency, then minimal non-realism would seem to force us to either reject or revise our folk notion of intentional agency.

This connection between the issue of belief realism and the issues of intentional agency and free will has recently been underscored by List (2019). According to List, we might only retain our current folk-psychological framework, in which we are intentional agents capable of free actions, if we treat beliefs (along with similar higher-level intentional states) as being genuine causes of human behaviour. List identifies three main challenges to the idea of free will. Apart from the traditional challenge of determinism, he analyses another two: the challenge stemming from the denial of the reality of intentional agency, and the challenge based on epiphenomenalism. In relation to both these challenges, List argues that in order to defend the idea of humans being free intentional agents, we must defend our common-sense realism about higher-level intentional states and their causal relevance.

Although List's objectives are very different from those I am pursuing here, his appraisal of the dialectics of the debate seems correct to me: our folk-psychological framework of free actions and intentional agency relies on the assumption that higher-level intentional states are real and are genuine causes of behaviour. However, I would like to deny List's other claim, namely that rejecting these folk assumptions must lead us to an intolerable form of eliminativism about free will and agency. In my view, we should instead make some substantial revisions to both these concepts.

It would be impossible to present a detailed description of how we should reconceptualize the notions of intentional agency and free will in the present book: this is a herculean task that the writer of these words feels unable to complete. Nor will I try to assess the feasibility of the aforementioned alternative non-causal theories of agency. This is because, among other things, these concepts are important from a normative standpoint. Agency and free will are connected to the concept of personal responsibility; therefore, revising the concept of agency would have to include a revision of the concept of responsibility. Inquiring into such a notion would take us too far from the subject of the present book. What I can do here is express hope that this project is a feasible one.

What is important for our purposes is the conclusion that although there are serious reasons to be sceptical about the possibility of mechanically extending minimal non-realism to all folk-psychological notions, the adoption of minimal non-realism about belief is not entirely inconsequential. Revising the concept of belief in such a way as to reject the idea of beliefs being substantially real and capable of causing actions must lead us to a serious rethink of large parts of our mentalist framework.

How broad such changes must be is, however, a question that would have to be answered by future research. To see whether minimal non-realism actually applies to a given folk-psychological notion (other than 'belief'), it would be necessary to get involved in detailed inquiry into both the content of this notion and into mental reality, which this concept aims to represent. It seems that the most apt candidates for such an attempt to apply minimal non-realism would be those of the mental concepts which involve the idea of content-based causation; however, the possibility that the framework would apply to a broader spectrum of cases cannot be *a priori* excluded.

In the next section, I will focus on the consequences of adopting the minimal non-realist stance for the question of the relation between folk psychology and the scientific approach to the human mind. In doing this, for the sake of simplicity of exposition, I will accept the claim that minimal non-realism applies to all folk-psychological notions, not only to beliefs. Obviously, this assumption is not warranted by the considerations presented in this section, but as we have reason to suspect that enough important folk-psychological concepts might be apt for the minimal non-realist treatment, asking this question in a simplified, general manner might be instructive.

9.2 Folk psychology vs cognitive science

One of the most problematic features of the original eliminativist version of anti-realism about beliefs (and folk psychology in general) was its commitment to the idea of eliminating folk psychology (see, e.g., Collins 2007). The thrust of this idea was that, at some unspecified point in the future, humanity would stop attributing beliefs and desires and would start to describe their own and each other's behaviours solely in terms of neuro-physiological states. This idea was sometimes seen as a factual prediction (that such a development would actually take place in the future), or as an indication of a possible course of events, or even as a normative statement (that humanity should undertake such an elimination in the future). Either interpretation makes this idea hardly believable. It does not seem plausible that humans could effectively describe, predict and explain their behaviour using only the language of neuronal events. We seem to be unable to get rid of the language of folk psychology and replace it with anything 'more basic'.

This is primarily due to the fact – often underscored by Dennett – that descriptions of the workings of the human neuronal systems are so extremely complex that we would not be able to use them effectively in the time scale of quotidian interactions (see, e.g., Dennett 1991). Consequently, folk psychology (or something very near to it) is practically indispensable for ensuring our everyday living together. We need a way of describing humans and making sense of their actions that is easily acquired and not too demanding of our cognitive capacities. The way we use folk psychology is indeed seemingly effortless and natural. There is nothing we can realistically think of as playing the very same role as folk psychology does.

The second problem with the idea of eliminating folk psychology and replacing it with the language of neuroscience was raised by Davidson. As he noted, the language of neuroscience that is postulated to replace the old folk-psychological categories might turn out to be the old language in disguise. We might use notions that look like they belong to the neurobiological framework, but in fact we will just rename our psychological notions. As Davidson put it:

> Suppose that in my office of Minister of Scientific Language I want the new man to stop using words that refer, say, to emotions, feelings, thoughts, and intentions, and to talk instead of the physiological states and happenings that are assumed to be more or less identical with the mental riff and raff. How do I tell whether my advice has been heeded if the new man speaks a new language? For all I know, the shiny new phrases, though stolen from the old language in which they refer to physiological stirrings, may in his mouth play the role of the messy old mental concepts.
>
> (Davidson 2001, p. 187–8)

The crux here is that the mere switch to language which uses neurobiological vocabulary does not mean that the folk-psychological categories have truly been eliminated: what could have happened is that we just relabelled the old category with new, fancy-sounding and superficially scientific terms. This is because the principles of property individuation that we use in our seemingly scientific framework might still be tacitly guided by psychological principles.

We might replace 'fear' by some sort of description of the neural states we associate with fear, but as long we identify these neural states by way of looking at the psychological functions which we use to define 'fear' we are still using the old notion in disguise. A genuine elimination of folk-psychological categories would require a strong reorganization of our conceptual scheme, not just a mere relabeling of existing categories, but such a deep re-conceptualization is not something that we can easily envisage.

These two arguments are, in my view, enough to show that the project of getting rid of folk psychology is most probably unrealistic. Fortunately, minimal non-realism does not carry any such problematic eliminativist commitments. One of the consequences of minimal non-realism is that we will be perfectly justified to continue to use folk-psychological vocabulary to describe ourselves and others, provided we are ready to make the necessary conceptual change.

The question of the relation between folk psychology and the scientific description of the human mind is one of the most important and vexed issues in contemporary philosophy of mind. Still, minimal non-realism has to answer this question: it is not enough to say we oppose the elimination of folk psychology; we must provide some positive account of how the folk-psychological description of the mental relates to the science of the mind.

Before we answer this question, it is important to note that the issue at hand is, nowadays, rarely framed as being caused by the question of what the relation is between (1) mental states that are postulated by folk psychology and (2) neuronal states. The current debate seems to assume a picture that includes (at least) three levels of description of the human mind (see, e.g., Dewhust 2021, Francken & Slors 2014, 2018). On the highest level, we have the mental categories postulated within the folk-psychological scheme. On the lowest level, we have brain states. The space in between these two levels is occupied by what Francken and Slors call 'scientific cognitive concepts', i.e., states postulated within the contemporary cognitive sciences. Examples of such concepts include 'working memory', 'response inhibition', etc.

Such middle-level posits of cognitive science have two important features. First, they are defined in a functional way: cognitive science postulates such states in order to explain certain cognitive functions and does so without explicit commitments to neural realizers (although it is important to note that the idea that cognitive states are defined with no regard to neuroscience is currently subject to strong criticism [see, e.g., Boone & Piccinini (2016)]). Second, such states are sub-personal in the simple sense that, in our everyday pre-scientific self-reflection, we are not aware of having any such states.

There are several important questions that arise with regard to these middle-level states. The first is that of whether such states can be mapped onto specific regions in the brain: this is a question of whether there is a one-to-one mapping between psychological function and brain structure (see, e.g., Price & Friston 2005). The other question is whether such sub-personal states can be thought of as having representational properties (see, e.g., Ramsey 2007). Although these two questions are certainly some of the most important in contemporary philosophy of mind, the position I develop here is neutral with regard to them: nothing here hinges on the question of whether sub-personal cognitive functional states are 'genuinely' representational or whether they can be easily mapped onto brain structures.

What matters for minimal non-realism, however, is the question of how folk-psychological states (especially beliefs) that are conceptualized as non-natural properties relate to the sub-personal posits of contemporary cognitive science. Murphy (2017, see also Dewhurst 2021) aptly identifies three possible approaches to this issue: integration, elimination or autonomy. The main idea of the integration approach is that the aim of folk psychology is to posit certain internal mechanisms that explain human behaviour. Proponents of this view assume (or hope) that future cognitive science will explain which cognitive states underlie these mechanisms. The eliminativist perspective is similar to the integrationist one, as it accepts the same idea about the aims of folk psychology but predicts that cognitive science will construe a different typology of functional mental states. For this reason, according to proponents of elimination, the current folk psychology would either be eliminated or be reformed to the point at which it would become obsolete in its present form. It is important to note that the eliminativism conceptualized by Murphy and Dewhurst does not envisage that folk psychology will be replaced by neuroscience. Rather, the claim is that contemporary cognitive science will create new theoretical constructs which will not be closely related to the posits of folk psychology. These new posits would be better at explaining behaviour, and they could also be integrated with neuroscience. As a result, folk-psychological categories would be, as it were, crowded out from explanations by the new taxonomy developed by cognitive science.

The last approach to this issue is the autonomy approach. This view has had many important predecessors, including McDowell (1996), and perhaps it can be traced back to at least Wittgenstein (1953). A contemporary version of this proposal can be found in Dewhurst (2021). The main idea is that attributions of attitudes such as beliefs should be seen as descriptions of 'whole persons' and that such attributions do not involve any descriptions of the brain and its parts. Additionally, the development of the conceptual repertoire of modern cognitive science should not be bounded by the idea that it is some sort of a duty to provide conceptual counterparts for folk-psychological notions. Folk psychology serves many functions: not only the epistemic one, but also regulative and normative ones (see McGeer 2007, Zawidzki 2008, 2013). For these reasons, folk psychology will remain useful even when cognitive science has developed its own independent conceptual scheme.

The programme of autonomy is certainly congenial to the project of minimal non-realism, but a caveat is needed at this point. The proponents of the autonomy of folk psychology, in my opinion, seriously undervalue the commitments that are made in our current, actual folk-psychological attributions. As I see it, in our present framework we assume that our attributions of beliefs track actual causes of behaviour (this idea was spelled out in more detail in Chapter 7, section 2). For this reason, the programme of autonomy cannot be applied to existing folk psychology.

The important aspect of minimal non-realism is the idea that our concept of belief (along with several others) is in need of revision. If we were to stick to our current understanding of beliefs (and perhaps other folk-psychological notions), then some version of eliminativism might be unavoidable. However, as has already been noted, the idea of elimination is unworkable, so we need to adopt a revisionary-preservationist approach. This revised folk-psychological framework – stripped of the unrealistic assumptions of the one we are using now – would be seen as being autonomous from cognitive science. If we do away with the idea that ascribing folk-psychological states provides insight into the internal structure of the mind and into the causal order of things, then we might start to see folk-psychological attributions as descriptions of whole persons that do not compete with cognitive scientific descriptions of sub-personal states. In this way, the autonomy approach becomes a regulative ideal: we should strive to see folk psychology as being a distinct and independent form of describing human persons.

The fact that the autonomy approach can be maintained only if we revise our current notion of belief (and other elements of our folk-psychological framework) might also be seen as providing a normative reason to support the project of revising folk psychology. It is often stressed that conceptual revisions usually (although perhaps not necessarily) require normative support: before we decide to revise a concept, we need to know why it would be advisable. For example, Haslanger's (2012) project of amelioration which was presented in Chapter 7, section 4 was explicitly based on normative considerations. In our case, it might be said that if we consider the project of the autonomy of psychology to be a normative ideal, then we might gain additional motivation to revise the notion of belief so as to achieve this normative ideal of the autonomy of folk psychology.

It is also worth noting that there is a strong methodological aspect to the idea of autonomy which results in the postulate that cognitive science and reflection on the folk-psychological conceptual repertoire should part ways. Cognitive science, in its pursuit of providing the 'middle-level' description of human cognition, should focus on two things: providing good descriptions of functions; and possible integration of its postulates with more basic levels of descriptions without paying much attention to the question of whether its theories would have anything to say about the folksy categories. In this way, we should not see cognitive science as being 'constrained from above': the mature science of human cognition has other aims than providing us with any illuminating account of our pre-theoretical notions, such as belief, self, agency or free will. In this way, the postulated autonomy of psychology (put forward a long time ago by people such as Fodor [1974]) gains new meaning. Not only do the functional concepts that psychology introduces not have to be constrained by their relation to neural correlates, but they also do not need to be constrained by the pre-theoretical personal framework of folk psychology.

Moreover, inquiries into folk-psychological notions, primarily including the notion of belief, would have to be conducted in a manner which would not assume that the sciences would provide us with any deep knowledge about the mechanisms that underwrite these categories. A better way of looking into these concepts would start with the assumption that they are, in a way, constructed (see also Chapter 8, section 6). Even though it is currently suspected that folk psychology is more a product of evolutionary pressures than an arbitrary cultural creation (although see Hutto 2012 for a defence of the cultural roots of folk psychology), seeing the concepts in question as somehow constructed might be illuminating. The practice of attributing beliefs would then be seen as part of the symbolic, broadly understood 'cultural' heritage of human kind (this idea is hardly new: its origins can be seen in Sellars's [1956] famous 'myth of Jones', although Sellars was more focused on the theoretical status of folk psychology).

If we treat folk psychology in this way, we will not expect its concepts to provide us with a reliable understanding of the causal structure of the human mind. Rather, we should see them as constituting a certain vision of what it is to be human: in this vision, humans would be seen as being capable of having internal states which are capable of representing the world and aiming at the truth, etc. The proper methodology to study this vision would be akin to the methodology we use to study other social constructs, and some version of conceptual analysis would most probably be useful in this venture. Although the method of conceptual analysis has been the subject of fierce criticism in recent decades, I think that analytical methodology might prove useful in this specific context of inquiry, at least to some extent: it might help us clarify the concept of belief and its relation to other folk-psychological concepts, such as the concepts of autonomy and agency. Moreover, conceptual analysis might also help us answer the question of whether there is any normativity involved in this concept.

What is important to note is that this idea of autonomy thwarts any hope of us solving our philosophical worries regarding the concept of belief (and other folk-psychological notions) by means of simple deference to cognitive science. If, in order to avoid irrealism about belief, we need to revise this concept in the way proposed in this book, then philosophy of mind cannot hope to solve its central problems (like the issue of realism) by looking into the developments of cognitive science. This is not to say that such developments are completely irrelevant to all questions of philosophy of mind – quite the contrary.

How this methodology might work in practice will be shown in the next section, in which I will apply this approach to one specific albeit important question in metaphysics of beliefs. This should show how we might want to approach specific questions regarding the category of belief once we buy into the picture presented here.

9.3 Pragmatic metaphilosophy of beliefs

One of the main philosophical issues regarding the notion of belief can be labelled as the question of the 'boundaries of belief'. In many sub-fields of philosophy of mind, the question arises of whether certain mental states can be properly classified as beliefs. One aspect of this broad question is the issue of whether certain systems other than humans can be treated as having beliefs. We are faced, for example, with a problem of whether non-human animals might be classified as having genuine beliefs (see, e.g., Davidson 1982 for a classic example of a sceptical position in this debate). There is also the question of whether artificial systems might be considered true believers: although for many (see, e.g., Dennett 1991) the positive answer is, at least in principle, obvious, some (see, e.g., Searle 1980) remain unconvinced. Also, there has been a recent surge in interest in the bold hypothesis that certain pan-individual entities such as corporations might be taken to hold genuine beliefs (see, e.g., List & Pettit 2011 for defence, and Ludwig 2017 for criticism).

When we focus on individual humans, the question of the boundaries of beliefs also arises in many contexts. We might, for example, wonder whether the hypothesis of extended minds can be applied to the notion of belief, or whether beliefs are necessarily embodied or located in the metaphorical skull (see, e.g., Weiskopf 2008). We might also wonder whether mono-thematic delusions such as the Capgras delusion should be classified as cases of beliefs (see, e.g., Bortolotti 2010). Another issue is whether religious convictions should be classified as beliefs (see Van Leeuwen 2014 for an example critical approach). Although religious convictions and delusions are certainly very different types of mental states, the question of whether they can be correctly classified as beliefs arises in both cases as both share many traits with paradigmatic beliefs but are dissimilar to them in many important respects.

This issue of whether certain mental states are 'genuine' beliefs also arises in more quotidian contexts. Many philosophers have been interested in the issue (discussed already in Chapter 5, section 1) of whether we should attribute beliefs in situations of discrepancy between professed opinions and actions. A popular example of such a discrepancy is the skywalk case (see, e.g., Gendler 2008, Schwitzgebel 2010), in which we are invited to imagine a clever engineer, who, after designing a skywalk and performing all the necessary tests and calculations, is willing to honestly say that the skywalk is perfectly safe; however, when confronted with the opportunity to walk on the skywalk herself, she is rather unwilling to do so. The question is whether in such a situation we should attribute the outwardly professed belief to the person in question. Alternatively, we might think that it would be appropriate to attribute a different kind of mental state to this person (as Gendler 2008 suggests), or to claim that the boundaries of the category of beliefs are fuzzy and in such a situation we are dealing with an in-between belief (see Schwitzgebel 2010).

I do not intend to try to answer any of these questions here. Rather, I want to focus on the meta issue. What are we doing when we ask such questions? What is the meaning of the various claims that people make when they take positions in the various debates about the boundaries of belief? What is the proper method of dealing with these issues?

It might be natural to suspect that the questions that fall under the category of 'boundaries of beliefs' have objective answers, i.e., that there are some facts about the world that determine the issue of whether, say, animals can have beliefs, or whether delusions should count as beliefs. It might also seem obvious that there is some 'objective' methodology which we need to use to answer such questions. For example, one might think that the proper way to gain access to these objective answers is by way of determining some sort of essence of the category of belief, either by means of purely *a priori* analysis or by deferring to contemporary cognitive science.

Minimal non-realism implies that both these ideas are mistaken. If we adopt the view that belief properties are not natural ones, then we should hold no presumption that there are any objective answers to questions about the boundaries of belief. It is one of the defining features of non-natural properties that they do not ground objective similarities; this justifies the claim that there is no such thing as the 'objective nature' of beliefs which could be taken to ground the fact that certain mental states are 'genuine' beliefs and others are not.

This claim is much stronger than the (perhaps less controversial) idea that the category of belief has fuzzy boundaries (which has been endorsed by Schwitzgebel 2010). The idea of the vagueness of beliefs is the simple thought that there are some cases in which we cannot classify a given mental state as belonging to the category of belief (or not). This is most probably true, but in my view the claim about the non-objectivity of the category of belief is significantly deeper.

As I see it (the following ideas are more deeply developed in my recent paper [Poslajko 2022]), the best way to characterize this non-objectivity of the notion of belief is by way of claiming that the concept of belief is 'plastic' in the sense of semantic plasticity (see Cappelen 2018, Dorr & Hawthorne 2014). The notion of semantic plasticity is defined as follows: a given concept is plastic if we might use the term related to the concept in question with a changed extension (and probably intension), yet it seems we are talking about the same thing. A useful example is the concept of salad. The concept of 'salad' might be considered plastic as, arguably, both the extension and the intension associated with it have significantly varied through history.

The claim I put forward that the concept of belief is plastic entails the claim that this category is apt for serious semantic changes. Most importantly, we are perfectly able to decide how to precisify the concept in question and to choose from many possible meanings of this concept. In other words, if the concept of 'belief' is plastic, then there are certain conceptual decisions regarding this concept which we are capable of making. Questions about the applicability of the category of belief to each specific problematic case should be seen as being questions about which precisification of the concept of belief we should or will choose. In this way, the question about the boundaries of belief turns out to be best treated as belonging to the area of conceptual ethics (see Burgess & Plunkett 2013). The answers to questions of this sort have more to do with our preferences regarding the conditions of the applicability of folk-psychological terms than with any objective facts.

This way of looking at the issue of meta-philosophy and the methodology of the question of the boundaries of belief is not entirely unprecedented. The idea that such questions (especially those which concern the phenomenon of discrepancy) should be answered in a pragmatic manner was put forward by Zimmerman (2018) and Schwitzgebel (2021). What differentiates my approach from those presented by Zimmerman and Schwitzgebel is that my postulate is located solely on the meta level. Even though Zimmerman and Schwitzgebel offer distinct theories, they both combine the commitment to the idea that such questions should be answered by using pragmatic methodology with what they call a 'pragmatic' account of beliefs. Broadly speaking, for them a pragmatic account of beliefs is a view which prioritizes behavioural clues over 'intellectualist' premises in cases in which we have to decide whether to attribute a certain belief to a person; for first-order pragmatists about belief, it is what we do rather than what we 'think' which is important for our belief profile. I wish to neither accept nor reject such a first-order pragmatism. Rather, I want to commit myself to pragmatism on a meta-level, namely to the postulate that when dealing with the question of boundaries of belief, we should treat these questions as pragmatic. Such meta-level pragmatism might but doesn't have to lead to first-level pragmatism. It all depends on which option turns out to be pragmatically preferable in particular contexts, but to settle this issue we must engage in actual philosophical arguments.

If we adopt this so-defined pragmatic meta-philosophy, then reflection about folk-psychological terms will differ from the inquiry that takes place in the subfields of the philosophy of mind that reflect on cognitive science. In the latter area, we are dealing with questions that have a much stronger claim to objective factuality. The issue of whether it is necessary to posit cognitive states that have representational properties to explain human cognition might be of a different status than the question of whether we might apply the category of belief to religious convictions, for example. The first question might be described as dealing with a fact that is independent of our conceptual choices; the second is ultimately about the way want to use the notion of belief.

The meta-philosophical view that is presented here about the status of the question of the boundaries of beliefs has important consequences for the methodology of dealing with this question. If pragmatic meta-philosophy is right in this context and the search for objective facts must be forlorn, then we should not expect that either conceptual analysis or deference to cognitive science is able to answer the questions that we are asking. Conceptual analysis, even if it is possible in principle and genuinely helpful in the project of understanding our folk psychology, is not able to provide us with objective and *a priori* answers about the boundaries of belief. This is because there are many possible analyses of the concept of belief that are in principle consistent with our pre-theoretical intuitions regarding this concept. The reason for this is that the concept in itself has no essence to speak of, and the current use of the notion of 'belief' is compatible with many possible precisifications and corrections.

The idea of deference to science also does not seem promising in this context. If belief properties are not natural ones, then they do not play a causal-explanatory role and thus the concept of belief would not play an important role in mature cognitive science (this is not to say that this concept would have no use at all, but it would not have an important explanatory role). However, if beliefs do not play an important role in mature cognitive science, then we have little reason to suspect that cognitive science will come up with a precise definition of the concept of belief.

In order to solve the issue of the boundaries of belief, instead of engaging in *a priori* conceptual analysis or reflection upon cognitive science, we should adopt an explicitly pragmatic and normatively oriented methodology. If the question of the boundaries of beliefs is about our conceptual choices, then we should be explicitly interested in the issue of what is the best way to conceptualize belief. The real question is not whether non-human animals really harbour beliefs; rather, is the conceptualization of the concept of belief which allows beliefs to be attributed to non-human animals pragmatically and normatively useful? Does such a notion of beliefs really improve our understanding of non-human animal minds? Or maybe the human-centred notion is better as it allows us to see the peculiarities of the human mind? Does extension of this notion to include the mental states of non-human animals help us in making normative decisions?

It is important to emphasize that this way of seeing things does not have to and should not lead us to a vulgar picture in which questions about the boundaries of beliefs would be resolved by ideologically motivated conceptual fiat. The pragmatic and normative considerations should be thoughtfully balanced and reflected upon, and we should be wary of knee-jerk reactions. The idea of a reflective equilibrium which takes into account various epistemic and normative goals should be our guiding principle here.

All in all, as folk psychology parts ways with cognitive science, there seems to be room for two paradigms in philosophy of mind. The first is philosophical reflection on the current state of cognitive science and its ontological commitments. The second is a pragmatically and normatively oriented project that deals with the precisification and amelioration (in Haslanger's [2012] sense) of our current folk-psychological conceptual scheme. Although it would be unwise to postulate a complete disintegration of these two approaches, they should be seen as largely autonomous. Thus, the optimistic conclusion is that even though minimal non-realism in itself is largely a negative view, there are still many important philosophical questions to engage with once we adopt this position.

10

Conclusion

Denying the reality of beliefs used to be considered a sort of radical intellectual act. A theorist who put forward the claim that beliefs are not real was to be taken as committing themselves to a series of contestable views: that all ascriptions of beliefs are uniformly false, that folk psychology will (or should) be completely eliminated, and that we will be left with only a neurobiological level of description and explanation of what was formerly known as the human mind. These pronouncements were met with widespread disbelief.

My aim in this book has been to present and justify a way of denying the reality of beliefs which would be less dramatic and perhaps more palatable. We are able to declare that beliefs fail to be real without committing ourselves to such ostensibly outrageous claims. We are also entitled to assert that the folk-psychological practice of belief attributions contains a grave error of a metaphysical sort: we take beliefs to be more real than they actually are. However, if we accept this idea, we might continue to see folk-psychological attributions of beliefs as capable of being true. We do not need to postulate any sort of elimination of folk-psychological vocabulary, and certainly there is no need to subscribe to any sort of fantastic scenario in which we stop using psychological vocabulary and replace it with neuroscience. What is needed, however, is that we revise our existing notion of belief so as to get rid of unrealistic presumptions. We must do away with the idea that by ascribing beliefs we are describing any sort of deep mental reality; and we should get rid of the view that by ascribing beliefs we are identifying the causes of actions. The real explanations of our behaviour would be found on a sub-personal level (which does not necessarily mean the neuro-biological one).

This is certainly a much more modest and pedestrian set of conclusions than the one that the original eliminativists were trying to promote. Still, many philosophers who are used to more realistic approaches might find them counter-intuitive and hard to swallow. However, in my view the evidence we have at this moment supports the non-realist view, as any stronger view simply lacks adequate justification. In such a situation, the considerations of parsimony and methodological caution should lead us to prefer the weaker view of moderate anti-realism.

Even though the approach of minimal non-realism is not as revolutionary in spirit as the original eliminativism, it has some important consequences for the way we should conduct inquiry in many areas of philosophy of mind. It postulates that philosophical inquiries into our folk-psychological schema of belief attributions should be seen as autonomous from cognitive science, which is in the business of providing us with genuine causal explanations. The philosophical questions which arise with regard to the folk practice of ascribing beliefs should be dealt with using pragmatic methodology: instead of hoping that we can somehow discover the 'essence of belief', we should focus on how we should be using the concept of belief.

The austere picture of eliminativism – according to which only neuroscience provides us with a proper description of the human mind, and folk psychology should be discarded – is not something that we have any reason to embrace. The proper picture assumes that we are indeed minded creatures and that our mind comprises several more or less independent levels. Above the basic neurological level there is a middle level of sub-personal states which are postulates of empirical cognitive science and whose function is to provide us with higher-level explanations of behaviour. These middle-level posits might or might not prove reducible to neuronal events: this question must be settled by further research into the status of cognitive science. Above this level there is a level of description of people in terms of their beliefs and desires. This personal-level description of a human person is irreducible to the description of sub-personal cognitive mechanisms that is provided by cognitive science.

There are many other mental phenomena which I have left entirely out of the picture in the present book: emotions, qualitative feelings, moods, imagination and so on. Their status and relation to the concept of belief is something that must be left for another occasion. Similarly, I have not touched upon many important questions that need attention in the context of the presented proposal. I have said nothing about how to think about self-knowledge, mindreading, linguistic understanding and many other issues that are related to the notion of belief: these must also wait for future occasions or thinkers who are more able.

What is important, however, is the idea that folk psychology – narrowly understood as the practice of explaining human action by way of attributing beliefs to humans – should be seen as a peculiar way of looking at humans that we should disentangle from the scientific approach to human psychology. The guiding thought of this book was that we should stop treating belief attributions as guiding us in our search for internal causes of our behaviour; we might truly ascribe beliefs to ourselves and others, but these ascriptions do not reveal any deep truths about our cognitive makeup. We should instead treat folk-psychological discourse as being a certain story about what we do and why we do it. This story might well have an evolutionary genesis, but this does not change the fact that we should treat it as a story: something we tell ourselves that might have several values but which we might also wish to change.

This picture is far less dramatic than the one we might expect to get from a book devoted to exposition of anti-realism about beliefs, but I feel it supports the view that beliefs are, in an important sense, not real. There are no internal, causally active states that bear semantic content. There is nothing that links the sphere of reasons with the realm of causes, at least there is nothing of the sort that many philosophers wish there were. Still, such a realization might not be the worst of news for philosophy, and there are many vital issues that we might try to engage with if we adopt the idea of unreal beliefs.

References

Adams, F., & Aizawa, K. (2017). 'Causal Theories of Mental Content', *The Stanford Encyclopedia of Philosophy* (Summer 2017 Edition), Edward N. Zalta (ed.), URL = <https://plato.stanford.edu/archives/sum2017/entries/content-causal/>.
Alexander, S. (1920). *Space Time, and Deity*, vol. 2. London: Macmillan.
Alvarez, M. (2017). 'Reasons for Action: Justification, Motivation, Explanation', *The Stanford Encyclopedia of Philosophy* (Winter 2017 Edition), Edward N. Zalta (ed.), URL = <https://plato.stanford.edu/archives/win2017/entries/reasons-just-vs-expl/>.
Andrews, K. (2008). It's in your nature: A pluralistic folk psychology. *Synthese*, 165(1), 13–29.
Andrews, K. (2015). Pluralistic folk psychology and varieties of self-knowledge: An exploration. *Philosophical Explorations*, 18(2), 282–96.
Annas, J., & Barnes, J. (eds.) (2000). *Sextus Empiricus: Outlines of Scepticism*. Cambridge: Cambridge University Press.
Arico, A., Fiala, B., Goldberg, R. F., & Nichols, S. (2011). The folk psychology of consciousness. *Mind & Language*, 26(3), 327–52.
Ayer, A. J. (1936). *Language, Truth and Logic*. London: Victor Gollancz Ltd.
Baker, L. (1987). *Saving Belief*. Princeton: Princeton University Press.
Bar-On, D. (2012). Expression, Truth, and Reality: Some Variations on Themes from Wright. In C. Wright & A. Coliva (eds.), *Mind, Meaning, and Knowledge: Themes from the Philosophy of Crispin Wright*. Oxford: Oxford University Press. pp. 162–94.
Baumgartner, M. (2009). Interventionist causal exclusion and non-reductive physicalism. *International Studies in the Philosophy of Science*, 23(2), 161–78.
Beebee, H., & Sabbarton-Leary, N. (2010). Are psychiatric kinds real? *European Journal of Analytic Philosophy*, 6(1), 11–27.
Bennett, K. (2008). Exclusion Again. In J. Hohwy & J. Kallestrup (eds.), *Being Reduced: New Essays on Reduction, Explanation, and Causation*. Oxford: Oxford University Press. pp. 280–305.
Besson, C. (2012). Empty natural kind terms and Dry-Earth. *Erkenntnis*, 76(3), 403–25.
Blackburn, S. (1993). *Essays in Quasi-Realism*. Oxford: Oxford University Press.
Block, N. (1978). Troubles with functionalism. *Minnesota Studies in the Philosophy of Science*, 9, 261–325.
Block, N. (1995). An Argument for Holism. In *Proceedings of the Aristotelian Society* (Vol. 95, No. 1, pp. 151–70). Oxford: Oxford University Press.
Bogdan, R. J. (1993). The architectural nonchalance of commonsense psychology. *Mind and Language*, 8(2), 189–205.
Boghossian, P. A. (1990). The status of content. *The Philosophical Review*, 99(2), 157–84.

Boone, W., & Piccinini, G. (2016). The cognitive neuroscience revolution. *Synthese*, 193(5), 1509–34.

Bortolotti, L. (2010). *Delusions and Other Irrational Beliefs*. Oxford: Oxford University Press.

Bourget, D. (2010). Consciousness is underived intentionality. *Noûs*, 44(1), 32–58.

Bourget, D. (2019). Anomalous Dualism: A New Approach to the Mind-Body Problem. In W. Seager (ed.), *The Handbook of Panpsychism*. New York: Routledge. pp. 168–80.

Boyd, R. (1991). Realism, anti-foundationalism and the enthusiasm for natural kinds. *Philosophical Studies*, 61(1/2), 127–48.

Braddon-Mitchell, D., & Jackson, F. (2007). *The Philosophy of Mind and Cognition (2nd ed.)*. Oxford: Blackwell.

Brandom, R. (1994). *Making It Explicit*. Cambridge, MA: Harvard University Press.

Brandom, R. (2008). *Between Saying and Doing: Towards an Analytic Pragmatism*. Oxford: Oxford University Press.

Burge, T. (1979). Individualism and the mental. *Midwest Studies in Philosophy*, 4(1), 73–121.

Burge, T. (2010). *Origins of Objectivity*. Oxford: Oxford University Press.

Burgess, A., & Plunkett, D. (2013). Conceptual ethics I. *Philosophy Compass*, 8(12), 1091–101.

Burgess, A., & Sherman, B. (2014). A Plea for the Metaphysics of Meaning. In A. Burgess & B. Sherman (eds.), *Metasemantics: New Essays on the Foundations of Meaning*. Oxford: Oxford University Press. pp. 1–16.

Butterfill, S. A., & Apperly, I. A. (2013). How to construct a minimal theory of mind. *Mind & Language*, 28(5), 606–37.

Byrne, A. (1998). Interpretivism. *European Review of Philosophy*, 3, 199–223.

Cappelen, H. (2018). *Fixing Language: An Essay on Conceptual Engineering*. Oxford: Oxford University Press.

Carnap, R. (1950). Empiricism, semantics, and ontology. *Revue internationale de philosophie*, 4(1950), 20–40.

Carruthers, P. (1996). *Language, Thought and Consciousness: An Essay in Philosophical Psychology*. New York: Cambridge University Press.

Chalmers, D. J. (1996). *The Conscious Mind: In Search of a Fundamental Theory*. New York: Oxford University Press.

Chalmers, D. J. (2011). Verbal disputes. *Philosophical Review*, 120(4), 515–66.

Chan, T. (2013). Introduction: Aiming at Truth. In T. Chan (ed.), *The Aim of Belief*. Oxford: Oxford University Press. pp. 1–16.

Chomsky, N. (2000). *New Horizons in the Study of Language and Mind*. New York: Cambridge University Press.

Chrisman, M. (2010). Expressivism, Inferentialism and the Theory of Meaning. In M. S. Brady (ed.), *New Waves in Metaethics*. Basingstoke: Palgrave Macmillan. pp. 103–25.

Churchland, P. M. (1981). Eliminative materialism and propositional attitudes. *The Journal of Philosophy*, 78(2), 67–90.

Churchland, P. M. (1986). Cognition and conceptual change: A reply to double. *Journal for the Theory of Social Behaviour*, 16(2), 217–21.

Churchland, P. M. (2007). The Evolving Fortunes of Eliminative Materialism. In B. P. McLaughlin & J. D. Cohen (eds.), *Contemporary Debates in Philosophy of Mind*. Oxford: Blackwell. pp. 160–81.

Collins, J. (2007). Meta-scientific eliminativism: A reconsideration of Chomsky's review of Skinner's verbal behavior. *The British Journal for the Philosophy of Science*, 58(4), 625–58.

Connors, M. H., & Halligan, P. W. (2015). A cognitive account of belief: A tentative road map. *Frontiers in Psychology*, 5, 1588.

Cooper, R. (2013). Natural Kinds. In K. W. M. Fulford, M. Davies, R. Gipps, G. Graham, J. Sadler, G. Stanghellini & T. Thornton (eds.), *Oxford Handbook of Philosophy and Psychiatry*. Oxford: Oxford University Press. pp. 950–65.

Corns, J. (2016). Pain eliminativism: scientific and traditional. *Synthese*, 193(9), 2949–71.

Crane, T. (2017). The unity of unconsciousness. *Proceedings of the Aristotelian Society*, 117(1), 1–21.

Curry, D. S. (2018). Beliefs as inner causes: The (lack of) evidence. *Philosophical Psychology*, 31(6), 850–77.

Curry, D. S. (2020). Interpretivism and norms. *Philosophical Studies*, 177(4), 905–30.

Curry, D. S. (2021). How beliefs are like colors. *Synthese*, 199(3–4), 7889–918. https://doi.org/10.1007/s11229-021-03144-1.

Daly, C. (2013). Psychology and indispensability. *The Monist*, 96(4), 561–81.

Damnjanovic, N. (2010). New Wave Deflationism. In C. Wright & N. Pedersen (eds.), *New Waves in Truth*. London: Palgrave Macmillan. pp. 45–58.

Davidson, D. (1963). Actions, reasons, and causes. *The Journal of Philosophy*, 60(23), 685–700.

Davidson, D. (1970). Mental events. *Experience and Theory*, 44, 43–64.

Davidson, D. (1974). Psychology as Philosophy. In S. Brown (ed.), *Philosophy of Psychology*. London: Palgrave Macmillan. pp. 41–52.

Davidson, D. (1982). Rational animals. *dialectica*, 36(4), 317–27.

Davidson, D. (1993). Thinking Causes. In J. Heil & A. Mele (eds.), *Mental Causation*. Oxford: Clarendon Press. pp. 3–17.

Davidson, D. (2001). On the Very Idea of a Conceptual Scheme. In D. Davidson (ed.), *Inquiries into Truth and Interpretation (Second Edition)*. Oxford: Clarendon Press. pp. 183–98.

Davidson, D. (2004). Problems in the Explanation of Action. In D. Davidson (ed.), *Problems of Rationality*. Oxford: Oxford University Press. pp. 101–16.

Demeter, T. (2009). Two kinds of mental realism. *Journal for General Philosophy of Science*, 40(1), 59–71.

Demeter, T. (2013). Mental fictionalism: The very idea. *The Monist*, 96(4), 483–504.

Dennett, D. C. (1989). *The Intentional Stance*. Cambridge, MA: MIT press.

Dennett, D. C. (1991). Real patterns. *The Journal of Philosophy*, 88(1), 27–51.

Dennett, D. C. (1998). Two Contrasts: Folk Craft versus Folk Science and Belief versus Opinion. In D. Dennett (ed.), *Brainchildren*. Cambridge, MA: MIT Press. pp. 135–48.

Dennett, D. C. (2009). Intentional Systems Theory. In B. McLaughlin, A. Beckermann & S. Walter (eds.), *The Oxford Handbook of Philosophy of Mind*. Oxford: Oxford University Press. pp. 339–50.

Dennett, D. C. (2018). Reflections on Tadeusz Zawidzki. In B. Huebner (ed.), *The Philosophy of Daniel Dennett*. Oxford: Oxford University Press. pp. 57–60.

Devitt, M. (2005). Scientific Realism. In F. Jackson & M. Smith (eds.), *The Oxford Handbook of Contemporary Philosophy*. Oxford: Oxford University Press. pp. 767–91.

Devitt, M., & Rey, G. (1991). Transcending transcendentalism: A response to Boghossian. *Pacific Philosophical Quarterly*, 72(2), 87–100.

Dewhurst, J. (2017). *From Folk Psychology to Cognitive Ontology*. Edinburgh: Dissertation, University of Edinburgh.

Dewhurst, J. (2021). Folk Psychological and Neurocognitive Ontologies. In F. Calzavarini & M. Viola (eds.), *Neural Mechanisms. Studies in Brain and Mind*, vol. 17. Cham: Springer. pp. 311–34.

Divers, J., & Miller, A. (1995). Minimalism and the unbearable lightness of being. *Philosophical Papers*, 24(2), 127–39.

Dorr, C., & Hawthorne, J. (2014). Semantic plasticity and speech reports. *Philosophical Review*, 123(3), 281–338.

Dreier, J. (2004). Meta-ethics and the problem of creeping minimalism. *Philosophical Perspectives*, 18, 23–44.

Dretske, F. (1981). *Knowledge and the Flow of Information*. Cambridge, MA: MIT Press.

Dupré, J. (1995). *The Disorder of Things: Metaphysical Foundations of the Disunity of Science*. Cambridge, MA: Harvard University Press.

Edwards, D. (2013). Truth as a substantive property. *Australasian Journal of Philosophy*, 91(2), 279–94.

Egan, F. (1995). Folk psychology and cognitive architecture. *Philosophy of Science*, 62(2), 179–96.

Egan, F. (2014). How to think about mental content. *Philosophical Studies*, 170(1), 115–35.

Egan, F. (2020). A Deflationary Account of Mental Representation. In J. Smortchkova, K. Dolega & T. Schlicht (eds.), *What Are Mental Representations*. New York: Oxford University Press. pp. 26–53.

Eklund, M. (2017). *Choosing Normative Concepts*. Oxford: Oxford University Press.

Eronen, M. I. (2020). Interventionism for the intentional stance: True believers and their brains. *Topoi*, 39(1), 45–55. https://doi.org/10.1007/s11245 017 9513 5.

Evans, M., & Shah, N. (2012). Mental Agency and Metaethics. In R. Shafer-Landau (ed.), *Oxford Studies in Metaethics, Volume 7*. Oxford: Oxford University Press. pp. 80–109.

Farkas, K. (2003). What is externalism? *Philosophical Studies*, 112(3), 187–208.

Fenici, M., & Zawidzki, T. W. (2021). The origins of mindreading: How interpretive socio-cognitive practices get off the ground. *Synthese*, 198(9), 8365–87.

Fine, K. (2001). The question of realism. *Philosophers' Imprint*, 1, 1–30.

Fodor, J. A. (1974). Special sciences (or: The disunity of science as a working hypothesis). *Synthese*, 28(2), 97–115.

Fodor, J. A. (1975). *The Language of Thought*. New York: Cromwell.

Fodor, J. A. (1985). Fodor's guide to mental representations. *Mind*, 94, 76–100.

Fodor, J. A. (1987). *Psychosemantics: The Problem of Meaning in the Philosophy of Mind (Vol. 2)*. Cambridge, MA: MIT press.

Fodor, J. A. (1990). *A Theory of Content and Other Essays*. Cambridge, MA: MIT press.

Fodor, J. A. (2008). Against Darwinism. *Mind & Language*, 23(1), 1–24.

Fodor, J. A., & Pylyshyn, Z. W. (2015). *Minds without Meanings: An Essay on the Content of Concepts*. Cambridge, MA: MIT Press.

Francken, J. C., & Slors, M. (2014). From commonsense to science, and back: The use of cognitive concepts in neuroscience. *Consciousness and Cognition*, 29, 248–58.

Francken, J. C., & Slors, M. (2018). Neuroscience and everyday life: Facing the translation problem. *Brain and Cognition*, 120, 67–74.

Frankish, K. (2016). Illusionism as a theory of consciousness. *Journal of Consciousness Studies*, 23(11–12), 11–39.

Frege, G. (1956). The thought: A logical inquiry. *Mind*, 65(259), 289–311.

Gauker, C. (2003). *Words without Meaning*. Cambridge, MA: MIT Press.

Gauker, C. (2021). Belief Attribution as Indirect Communication. In L. Koreň, H. B. Schmid, P. Stovall & L. Townsend (eds.), *Groups, Norms and Practices. Studies in the Philosophy of Sociality, vol 13*. Cham: Springer. pp. 173–87.

Gendler, T. (2008). Alief and belief. *The Journal of Philosophy*, 105(10), 634–63.

Gibbard, A. (2012). *Meaning and Normativity*. Oxford: Oxford University Press.

Glüer, K., & Wikforss, Å. (2018). 'The Normativity of Meaning and Content', *The Stanford Encyclopedia of Philosophy* (Spring 2018 Edition), Edward N. Zalta (ed.), URL = <https://plato.stanford.edu/archives/spr2018/entries/meaning-normativity/>.

Griffiths, P. E. (2004). Emotions as natural and normative kinds. *Philosophy of Science*, 71(5), 901–11.

Hacking, I. (1995). The Looping Effects of Human Kinds. In D. Sperber, D. Premack & A. Premack (ed.), *Causal Cognition: A Multidisciplinary Debate*. Oxford: Clarendon Press. pp. 35–94.

Hall, N. (2016). 'David Lewis's Metaphysics', *The Stanford Encyclopedia of Philosophy* (Winter 2016 Edition), Edward N. Zalta (ed.), URL = <https://plato.stanford.edu/archives/win2016/entries/lewis-metaphysics/>.

Harmon-Jones, E., & Mills, J. (1999). An introduction to cognitive dissonance theory and an overview of current perspectives on the theory. In E. Harmon-Jones & J. Mills (eds.), *Cognitive Dissonance: Progress on a Pivotal Theory in Social Psychology*. Washington, DC: American Psychological Association. pp. 3–21.

Haslanger, S. (2012). *Resisting Reality: Social Construction and Social Critique*. New York: Oxford University Press.

Hochstein, E. (2012). Minds, models and mechanisms: A new perspective on intentional psychology. *Journal of Experimental & Theoretical Artificial Intelligence*, 24(4), 547–57.

Hochstein, E. (2017). When does 'folk psychology' count as folk psychological? *The British Journal for the Philosophy of Science*, 68(4), 1125–47.

Holton, R. (1993). Minimalism about Truth. In B. Garrett & K. Mulligan (eds.), *Themes from Wittgenstein*. Canberra: ANU Working Papers in Philosophy 4.

Horgan, T. (1993). The austere ideology of folk psychology. *Mind and Language*, 8(2), 282–97.

Hume, D. (1748/51). *Enquiries Concerning Human Understanding and Concerning the Principles of Morals*. L. A. Selby-Bigge & P. H. Nidditch (eds.) 3rd edition (1975). Oxford: Clarendon Press.

Hutto, D. D. (2011). Presumptuous naturalism: A cautionary tale. *American Philosophical Quarterly*, 48(2), 129–45.

Hutto, D. D. (2012). *Folk Psychological Narratives: The Sociocultural Basis of Understanding Reasons*. Cambridge, MA: MIT press.

Hutto, D. D. (2013). Fictionalism about folk psychology. *The Monist*, 96(4), 582–604.

Hutto, D. D., & Myin, E. (2012). *Radicalizing Enactivism: Basic Minds without Content*. Cambridge, MA: MIT Press.

Hutto, D. D., & Satne, G. (2015). The natural origins of content. *Philosophia*, 43(3), 521–36.

Jackson, F. (1999). Non-cogntivism, normativity, belief. *Ratio*, 12(4), 420–35.

Jackson, F., & Pettit, P. (1990). In defence of folk psychology. *Philosophical Studies*, 59(1), 31–54.

Jackson, F., & Pettit, P. (1993). Folk belief and commonplace belief. *Mind and Language*, 8(2), 298–305.

Jenson, J. C. (2016). The belief illusion. *The British Journal for the Philosophy of Science*, 67(4), 965–95.

Joyce, R. (2001). *The Myth of Morality*. Cambridge: Cambridge University Press.

Joyce, R. (2013). Psychological fictionalism, and the threat of fictionalist suicide. *The Monist*, 96(4), 517–38.

Kennedy, C., & Stanley, J. (2009). On 'average'. *Mind*, 118(471), 583–646.

Khalidi, M. A. (2013). *Natural Categories and Human Kinds: Classification in the Natural and Social Sciences*. Cambridge: Cambridge University Press.

Khalidi, M. A. (2015). Three kinds of social kinds. *Philosophy and Phenomenological Research*, 90(1), 96–112.

Kim, J. (1989). The Myth of Nonreductive Materialism. In *Proceedings and Addresses of the American Philosophical Association* (Vol. 63, No. 3, pp. 31–47).

Kim, J. (1993). *Supervenience and Mind: Selected Philosophical Essays*. Cambridge: Cambridge University Press.

Kim, J. (1998). *Mind in a Physical World: An Essay on the Mind-Body Problem and Mental Causation*. Cambridge, MA: MIT press.

Kim, J. (2002). Mental Causation. In B. McLaughlin, A. Beckermann & S. Walter (eds.), *The Oxford Handbook of Philosophy of Mind*. Oxford: Oxford University Press. pp. 170.

Kim, J. (2005). *Physicalism, or Something near Enough*. Princeton: Princeton University Press.

Kim, J. (2006). *Philosophy of Mind (Second Edition)*. Boulder: Westview Press.

Knowles, J. (2002). Is folk psychology different? *Erkenntnis*, 57(2), 199–230.

Kovács, Á. M., Téglás, E., & Endress, A. D. (2010). The social sense: Susceptibility to others' beliefs in human infants and adults. *Science*, 330(6012), 1830–4.

Kriegel, U. (2003). Is intentionality dependent upon consciousness? *Philosophical Studies*, 116(3), 271–307.

Kriegel, U. (2010). Interpretation: Its Scope and Limits. In A. Hazlett (ed.), *New Waves in Metaphysics*. London: Palgrave Macmillan. pp. 111–135.

Kriegel, U. (2011). Cognitive Phenomenology as the Basis of Unconscious Content. In T. Bayne & M. Montague (eds.), *Cognitive Phenomenology*. Oxford: Oxford University Press. pp. 79–102.

Kripke, S. (1980). *Naming and Necessity*. Cambridge, MA: Harvard University Press.

Kripke, S. (1982). *Wittgenstein on Rules and Private Language: An Elementary Exposition*. Cambridge, MA: Harvard University Press.

Lahav, R. (1992). The amazing predictive power of folk psychology. *Australasian Journal of Philosophy*, 70(1), 99–105.

Lau, J., & Deutsch, M. (2019). 'Externalism about Mental Content', *The Stanford Encyclopedia of Philosophy* (Fall 2019 Edition), Edward N. Zalta (ed.), URL = <https://plato.stanford.edu/archives/fall2019/entries/content-externalism/>.

Laudan, L. (1981). A confutation of convergent realism. *Philosophy of Science*, 48(1), 19–49.

Lewis, D. (1970). How to define theoretical terms. *The Journal of Philosophy*, 67(13), 427–46.

Lewis, D. (1978). Truth in fiction. *American Philosophical Quarterly*, 15(1), 37–46.

Lewis, D. (1983). New work for a theory of universals. *Australasian Journal of Philosophy*, 61(4), 343–77.

Lewis, D. (1984). Putnam's paradox. *Australasian Journal of Philosophy*, 62(3), 221–36.

List, C. (2019). *Why Free Will Is Real*. Cambridge, MA: Harvard University Press.

List, C., & Menzies, P. (2017). My Brain Made Me Do It: The Exclusion Argument against Free Will, and What's Wrong with It. In H. Beebee, C. Hitchcock & H. Price (eds.), *Making a Difference: Essays on the Philosophy of Causation*. Oxford: Oxford University Press. pp. 269–85.

List, C., & Pettit, P. (2011). *Group Agency: The Possibility, Design, and Status of Corporate Agents*. Oxford: Oxford University Press.

Ludwig, K. (2017). *From Plural to Institutional Agency: Collective Action II*. Oxford: Oxford University Press.

Lycan, W. (1988). *Judgement and Justification*. Cambridge: Cambridge University Press.

Lycan, W. G. (2012). Desire considered as a propositional attitude. *Philosophical Perspectives*, 26, 201–15.
Machery, E. (2009). *Doing without Concepts*. New York: Oxford University Press.
Machery, E. (2017). *Philosophy within Its Proper Bounds*. Oxford: Oxford University Press.
Mackie, J. L. (1977). *Ethics: Inventing Right and Wrong*. London: Penguin Books.
Malcolm, N. (1968). The conceivability of mechanism. *The Philosophical Review*, 45–72.
Mallon, R. (2016). *The Construction of Human Kinds*. Oxford: Oxford University Press.
Mallon, R., Machery, E., Nichols, S., & Stich, S. (2009). Against arguments from reference. *Philosophy and Phenomenological Research*, 79(2), 332–56.
Matthews, R. J. (2013). Belief and Beliefs Penumbra. In N. Nottelmann (ed.), *New Essays on Belief*. London: Palgrave Macmillan. pp. 100–23.
McCulloch, G. (1990). Dennett's little grains of salt. *The Philosophical Quarterly*, 40(158), 1–12.
McDowell, J. (1996). *Mind and World*. Cambridge, MA: Harvard University Press.
McGeer, V. (2007). The Regulative Dimension of Folk Psychology. In D. D. Hutto & M. Ratcliffe (eds.), *Folk Psychology Re-assessed*. Dordrecht: Springer. pp. 137–56.
McHugh, C., & Whiting, D. (2014). The normativity of belief. *Analysis*, 74(4), 698–713.
McPherson, T. (2015). What is at stake in debates among normative realists? *Noûs*, 49(1), 123–46.
Mendelovici, A. (2013). Reliable misrepresentation and tracking theories of mental representation. *Philosophical Studies*, 165(2), 421–43.
Mendelovici, A., & Bourget, D. (2014). Naturalizing intentionality: Tracking theories versus phenomenal intentionality theories. *Philosophy Compass*, 9(5), 325–37.
Menzies, P. (2008). The Exclusion Problem, the Determination Relation, and Contrastive Causation. In J. Hohwy & J. Kallestrup (eds.), *Being Reduced: New Essays on Reduction, Explanation, and Causation*. Oxford: Oxford University Press. pp. 196–217.
Miłkowski, M. (2015). The hard problem of content: Solved (long ago). Studies in logic. *Grammar and Rhetoric*, 41(1), 73–88.
Mill, J. S. (1843/1882). *A System of Logic (8th ed.)*. New York: Harper & Brothers.
Miller, A. (2016). 'Realism', *The Stanford Encyclopedia of Philosophy* (Winter 2016 Edition), Edward N. Zalta (ed.), URL = <https://plato.stanford.edu/archives/win2016/entries/realism/>.
Millikan, R. G. (2000). Naturalizing Intentionality. In *The Proceedings of the Twentieth World Congress of Philosophy* (Vol. 9, pp. 83–90).
Mölder, B. (2010). *Mind Ascribed. An Elaboration and Defence of Interpretivism*. Amsterdam: John Benjamins.
Moore, G. E. (1939). Proof of an external world. *Proceedings of the British Academy*, 25(5), 273–300.
Murphy, D. (2017). Brains and Beliefs. In D. M. Kaplan (ed.), *Explanation and Integration in Mind and Brain Science*. Oxford: Oxford University Press. pp. 119–45.

Pagin, P. (2016). 'Assertion', *The Stanford Encyclopedia of Philosophy* (Winter 2016 Edition), Edward N. Zalta (ed.), URL = <https://plato.stanford.edu/archives/win2016/entries/assertion/>.

Paprzycka, K. (2014). The Social Re-construction of Agency. In M. C. Galavotti et al. (eds.), *New Directions in the Philosophy of Science*. Cham: Springer. pp. 323–38.

Perez, D. (2004). Mental concepts as natural kind concepts. *Canadian Journal of Philosophy*, 34(sup1), 201–25.

Pietroski, P. (1992). Intentionality and teleological error. *Pacific Philosophical Quarterly*, 73(3), 267–82.

Plebani, M. (2018). Fictionalism versus deflationism: A new look. *Philosophical Studies*, 175(2), 301–16.

Plunkett, D. (2015). Which concepts should we use? Metalinguistic negotiations and the methodology of philosophy. *Inquiry: An Interdisciplinary Journal of Philosophy*, 58(7–8), 828–74.

Polger, T. (2004). *Natural Minds*. Cambridge, MA: MIT Press.

Porot, N., & Mandelbaum, E. (2020). The science of belief: A progress report. Wiley Interdisciplinary Reviews: Cognitive Science, e1539.

Poslajko, K. (2016). From Epiphenomenalism to Eliminativism? In A. Kuźniar & J. Odrowąż-Sypniewska (eds.), *Uncovering Facts and Values: Studies in Contemporary Epistemology and Political Philosophy*. Boston: Brill | Rodopi. pp. 192–203.

Poslajko, K. (2017). Semantic deflationism, public language meaning and contextual standards of correctness. *Studia Semiotyczne*, 31(1), 45–66.

Poslajko, K. (2019). Eliminativism: The problem of representation and Carnapian metametaphysics. *Acta Analytica*, 34(2), 181–95.

Poslajko, K. (2020). Can deflationism save interpretivism? *Philosophia*, 48(2), 709–25.

Poslajko, K. (2022). The Lycan–Stich argument and the plasticity of 'belief'. *Erkenntnis*, 87, 1257–73. https://doi.org/10.1007/s10670-020-00242-3.

Poslajko, K. (2024). Expressivism, inferentialism, and the status of attitudes. *Inquiry*, 67(1), 171–98. https://doi.org/10.1080/0020174X.2021.1886982.

Price, C. J., & Friston, K. J. (2005). Functional ontologies for cognition: The systematic definition of structure and function. *Cognitive Neuropsychology*, 22(3–4), 262–75.

Price, H. (2013). *Expressivism, Pragmatism and Representationalism*. Cambridge: Cambridge University Press.

Putnam, H. (1975). The meaning of 'meaning'. *Minnesota Studies in the Philosophy of Science*, 7, 131–93.

Putnam, H. (1981). *Reason, Truth and History*. New York: Cambridge University Press.

Putnam, H. (1987). *The Many Faces of Realism*. LaSalle, IL: Open Court.

Quilty-Dunn, J., & Mandelbaum, E. (2018). Against dispositionalism: Belief in cognitive science. *Philosophical Studies*, 175(9), 2353–72.

Quine, W. V. (1948). On what there is. *The Review of Metaphysics*, 2(1), 21–38.

Quine, W. V. (1960). *Word and Object*. Cambridge, MA: MIT Press.

Ramsey, W. M. (2007). *Representation Reconsidered*. Cambridge: Cambridge University Press.

Ramsey, W. M. (2019). 'Eliminative Materialism', *The Stanford Encyclopedia of Philosophy* (Spring 2019 Edition), Edward N. Zalta (ed.), URL = <https://plato.stanford.edu/archives/spr2019/entries/materialism-eliminative/>.

Rellihan, M. (2020). Functional properties are epiphenomenal. *Philosophia*, 48, 1171–195. https://doi.org/10.1007/s11406-019-00118-z.

Rorty, R. (1965). Mind-body identity, privacy, and categories. *The Review of Metaphysics*, 19(1), 24–54.

Rosenberg, A. (2013). How Jerry Fodor slid down the slippery slope to anti-Darwinism, and how we can avoid the same fate. *European Journal for Philosophy of Science*, 3(1), 1–17.

Rosenberg, A. (2015). The genealogy of content or the future of an illusion. *Philosophia*, 43(3), 537–47.

Rupert, R. D. (2018). Representation and mental representation. *Philosophical Explorations*, 21(2), 204–25.

Ryle, G. (1949/2009). *The Concept of Mind*. New York: Routledge.

Scharp, K. (2021). Conceptual engineering for truth: Aletheic properties and new aletheic concepts. *Synthese*, 198(Suppl 2), 647–88.

Schiffer, S. (1996). Language-created language-independent entities. *Philosophical Topics*, 24(1), 149–67.

Schiffer, S. (2003). *The Things We Mean*. Oxford: Oxford University Press.

Schlosser, M. (2010). Agency, Ownership, and the Standard Theory. In A. Buckareff, J. Aguilar & K. Frankish (eds.), *New Waves in Philosophy of Action*. New York: Palgrave Macmillan. pp. 13–31.

Schwitzgebel, E. (2002). A phenomenal, dispositional account of belief. *Noûs*, 36(2), 249–75.

Schwitzgebel, E. (2010). Acting contrary to our professed beliefs or the gulf between occurrent judgment and dispositional belief. *Pacific Philosophical Quarterly*, 91(4), 531–53.

Schwitzgebel, E. (2013). A Dispositional Approach to Attitudes: Thinking outside of the Belief Box. In N. Nottelmann (ed.), *New Essays on Belief*. London: Palgrave Macmillan. pp. 75–99.

Schwitzgebel, E. (2021). The Pragmatic Metaphysics of Belief. In C. Borgoni, D. Kindermann & A. Onofri (eds.), *The Fragmented Mind*. Oxford: Oxford University Press. pp. 350–75.

Searle, J. R. (1980). Minds, brains, and programs. *Behavioral and Brain Sciences*, 3(3), 417–24.

Searle, J. R. (1991). Consciousness, unconsciousness and intentionality. *Philosophical Issues*, 1, 45–66.

Segal, G. M. (2000). *A Slim Book about Narrow Content*. Cambridge, MA: MIT Press.

Sehon, S. (2016). *Free Will and Action Explanation: A Non-causal, Compatibilist Account*. Oxford: Oxford University Press.

Sellars, W. (1956). Empiricism and the philosophy of mind. *Minnesota Studies in the Philosophy of Science*, 1(19), 253–329.

Shea, N. (2013). Naturalising representational content. *Philosophy Compass*, 8(5), 496–509.

Sider, T. (2011). *Writing the Book of the World*. Oxford: Oxford University Press.

Slors, M. (2007). Intentional systems theory, mental causation and empathic resonance. *Erkenntnis*, 67(2), 321–36.

Slors, M., De Bruin, L., & Strijbos, D. (2015). *Philosophy of Mind, Brain and Behaviour*. Amsterdam: Boom.

Spaulding, S. (2018). Mindreading beyond belief: A more comprehensive conception of how we understand others. *Philosophy Compass*, 13(11), e12526.

Stich, S. P. (1981). Dennett on intentional systems. *Philosophical Topics*, 12(1), 39–62.

Stich, S. P. (1983). *From Folk Psychology to Cognitive Science: The Case against Belief*. Cambridge, MA: MIT press.

Stich, S. P. (1993). The Future of Folk Psychology. In S. M. Christensen & D. R. Turner (eds.), *Folk Psychology and the Philosophy of Mind*. Hillsdale, NJ: L. Erlbaum. p. 93.

Stich, S. P. (1996). *Deconstructing the Mind*. Oxford: Oxford University Press.

Stoljar, D. (2014). Chomsky, London and Lewis. *Analysis*, 75(1), 16–22.

Streumer, B. (2017). *Unbelievable Errors: An Error Theory about All Normative Judgements*. Oxford: Oxford University Press.

Strijbos, D. W., & de Bruin, L. C. (2013). Universal belief-desire psychology? A dilemma for theory theory and simulation theory. *Philosophical Psychology*, 26(5), 744–64.

Taylor, K. (1994). How not to refute eliminative materialism. *Philosophical Psychology*, 7(1), 101–25.

Thomasson, A. L. (2003a). Fictional characters and literary practices. *The British Journal of Aesthetics*, 43(2), 138–57.

Thomasson, A. L. (2003b). Realism and human kinds. *Philosophy and Phenomenological Research*, 67(3), 580–609.

Thomasson, A. L. (2013). Fictionalism versus deflationism. *Mind*, 122(488), 1023–51.

Thomasson, A. L. (2014). Deflationism in Semantics and Metaphysics. In A. Burgess & B. Sherman (eds.), *Metasemantics: New Essays on the Foundations of Meaning*. Oxford: Oxford University Press. pp. 185–213.

Thomasson, A. L. (2015). *Ontology Made Easy*. Oxford: Oxford University Press.

Tollefsen, D. (2015). *Groups as Agents*. Cambridge: Polity Press.

Toon, A. (2016). Fictionalism and the folk. *The Monist*, 99, 280–95.

Toppinen, T. (2015). Expressivism and the Normativity of Attitudes. *Pacific Philosophical Quarterly*, 96(2), 233–55.

Tumulty, M. (2014). Managing mismatch between belief and behavior. *Pacific Philosophical Quarterly*, 95, 261–92.

Van Leeuwen, N. (2014). Religious credence is not factual belief. *Cognition*, 133(3), 698–715.

Vargas, M. (2004). Libertarianism and skepticism about free will: Some arguments against both. *Philosophical Topics*, 32(1/2), 403–26.

Vargas, M. (2005). The revisionist's guide to responsibility. *Philosophical Studies*, 125(3), 399–429.

Vargas, M. (2009). Revisionism about free will: A statement & defense. *Philosophical Studies*, 144(1), 45–62.

Vargas, M. (2013). If Free Will Doesn't Exist, Neither Does Water. In G. D. Caruso (ed.), *Exploring the Illusion of Free Will and Moral Responsibility*. Lanham, MD: Lexington Books. pp. 177–202.

Voltolini, A. (2013). There are intentionalia of which it is true that such objects do not exist. *International Journal of Philosophical Studies*, 21(3), 394–414.

Wallace, M. (2016). Saving mental fictionalism from cognitive collapse. *Res Philosophica*, 93(2), 1–20.

Walton, K. L. (1993). Metaphor and prop oriented make-believe. *European Journal of Philosophy*, 1(1), 39–57.

Warren, M. D. (2018). Building bridges with words: An inferential account of ethical univocity. *Canadian Journal of Philosophy*, 48(3–4), 468–88.

Weiskopf, D. A. (2008). Patrolling the mind's boundaries. *Erkenntnis*, 68(2), 265–76.

Williams, M. (2010). Pragmatism, minimalism, expressivism. *International Journal of Philosophical Studies*, 18(3), 317–30.

Williams, M. (2013). How Pragmatists Can Be Local Expressivists. In H. Price (ed.), *Expressivism, Pragmatism and representationalism*. Cambridge: Cambridge University Press. pp. 128–44.

Wilson, G. M. (1980). *The Intentionality of Human Action*. Stanford: Stanford University Press.

Wimsatt, W. (1981). Robustness, Reliability, and Overdetermination. In M. Brewer & B. Collins (eds.), *Scientific Inquiry and the Social Sciences*. San Francisco, CA: Jossey-Bass Publishers. pp. 124–63.

Wittgenstein, L. (1953). *Philosophical Investigations*, G. E. M. Anscombe and R. Rhees (eds.), G. E. M. Anscombe (trans.). Oxford: Blackwell.

Woodward, J. (2008). Mental Causation and Neural Mechanisms. In J. Hohwy & J. Kallestrup (eds.), *Being Reduced: New Essays on Reduction, Explanation, and Causation*. Oxford: Oxford University Press. pp. 218–62.

Woodward, J. (2015). Methodology, ontology, and interventionism. *Synthese*, 192(11), 3577–99.

Wright, C. (1992). *Truth and Objectivity*. Cambridge, MA: Harvard University Press.

Wright, C. (1995). Can there be a rationally compelling argument for anti-realism about ordinary ('folk') psychology? *Philosophical Issues*, 6, 197–221.

Wright, C. (2002). What could antirealism about ordinary psychology possibly be? *The Philosophical Review*, 111(2), 205–33.

Yablo, S. (1992). Mental causation. *The Philosophical Review*, 101(2), 245–80.

Zangwill, N. (2010). Normativity and the metaphysics of mind. *Australasian Journal of Philosophy*, 88, 21–39.

Zawidzki, T. W. (2008). The function of folk psychology: Mind reading or mind shaping? *Philosophical Explorations*, 11(3), 193–210.

Zawidzki, T. W. (2013). *Mindshaping: A New Framework for Understanding Human Social Cognition*. Cambridge, MA: MIT Press.

Zawidzki, T. W. (2018). The Many Roles of the Intentional Stance. In B. Huebner (ed.), *The Philosophy of Daniel Dennett*. Oxford: Oxford University Press. pp. 36–56.

Zawidzki, T. W. (2021). A new perspective on the relationship between metacognition and social cognition: Metacognitive concepts as socio-cognitive tools. *Synthese*, 198(7), 6573–96.

Zimmerman, A. Z. (2018). *Belief: A Pragmatic Picture*. Oxford: Oxford University Press.

Index

a priori 3, 58, 60, 112, 145–7, 168, 176, 178
action 24, 78, 100, 125, 149, 175
   and free will 129–30
   causes of 56–7, 86–8, 103–5, 153–4, 181–2
   explanation of 4–5, 59, 98, 165–9
agency 17, 120, 129–30, 166–7, 173–4
application criteria 35, 37, 70, 102, 125, 131, 134

behaviourism/neo-behaviourism 117, 122–3
Blackburn, S. 13, 39–40
Block, N. 87, 102
Boghossian, P. 18–19, 30, 70, 144–7
Burge, T. 88, 101–2

Carnap, R. 21, 129
causal exclusion 57, 59, 98–100, 105
causal explanation 59, 64–5, 78, 119–20, 153, 182
   and natural properties 2, 9, 48, 51, 55–6
Chomsky, N. 14, 45, 81–5, 134
Churchland, P. 6–7, 15, 21, 53, 81, 134
cognitive science 37–8, 63, 125, 142, 176–9, 182
   and folk psychology, *see* folk psychology and (cognitive) science
   elimination/eliminativism 15, 24–5, 53
   of belief 95
common-sense functionalism 17, 23–4, 36, 86–7
concept acquisition 102, 106
conceptual analysis 34–5, 37, 118, 174, 178
conceptual engineering 129
Curry, D. 66, 76, 119, 122

Davidson, D. 37, 56, 76–9, 166, 169, 174
deflationary account of/deflationism about
   existence 33, 35–8, 42–3, 49, 80, 134, 137
   meaning 43–5
   truth 13, 19, 42, 46, 48–9, 144–5
Dennett, D. 68, 37, 152, 169
   artificial systems 174

folk craft 124–5, 149
   intentional stance 116–17, 138
   interpretivism 76, 79, 81–2, 121
Dewhurst, J. 97, 171
difference-making 98–100, 103, 105–6

Egan, F. 62–3, 118–19
eliminativism/eliminative materialism 6–10, 14–25, 29, 38, 136, 139, 144, 182
   about free will 130, 133, 167
   and austere folk psychology 151, 154
   and fictionalism 27–9, 68
   and mental causation 58
   inconsistency 31, 69–70
   mild 81, 84
   scientific 53
   versus autonomy and integration 171–2
error theory 15, 18–19, 69, 132

fictional characters 29, 135, 138
fictionalism 16, 25–8, 30, 68, 137–40
Fodor, J. 54, 58, 107–9, 111, 152, 173
   Industrial-strength-realism 6, 37
   language of thought 85–6
   multiple realizability 66–7
   non-reductive physicalism 56
   success argument 147–9
folk psychology
   and (cognitive) science 3, 6–7, 10, 81–4, 134, 168–74, 179
   as theory 15–16, 20, 22
   empirical assumptions 82, 84, 134, 151–2
   posits 147–9, 171
   regulative 133, 172
free will 128–31, 133, 141, 167, 173

Gauker, C. 153–4
gender 128–32, 141

Haslanger, S. 129, 131–3, 179
Hutto, D. 79, 111, 123–5, 138, 173

inferentialism 126, 143
intentional stance 79, 81, 116–7, 121, 125, 127, 138
interpretivism 9, 37, 42, 76–7, 79–80, 115, 117, 121–3
interventionist causation 99–100, 103–5, 123
irrealism 33, 42, 70, 80, 136, 153, 174
    arguments against 30–1, 144–5
    gender and race 133
    inconsistency 2–3

Jackson, F. 11, 23, 79, 86, 138

Khalidi, M. 55, 93, 160
Kim, J. 56–8, 78, 98, 104, 155, 158

language of thought 85–6, 151–2
Lewis, D. 97, 107, 165
    fiction 26
    natural properties 43–9, 54, 60, 67–9, 73, 83, 97, 107, 112, 117, 165
    theoretical terms 21
List, C. 98–9, 167, 175

Mandelbaum, E. 85–7, 93, 123
Matthews, R. 54–5, 76
meaning 17, 21, 83, 108, 119, 126–8, 142–5, 147
meaning-intentions 102, 106
mental causation 56, 58, 103–6, 123, 125, 155, 157–8
Millikan, R. 109
mindreading 16, 118, 120–2, 161–3
Mölder, B. 36, 42, 77, 89
multiple realizability 66–7

natural kinds 67, 91–7, 102, 112–13, 146
    and natural-kind terms 21–3, 124
    realism 53–5, 64–5, 71, 87–8
    social kinds 159–63
natural properties 43–9, 56, 60–1, 73, 83, 101, 107
    causation 54, 56
    pleonastic properties 42
    realism 64, 68–9, 73, 81, 91, 113, 115, 137
    similarity 51, 54
natural-kind terms 21–3, 113, 124
naturalism 46, 61, 64, 157
naturalization of content 6, 61–2, 71, 106–7, 112

neo-dispositionalism 37, 75–6, 115, 117
normative statements 11–14, 27, 39

phenomenal intentionality 63–4, 156–9
physicalism 45, 56–7, 67, 107, 155
Putnam, H. 21, 31, 54, 92, 101, 124, 159

Quilty-Dunn J. 85–7, 93, 123
Quine, W. V. 14
    approach to ontology 8, 28–31, 34

race 131–2
reduction/reductionism 46, 58, 61, 106
representationalism 6–7, 85–8, 92
revision of concepts 2–3, 10, 125, 128–31, 136, 141, 158, 167, 172
Rosenberg, A. 14, 61–2, 109, 111
Rupert, R. 6–7
Ryle, G. 37, 73–5, 119

Schiffer, S. 33–4, 36, 80
Schwitzgebel, E. 37, 73, 75, 115–16, 175–7
Searle, J. 142, 156, 175
Sellars, W. 5, 173
semantic properties 4, 61, 85, 104, 121, 143, 146, 157
Slors, M. 16, 76–7, 170
Stich, S. 52, 134
    eliminativism 9, 14, 71, 81–2, 84–5
    Lycan-Stich argument 17, 20–3
    naive Quineanism 29–30
sub-personal states/level 63, 65–6, 91, 105, 154, 170–2, 181–2

Thomasson, A. 33–6, 39, 135, 140, 144, 161
Toon, A. 25–6, 137

Vargas, M. 129–30, 132–3
velociraptors 134–5

Wallace, M. 25–8, 137
Wittgenstein, L. 17, 44, 171
Woodward, J. 99–100, 104
Wright, C. 58, 138–9, 141
    Boghossian-Wright argument 70, 144–7
    deflationism/minimalism 33–4, 40–1
    non-cognitivism 11, 13

Zawidzki, T. 4, 120–1, 125, 133, 149, 161, 172

www.ingramcontent.com/pod-product-compliance
Lightning Source LLC
Chambersburg PA
CBHW052116300426
44116CB00010B/1690